THE PRESENT AS HISTORY I

NERMEEN SHAIKH ▮

THE PRESENT AS HISTORY

CRITICAL PERSPECTIVES

ON CONTEMPORARY GLOBAL POWER

Columbia University Press New York

Columbia University Press
Publishers Since 1893
New York, Chichester, West Sussex
Copyright © 2007 Columbia University Press
All rights Reserved

A Caravan book. For more information, visit
www.caravanbooks.org

Library of Congress Cataloging-in-Publication Data

Shaikh, Nermeen.
The Present as history : critical perspectives on
contemporary global power / by Nermeen Shaikh.
    p. cm.
Includes bibliographical references and index.
ISBN 978-0-231-14298-4 (clothbound : alk. paper) —
ISBN 978-0-231-14299-1 (pbk. : alk. paper) —
ISBN 978-0-231-51241-1 (e book)
    1. International relations. 2. World politics—1989–
3. Postcolonialism. 4. Developing countries—
Politics and government. 5. Developing countries—
Economic conditions. 6. Developing countries—
Social conditions. 7. Intellectuals—Interviews.
I. Title.

JZ1310.S47   2008
327.1—dc22   2007003408
♾
Columbia University Press books are printed on
permanent and durable acid-free paper

Printed in the United States of America
Designed by Audrey Smith

c 10 9 8 7 6 5 4 3 2 1
p 10 9 8 7 6 5 4 3 2

For Raana Shaikh,
my Amma

CONTENTS I

Acknowledgments   ix
Introduction   xi

PART 1 I THE GLOBAL ECONOMY   **1**
1. Amartya Sen   3
2. Helena Norberg-Hodge   17
3. Sanjay Reddy   27
4. Joseph Stiglitz   54

PART 2 I POSTCOLONIALISM AND THE NEW IMPERIALISM   **69**
5. Partha Chatterjee   71
6. Mahmood Mamdani   94
7. Anatol Lieven   109

PART 3 I FEMINISM AND HUMAN RIGHTS   **137**
8. Shirin Ebadi   139
9. Lila Abu-Lughod   143
10. Saba Mahmood   148
11. Gayatri Chakravorty Spivak   172

PART 4 I SECULARISM AND ISLAM   **203**
12. Talal Asad   205
13. Gil Anidjar   225

Notes   255
Notes on Interviewees   259
Index   263

ACKNOWLEDGMENTS I

I am grateful for the time that the people in this volume gave me for interviews, and to the Asia Society for permission to reprint some of the interviews. This book would not have been possible without the dedication and unwavering support of my editor, Peter Dimock. With help on the initial proposal, I am grateful to Brenda Coughlin, Yogesh Chandrani, Amy Scholder, and Adam Shatz. The interviews were conducted over the course of a few years, and during this time, the idea for this anthology took shape in discussions with much beloved friends and interlocutors: Nauman Naqvi, Gil Anidjar, James Ingram, Ninon Vinsonneau, Jonathan Magidoff, Amy Rosenberg, Sanjay Reddy, Asad Ahmed, Iram Khandwala, Barnett Rubin, and Ritu Birla. To James Ingram I am especially thankful for fifteen years of incredible conversation on politics, modernity, and much else. My father, Najmuddin Shaikh, and my grandfather, Iftikhar Ahmed Sharwani, have always nurtured my intellectual aspirations, for which they have my inexpressible gratitude. For supporting this project, despite obvious ideological differences, I am grateful to my brother Nadir Shaikh. For their unquestioning love, I will forever be indebted to Ammi and Abu (Najma and Riaz Naqvi), to my dear sister Naveen Naqvi, and to my little brother Nofil Naqvi. My parents, Najmuddin and Raana Shaikh, have made everything possible, from the beginning.

Gil Anidjar has blessed me with his intense passion, conviction, and love from the moment we first spoke, and it is only in conversation with him and Nauman that another life has become imaginable.

Nauman Naqvi, my home in all worlds, is for me an exemplary model of a critical, just, and ethical being in the world, and it is from him that I have learned more than I can ever acknowledge, in words or otherwise.

This book is dedicated to my mother, Raana Shaikh, whose example of justice and love continues to guide me, and whose encouragement and devotion gave me the strength to think, and to live, differently.

INTRODUCTION I

This anthology provides an introduction to the thought of several important scholars writing on the present global configuration of power and
international politics.[1] I have chosen intellectuals in various fields in the
social and human sciences whose work puts them in a position to give
first-hand reports on how the tradition of scholarship within which they
work can provide critical angles of vision not otherwise available with
which to understand and assess contemporary events. The interview
format enables these intellectuals to articulate the often difficult concepts they deploy in their professional work in more accessible ways for
a nonspecialist audience, bringing out the urgency and political significance of theoretical and often abstract ideas in economics, anthropology,
political science, religion, history, law, and comparative literature. These
voices enable us to better apprehend the broader historical, political, and
economic contexts that have given rise to the global order as we live it
by engaging some of the most urgent questions of our times: imperialism, the legacy of colonialism, economic inequality, global institutional
frameworks, political Islam, secularism, feminism, and human rights.
They also impart a broad overview of the historical context in which
these issues have emerged and taken shape: from colonialism to development, from postcolonialism to modernity and beyond.

Foregrounding the significance of large and often increasing inequalities, both within and across nation states, the anthology opens with a
section on the Global Economy, which includes interviews with Nobel
laureates Amartya Sen and Joseph Stiglitz, as well as Sanjay Reddy and

development critic Helena Norberg-Hodge. Sen discusses the short-comings of the development agenda as it was conceived at the close of the Second World War, as well as the role of the institutions entrusted with the task of development, specifically the World Bank and the International Monetary Fund (IMF). He elaborates his contribution to the global debate, namely, the capabilities approach and, with it, the inauguration of the human development agenda, which expanded the field, narrowly focused on economic indicators, to include social issues such as education and health in the measure of development. Stiglitz discusses economic globalization and the overwhelming power of the IMF in particular in guiding its trajectory. He elaborates how international economic institutions are often dominated by financial and commercial interests in the wealthiest countries and the implications of this for developing economies. Helena Norberg-Hodge uses her experience in Ladakh, Tibet, as a way of advancing a critique of the development agenda as it has been conceived and practiced in the postwar era and its relation to similar practices in the colonial period. She discusses the shortcomings of the World Bank and the IMF, as well as the often adverse consequences of development policies for local populations in recipient countries.

In the next section, Postcolonialism and the New Imperialism, political scientists Partha Chatterjee, Mahmood Mamdani, and Anatol Lieven chart the trajectory of hegemonic power from the colonial to the postcolonial period. Elaborating on his earlier work on India, Chatterjee discusses the significance of the Subaltern Studies school of history writing, a history from below, as it were, of the nationalist struggle against British colonialism. He discusses the implications of the continuation of colonial government administration following decolonization, and the peculiar forms of modernity bequeathed to the former colonies. Mahmood Mamdani also elaborates the continuation of colonial practices in the context of Africa and in much of the developing world. Focusing on the consequences of the Cold War, he discusses the growth of terrorist movements around the world during that period, and the increasing politicization of Islam, together with the global impact of the continuities in American foreign policy with respect to the Third World. Anatol Lieven, a journalist as well as a researcher, focuses on the different strains of American nationalism. He discusses the continuities and the ruptures between nineteenth-century empires and the American one, elaborating on the use of concepts such as the civilizing mission and indirect rule.

The section on Feminism and Human Rights includes interviews with Iranian human rights lawyer and Nobel laureate Shirin Ebadi, as well as anthropologists Lila Abu-Lughod and Saba Mahmood, and Gayatri Chakravorty Spivak, literary theorist and cultural critic. Ebadi discusses her work in the field of human rights, and the relationship between Islam, democracy, and human rights, as well as the consequences of the present and continuing war on terror. Lila Abu-Lughod explains how women have historically been used as an excuse for imperial interventions, and how best to understand the situation of Muslim women in that context. Saba Mahmood discusses the relationship between liberalism, Islam, and secularism. In elaborating the place of Muslim women, Mahmood discusses the significance of the veil and provides an account of the growth of Islamist movements around the world. Gayatri Spivak highlights the problems associated with human rights discourse and practice and discusses representations of women from the non-Western world. She also elaborates some of the important concepts in her work on colonialism.

In the final section, on Secularism and Islam, Talal Asad traces the genealogy of the term secularism, its relationship to modernity, and the particular forms it has taken in different contexts. He discusses as well the question of human rights, and the special place of Islam in debates about secularism. Gil Anidjar discusses the distinction between the theological and the political, corresponding to the crucial modern opposition between the religious and the secular, and elaborates the historical links between secularism and Christianity.

Read together, these interviews contribute a valuable understanding of world history and a corrective, as well, to some of the predominant conventional discourses on issues of global power and justice.

THE PRESENT AS HISTORY I

PART ONE | THE GLOBAL ECONOMY

ONE I Amartya Sen

Some critics have suggested that development as it has been pursued in the last fifty years was poorly conceived and narrowly defined. What biases in the development agenda were you trying to address and why?

The idea of development is a complex one: it is not surprising that people think that the way development is defined could be improved. When the subject began in the 1940s it was primarily driven by the progress in economic growth theory that had occurred through the preceding period in the 1930s as well as the 1940s. It was dominated by the basic vision that poor countries are just low-income countries, and the focus was simply on transcending the problems of underdevelopment through economic growth, increasing GNP, and so on. That proved to be a not very good way of thinking about development, which has to be concerned with advancing human well-being and human freedom.

Income is one of the factor that contributes to welfare and freedom, but not the only factor. The process of economic growth is a rather poor basis for judging the progress of a country; it is not, of course, irrelevant, but it is only one factor among many.

It is interesting to remember that if we go back a long time, the development agenda, right from the beginning, had a concern with human life, extending well back to Adam Smith, John Stuart Mill, Karl Marx, and others. But all this had to be reasserted in the contemporary development literature. This is an issue in which I have felt quite involved. I should explain that I am not primarily a development economist. I should not pretend to be one! (Even though I feel flattered when I read that I got the Nobel Prize for contributions to development economics, it was in fact awarded for work on "welfare economics" and "social choice theory.") But insofar as I have been involved in development, I have been concerned quite a bit with the nature of development and the causal mechanisms that contribute to it.

The Human Development Report, *published annually by the UNDP since 1990, draws substantially on your work on capabilities. Could you explain the importance of this approach and its policy implications?*

Human development, as an approach, is concerned with what I take to be the basic development idea: namely, advancing the richness of human life, rather than the richness of the economy in which human beings live, which is only a part of it. That is, I think, the basic focus of the human development approach. It was pioneered by Mahbub ul-Haq, and the first report came out in 1990. Mahbub started working on this in the summer of 1989. I remember his ringing me in Finland where I was living at the time. Mahbub, of course, was an extremely close friend: we were students together, we maintained close contact until his untimely death, and I always enjoyed talking and arguing with him, which we did throughout our friendship.

Regarding your question, I would say it is not quite correct to say that the *Human Development Report* draws on my ideas in particular; it draws on the ideas of a lot of us, and Mahbub himself was a great pioneer of this. We could see the expressions of frustration Mahbub had in his early work. For example, in his 1963 book on Pakistan, *The Strategy of Economic Planning*, he mentions that if India and Pakistan were to grow at what were then thought to be the most rapid rates experienced in the world, then in about twenty-five years or so, India or Pakistan would be where Egypt was at that time. Mahbub was, obviously, not anti-Egyptian in any sense! But he was arguing that it is just not good enough for India and Pakistan, after twenty-five years of maximum growth, only to get where Egypt already was. This basic concern can be seen as the beginning of human development thought, and it had much to do with the way Mahbub's mind was working already in 1963.

He was arguing that we should be able to make human life much richer by going directly at the determining factors that influence the quality of our lives. However, in his professional life in Pakistan, Mahbub got involved, first, with administration, and then for a while with politics, as Pakistan's finance minister, and in between he was advising and working with the World Bank. So he was not master of his own time in the way I was, being an academic. I thus had more opportunity to work freely to pursue the ideas that he and I shared. Mahbub was very interested indeed when I delivered my first Tanner Lecture in 1979 called "Equality of What?" at Stanford University (I gave two other Tanner Lectures on a related theme at Cambridge University in 1985). The 1979 essay was my first serious writing on what is now called "the capabilities approach." I remember seeing Mahbub not long after that in Geneva and we had a long conversation about it. Then my book, *Commodities and Capabilities*, came out in 1985, and a further study, *The Standard of Living*, came out in 1987, based on my 1985 Cambridge lectures. I was getting more and more involved in all this, and Mahbub was cheering me on.

When he called me in 1989, he told me that I was too much into pure theory and should drop all that now ("enough is enough"), and that he and I should work together on something with actual measurement, actual numbers, and try to make an impact on the world. He was very driven (as always!). He displayed the same kind of vigor I recollected he had in our undergraduate days together, a vigor that had been somewhat restrained by his official positions in the World Bank and in the government of Pakistan. I remember asking his wife—Khadija (or Bani to us, her friends)—whether I was right in thinking that Mahbub was back to his old high spirits, and she confirmed that he was. Absolutely.

To what extent do you believe that the institutions entrusted with development—the World Bank and the IMF foremost among them—have been equal to the task? In other words, do you think that the structural conditions exist for the realization of human equality, capabilities, and freedom as you envision them?

There are three things here that I should try to make clear. First, there were some policies emanating from the Bank and from the Fund that were clearly not, at least in my judgment, ideally suited for the advancement of an agenda of human development. If one is looking for a record of impeccable correctness—or even being "roughly correct"—throughout, I do not think I am able to put the World Bank and International Monetary Fund in that category.

The second point to note is that institutions, like all of us individually, also go through a learning process, and the Bank and the Fund did too. Sometimes one's learning is at one's own expense (like going to a costly private school), but in contrast, the Bank and the Fund had a very expensive education the costs of which were borne mostly by others, through unnecessary or misdirected economic hardship.

To look at things more positively, a lot has indeed been learned. Also there have been changes in the leadership of these institutions. Under the direction of James Wolfensohn, the Bank has certainly taken a much more pro–human development approach. Indeed, what was unthinkable many years ago has occurred with little fuss in the Bank, to wit, having a whole section dedicated to "human development." That quiet organizational change also reflects a shift in the Bank philosophy, bringing poverty removal to the center of the stage.

There are, of course, changes in the Fund too. Camdessus and Stanley Fisher took considerable interest in what we call human development, compared with what was the case earlier, even though the nature of the Fund's work, which is more financial and less oriented to long-run development, made the exercise rather different there. In any case, the change in the Fund has not been as big as in the Bank under Wolfensohn's leadership.

The third point to make is that the World Bank and IMF governing structures—fixed by their rules and protocol—are very unequal in terms of the influence of different perspectives. This reflects not only the fact that these are financial institutions, not primarily political ones, as the United Nations is. But there is something more than that in the systematic asymmetries of power of the different countries in the governance of the Bank and the Fund. The entire UN family, including the United Nations itself, came into being in the 1940s in a world that was very different. The Bank and the Fund emerged from the Bretton Woods Agreement in 1944. This was a world where more than half the countries were not self-governing. This was before the independence of India and many other countries in Asia and Africa. China was independent, but it was just emerging from a very long period of Western dominance followed by Japanese conquest. And Germany, Japan, and Italy were the defeated—or about to be defeated—nations, with little say in world governance.

There was not a single democratic poor country in the world. In addition, the understanding of such things as human rights was very limited. The United Nations itself played a big part in producing the Universal Declaration of Human Rights, a few years after Bretton Woods, but that entire approach was in its infancy.

Today there are nongovernmental organizations (NGOs) that are very powerful in the world, which was not the case then at all. OXFAM was founded in 1942, but it was a small relief organization then, with little voice in world affairs. That has changed over the years, and I know—having been honorary president of OXFAM for some years—how strong the commitment of this wonderful organization is to making the voices of the poor and the underprivileged heard. There are other organizations like that today, fighting for the underdogs of society, through work but also through advocacy, such as Amnesty International, Médecins Sans Frontières, Human Rights Watch, Save the Children, Actionaid, and so on, but in the world of the mid-1940s, they either did not exist or had a very limited role. CARE did exist (I remember teaching in makeshift night schools in neighboring villages in Bengal, when I was completing my own school education, using erstwhile food boxes of CARE as tables, chairs, and blackboard stands), but CARE was mainly a relief organization, primarily distributing food. The idea that NGOs could be vocal and influential participants in development dialogues is a much more recent one.

So in that context, the world that emerged had a tremendous concentration of power in the hands of what we may call the "establishment countries." For example, the president of the World Bank is always an American, while the president of the IMF can be an American or a European, but he or she is not going to be a Pakistani or an Ethiopian (irrespective of personal qualifications). The inequalities in the governing structure need to be reexamined, but it is unlikely that this will happen any time soon.

The United Nations itself faces a similar problem (particularly with asymmetries in the Security Council), and being a more political organization, it has undertaken attempts at reexamination (so far without much effect). I do not believe the World Bank and the IMF have really considered any major reform of governing arrangements, and given the fact that these are financial institutions, they probably will not. A pity, that, but also a reasonable subject for more global public discussion.

Some of the chapters in your highly acclaimed Development as Freedom *book were delivered as lectures to World Bank staff at the behest of James Wolfensohn. Do you believe that your collaboration with him led to substantive change in Bank practice?*

I cannot really claim that my lecturing the Bank has had any particular impact. But Jim Wolfensohn has introduced many new ideas and practices in the Bank that reflect his own thinking. I am very happy that his ideas have much similarity with my way of thinking, but he arrived at them on his own.

The World Bank had not been my favorite organization. I would not have liked to have been involved very much in the Bank without some basic change in its attitude to a number of these questions. This did occur with Jim Wolfensohn's arrival. He is also an old friend, and we had worked together as trustees of the Institute for Advanced Study at Princeton. He was then, and still is, the chairman of its Board. I was a member of the Board, and we worked there together. I developed a tremendous admiration for the way Jim ran the Board. I was delighted when he became the president of the World Bank.

When he asked me to give these lectures at the Bank, on any subject of my choice, I thought immediately that this was something I would like to do. And it was a good experience, with lots of useful comments on my lectures that I could use in finalizing the book, *Development as Freedom*. And it was good to have tried out the book on a large but critical and knowledgeable audience.

In an article in the Guardian *(UK) entitled "Freedom's Market," you suggested that "The real debate associated with globalization is, ultimately, not about the efficiency of markets, nor about the importance of modern technology. The debate, rather, is about inequality of power." Do you believe that this rather dramatic inequality in power within and between states can be altered without equally dramatic structural change?*

This is a difficult issue. Let me say three things. One is that the inequalities are monumental in the world today both in economic affluence and in political power. Any kind of analysis of globalization has to be alive to that fact. Now I do believe that greater global contact has been a very strong force for good, not just today but over thousands of years. The history of the global contact is sometimes underestimated by thinking of it primarily as a recent phenomenon, and in terms of influences going only from the West to the East, or from North to South. But historically the process of influence has not been unidirectional. Look, for example, at A.D. 1000, at the beginning of the millennium that finished just four years ago. In the fields of science and technology, there were a great many things known then in China that were not known in Europe. Similarly, Indian, Arab, and Iranian mathematicians knew a great deal about mathematics that the Europeans had no clue about, including the decimal system and a number of departures in trigonometry. These moved through globalization from East to West, just as science and technology easily move today from West to East. Europe would have been as silly to turn down wisdom coming from the East as the East would be today to turn down wisdom coming from the West. So despite the inequality of power, my first point is that you have to really see the positive contribution that a global movement of ideas—of knowledge and understanding—makes.

The second point is that economic globalization itself could be a source of major advancement of living conditions, and it often is. The main difficulty is that the circumstances in which it produces the maximum benefits for poorer people do not exist now. This is not, however, an argument for being against global economic contact, but rather an argument for working toward a better division of benefits from global economic contact.

It is not, by and large, the case that as a result of globalization the poor are getting poorer and the rich are getting richer, which is the rhetoric that is often used, and which I believe is mistaken. It may have happened in a few countries, but by and large this is not the case. The relative success or failure of globalization should not be measured by whether the poor are getting a little richer; the question is: could they have become a lot richer by the same process if the governing circumstances were different? And the answer is yes. This requires both national and local policies like advancing educational arrangements, particularly school education, advancing basic health care, advancing gender equity, undertaking land reforms. It can also be helped by a more favorable global trade situation and more equitable economic arrangements, for example, better access to the markets in the richer countries, which would help the poorer countries to benefit more from global economic contact. For that, patent laws have to be reexamined, arrangements have to be made whereby the richer countries are welcoming to commodities coming from poorer countries, and so on. Globalization can become more equitable and effective through these changes. So the issue is not whether economic globalization is ruining people. It may not be doing that, and yet it can actually benefit people much more—and this is the central issue—than it is doing now.

The third point is that the market economy is just one institution among many. Even though there is no such thing today as global democracy, one can still have an impact on these questions by speaking out and having one's voice heard: the practice of any kind of democracy is primarily about public reasoning. If, for example, the World Bank and the IMF have changed, they have in part been responding to plentiful criticisms that have come from different parts of the world. So one should not think of global democracy just as institutional global government. It is also the fostering of public reasoning—critical public reasoning. Happily, under Kofi Annan's leadership, the UN has often been able to be a vehicle for the expression of certain types of critiques that otherwise might not have received that attention. Newspapers, the media in general, play that part. The expansion of information technology, most notably the Internet, as well as the availability of news across the world—CNN or BBC or whatever—make a contribution to what I would call "global speech" and through that help to advance the pursuit of global democracy.

In order to make the division of benefits from globalization more favorable, there is something we can all do: we can pay attention to it, speak about it, and holler about it. That is a very important thing to do right now. Silence is a powerful enemy of social justice.

Martha Nussbaum has elaborated on your work and expanded the list of universal human capabilities to include issues such as being able to express "justified anger" and having "opportunities for sexual satisfaction." Do you believe there are limits to such an approach? In other words, is this not too subjective a conception of an allegedly objective way of measuring universal human well-being?

This is a difficult but excellent question. In terms of what we desire and what we regard to be important in our lives, our thinking must enter into that evaluation; to look for something that would be untouched by the human mind would be a mistake. On the other hand, the fact that it emanates from our thinking process does not indicate that the process itself would lack objectivity. Objectivity in matters of valuation and judgment demands open and unrestrained critique—it demands public reasoning and challenging discussion. If there is one thing that we have learned from the progress in political philosophy over the last half a century—to a great extent led by John Rawls—it is that objectivity in ethics and in political philosophy is basically linked to the need to subject beliefs and proposals to the scrutiny of public debates and discussions. What priority—if any—to give to any capability, like expressing justified anger, must depend on the valuations that emerge from critical assessment. Given everything else, if we could express "justified anger" that others too see as reasonable (this is the central exercise in the search for "truth and reconciliation" in contemporary South African politics), it would obviously be a good exercise of a significant capability. Similarly, if there are opportunities for sexual satisfaction involving consenting adults, there should be no particular reason to object to it. Difficulties arise only when one good thing conflicts with another. Then it is a question of relative evaluation, and that is where the discipline of public scrutiny of contentious matters comes in.

When, at a point of particular repression in British India, Mahatma Gandhi was asked by a journalist in London what he thought of British civilization, Gandhi replied, "It would be a good idea." That certainly was a quiet expression of critical anger (even if expressed rather gently), but objective public assessment could yield the conclusion that this anger was indeed justified (most people even in Britain today would accept that). It would have been a serious loss of freedom for Gandhi if the liberty to express such anger, under considerable provocation, were to be denied.

Martha Nussbaum has been a major contributor to the literature on capabilities. She has made the whole field much more vibrant as well as accessible. She has also created the context in which this field is taken seriously into account not by economists alone, but philosophers as well, and social scientists generally. We do, of course, have some differences on how the capability approach is to be used. Martha is more inclined to get use out of an agreed list of capabilities, whereas my leaning has been toward taking the relevant lists to be contingent on public discussion, and variable with context and circumstances. It is not a big difference, and I do see clearly the advantage of working with a preeminent list of capabilities (as Martha does) for many exercises, such as the assertion of human rights of the most basic kind.

On the other side, we come to learn the importance of some capabilities through intense public discussion. We learn certain things over time that we may not have known earlier—public discussion may bring this about. Just to give an example from the field of gender equity (since the issue of gender often comes up in this context), consider the understanding that women being induced to stick to their traditional role in the family may itself involve an oppression, even though they have accepted that role with little protest over thousands of years. This recognition is a new learning that has emanated to a great extent from the work of feminists and from public discussions based on new scrutiny. Similarly, the idea that neglecting women's identity in language (referring to everyone as a man) is not just a rhetorical problem, but is a part of a real deprivation of freedom, is again a new understanding. Now if one were listing the parameters of women's freedoms in the 1940s, I do not think these would have emerged as factors of great importance, because people did not fully understand the reach of these freedoms. We are always learning, and that is one of the reasons why public reasoning is so important.

Circumstances are also changing. Say for India, Pakistan, and Bangladesh today: people's ability to communicate with each other through e-mail or the Internet is a new development. Being able to communicate with each other has now become possible with the new electronic media, and it is important in terms of economic, social, and political relations. Again in the 1940s' list, this would not have figured because the capability in question was not easy to imagine then.

So we have to treat the list of capabilities as something that is not final and fixed, but which is contextual and dependent on the nature of the exercise and also on the extent of our understanding, based on public discussion. The Human Development Index of the United Nations uses capabilities in a very minimal form, but it has its value still, in its particular context. Martha Nussbaum too has made excellent use of a particular list of capabilities that made good sense for her evaluative exercise on gender equity and on human rights.

In Development as Freedom *you say, "It is the power of reason that allows us to consider our obligations and ideals as well as our interests and advantages. To deny this freedom of thought would amount to a severe constraint on the reach of our rationality." Having just emerged from a blood-drenched century with a widespread faith in human reason and evolutionary progress, how are you so optimistic about the possibilities enabled by rationality?*

Well, the bloodstains that you see were not, in fact, the results of exercising reasoning—indeed just the contrary. Whatever the Nazis in Germany could be credited with, it could not be said that they were impeccable models of human reasoning, nor great practitioners of open public discussion. The idea that there are whole groups of people, like Jews and gypsies, who are best exterminated cannot but offend elementary human reasoning in a major way. The same thing can be said of nearly all the blood-drenched events and experiences that occurred in the last century. There is often a peculiarly mistaken diagnosis suggesting that somehow it is the celebration of reason in the Enlightenment, beginning in the mid-eighteenth century, that is responsible for the Nazi concentration camps, the Japanese prisoner of war camps, and the Hutu violence against Tutsis in Rwanda. I really do not see why people take that view because these are quintessential examples of people being driven by passion rather than by reason. In fact reason could have played a major part in moderating such turmoil. When a Hutu, for instance, is being told that he is just a Hutu and he ought to kill Tutsis on grounds that Tutsis are an enemy lot, a Hutu could reason that he is not only a Hutu but also a Rwandan, an African, a human being, and all these identities make some demands on his attention. It is reason that could stand up against the imposition of unreasoned identities on people (such as, "You are just a Hutu and nothing else").

As a child, I saw the Hindu-Muslim riots in the 1940s, and I know how easy it is to make people forget their reasoning and the understanding of the basic plurality of their identities in favor of one fierce identity, whether fiercely Hindu or fiercely Muslim. There again the appeal has to be to reason. Indeed, precisely because we have emerged from such a blood-drenched century, it is extraordinarily important to fight for reason—to celebrate it, to defend it, and to help expand its reach.

It has been suggested that part of the reason for the form that religious movements have taken in much of the Third World, and in India's case specifically, has to do with the way in which these movements, integral to the anticolonial nationalist struggle, were repressed in the immediate aftermath of independence because they were seen to be inconsistent with the modern constitutional state. Are you familiar with this argument? Would you agree that this genealogy complicates the standard liberal secularist line?

I am familiar with the argument and I believe it to be false. I don't think anything like that happened. In those places where religion was given a bigger range in politics, for example in Pakistan, it is not the case that this had the effect of strengthening the secular bases of the society—quite the contrary.

Colonialism imprisons the mind. But the colonized mind often takes a deeply dialectical form. One of the forms that the colonized mind takes is rabid anti-Westernism: you judge the world in terms of having been dominated by the West for a hundred years or more, and this can become the overarching concern, drowning all other identities and priorities. Suddenly, for example, activist Arab Muslims might become persuaded that they must see themselves as people who are trying to settle scores with the West, and all other affiliations and associations are unimportant. The whole tradition of Arab science, Arab mathematics, Arab literature, music, painting would then have lost their informing and identifying role. That is the result of a colonized mind because you forget everything else other than your relation with the former colonial masters. I would link the outburst of some of the violence we see today to a deeply misguided reaction to colonialism; it is certainly not unconnected with colonialism.

When the Muslim kingdoms ran the centers of civilization in the old world, from Spain and Morocco to India to Indonesia, there was no feverish need to define oneself in negative terms, as being against something, seeing oneself as what my friend Akeel Bilgrami calls "the Other" ("We are not Western!"). This is because being Muslim or Arab at that time involved a very positive identity. They had a philosophy, they had an interest in science, they had interest in their own work, they had interest in other people's work. The Greek works—such as Aristotle and Plato—survived in the Arab world in a way they had not in Europe. Hindu mathematics became known in the Christian West mainly through Muslim Arab authors who translated them from Sanskrit, from which Latin translations were made. At the time when the Muslim kingdoms were in command over the world, there was no need for them to define themselves in negative terms as "the Other." We see a similar attempt to raise the banner of "Asian values" today—it was very strong in the 1990s—when East and Southeast Asia try to "Westernize" feverishly. These are particular reflections of the colonized mind.

You have noted how India has not suffered famine-related hunger since decolonization—given its vibrant democracy and free press—but has, on the other hand, not fared as well in dealing with endemic hunger, widespread mal/undernourishment, and high levels of illiteracy. How would you account for this? Do you believe there are structural impediments to reform, either nationally or globally? Is the existing form of liberal democracy—however informed in terms of participation, periodic elections, and so on—sufficient to guarantee change?

Again an excellent question. No institution is ever adequate on its own; everything depends on what use we make of these institutions. There is no substitute for political and social engagement. The success of India in preventing famines is an easy success because famines are extremely easy to politicize: all you have to do is to print a picture of an emaciated mother and a dying child on the front page and that in itself is a sting-ing editorial. It does not require much reflection. But in order to bring quiet but widespread hunger to public attention, in order to publicize the debilitating effects of lack of schooling and illiteracy, and similarly the long-term deprivations of not having land reform, you need a great deal more engagement and use of imagination.

The Indian practice of democracy in this respect has been relatively modest, and success has been relatively moderate. Though I would say here again that things are changing; for example, issues of women's inequality received almost no attention in the media and in the political process until recently. This has changed now. It would have been very hard to think even twenty or thirty years ago that one of the serious concerns in the Indian parliament would be the ways and means of making sure that at least one-third of the members of parliament are women. This kind of issue had not come up earlier at all. So I think it is a question of what we can make of the institutions of democracy. When you need more democ-racy by practicing it more, to say that democracy is at fault and let us have less democracy is to move exactly in the wrong direction.

There is a paper of mine that recently appeared in the *New York Review of Books* on India and China ("Passage to China," December 2, 2004). I address this issue there. I also point out why I think that China is now suffering a certain amount from not having a democratic, multi-party system. That is, the Chinese made major progress early on because of a visionary political leadership after the revolution. In terms of social change and progress in school education and health, they did much bet-ter than India even though they had a gigantic famine (they kept on making mistakes of that kind), but the basic commitment to universal school education and health care and employment for women served China extremely well. Much better than India's more hesitant process of democracy did.

On the other hand, if you look at the results today, despite the fact that since the economic reforms of 1979 Chinese economic growth has been much faster than India's, life expectancy in India has grown about three times as fast as that in China. To a great extent, this is connected with the avenues of public discussion and criticism that a democratic system provides to the health services. We know how terrible the Indian health services are, but the fact that we know it and the newspapers are constantly discussing it makes it hard for those things to continue in the way they could in a system that does not encourage public criticism.

In 1979 Chinese life expectancy was fourteen years longer than India's; today it is seven years longer. Some parts of the country, like Kerala, are now four years ahead of China in terms of life expectancy. Another comparison to look at: in 1979 China and Kerala both had exactly the same infant mortality rates—37 per 1,000. By now, while the Chinese have cut that down from 37 to 30, in Kerala the infant mortality rate has come down from 37 to 10—a third of the Chinese number. Kerala has the advantage here of combining, on the one hand, the kind of radicalism that helped the Chinese make immediate progress in the early years after their revolution, and on the other, the benefits of a multiparty democratic system.

The main point to appreciate is that what we make of democracy depends to a great extent on how much we are ready to put into it. One of the really big issues for me in India is that the intellectuals who could play a big role in the democratic political system tend, by and large, not to go into politics. They often regard that as a shady affair. To some extent that is changing, but it requires a much more dramatic change and much greater engagement to make a fuller success of democracy in India. There is also a strong need for the politics of the underdogs—involving the poorer sections and the lower castes—to be less divisive and more united in confronting old inequalities that still survive. This is one of the tasks, along with many others, that democratic practice has to address.

TWO I Helena Norberg-Hodge

You have said elsewhere that one "has to go back to precolonialism to understand development. Colonialism is part and parcel of a process which was later on called development." Could you please elaborate on this? What precisely are you talking about when you say development?

I'm talking about development as it was conceived following the Second World War, a program that was designed to lift people out of poverty; this is how it was perceived by the general public as well as by its authors. But what development entailed was essentially pursuing the same policies that had started under colonialism: for example, encouraging production for trade, as opposed to production for home needs. What happened under colonialism was that powers from Europe moved across the entire globe in search of resources, and they used force, and as we know, even killing, slaughtering, enslaving people, or carrying them to another part of the world, to work in monocultures for export. In the Western world, we came to identify countries according to what resource they provided for the center; so whole countries became tin countries, coffee countries, and so on.

These economic policies continued after the Second World War, following independence and formal decolonization, under the name of development. After independence, the colonial leaders left but were replaced by a local elite who had been trained to pursue the same policies. So if we look carefully at what happened to resources, to agriculture, or to money, we will find that fundamentally the same basic formula was used: encouraging larger- and larger-scale monocrops and encouraging production for export and import. So what was thought at that time in the development era (as it is today in the name of globalization) was that if you promote export-import you'll be better off. This goes back to the belief that the principle of comparative advantage is accurate, that this is the way to create prosperity. On the surface it has a great deal of appeal for many reasons.

First, local populations around the world have always identified goods from the outside with luxury, quite understandably, because they were a luxury: it was once the case that prices reflected the fact that goods had been carried halfway across the world (whether it was fine cotton or tea in Europe or turquoise in places like Ladakh). These were considered as luxuries, and local people were very happy to have them. So when you promote trade as a fundamental of economic development, it is quite easy to persuade people that this is going to be in their interest.

Second, this makes a lot of sense because no part of the world can produce everything that it would like to have, and so it appears as though increasing trade will increase prosperity and well-being. However, we should have noticed, even after the colonial era, that such a fundamental restructuring of the economy, particularly in food, was actually very damaging and created a lot of suffering and poverty while generating wealth for a tiny minority.

Is it not the case that you base most of your assumptions about what constitutes development, and more importantly, what its consequences are, on your experiences in Ladakh? But Ladakh, you must concede, is rather an anomaly, in the sense that it neither was colonized nor had a very large or heterogeneous population. How can you extrapolate from that to the rest of the South?

What Ladakh can help us do is to see what an economy can look like when it hasn't been colonized. In this way Ladakh is very important because it shows that in an area of very scarce resources, there is a remarkably high standard of living. An area geared toward fulfilling the basic needs of its population, and relegating trade to a secondary position, creates a prosperous local economy, and trade adds to it, which is the way it should be (which is also why we are in no way opposed to trade; we are opposed to economies enslaving themselves to the traders).

Let me go back to what I said about development and colonialism. It is important to keep in mind that when this process of Europe moving out across the world and seeing the whole world as its resource-base happened, governments favored and worked with large companies that were already very powerful. But because governments worked with them and aided and abetted trade, they were aiding and abetting the traders. So what we had was a process whereby these giant corporations became so powerful that they were able to help encourage and shape policy.

In effect when local, regional, national economies keep favoring trade, they are favoring the traders at the expense of the local producers and consumers. And since traders are in a much smaller number than the local producers and consumers, they are actually favoring a minority. That minority becomes so mobile that it becomes very hard to control its activities and its accumulation of wealth. Structurally it is actually a very shortsighted and counterproductive policy for nation-states to pursue.

What Ladakh offers us is a living example of what is possible if a country focuses on helping itself and its own people and uses trade to benefit them rather than benefiting the traders. Ladakh is a remarkable and powerful example because it is an exceptional area. It has very scarce resources, a harsh climate, and only a four-month growing season. Due to the harsh climate conditions, the yields in Ladakh in terms of agriculture were not as high as in many parts of India at the time that the conquistadors and colonials arrived. In India, there were areas where yields were as high as ten tons a hectare; in Ladakh they were on average three tons a hectare. Ladakh proves that even in such difficult circumstances people were very well off because their economic priorities were different.

When I criticize development, however, I am in no way basing it just on Ladakh. I am basing it on a mass of evidence from around the world, of the poverty that has been created, of the hardship and the madness of promoting the same formula (of trade for the sake of trade) without considering its wider or long-term implications.

As I am sure you know, a number of people argue that positions such as yours in fact deprive poor people of the "choice" to develop or not. Why, for instance, would a subsistence farmer continue wanting to be a subsistence farmer if s/he could instead own a VCR, potentially quadruple household income, and move out of a rural area into an urban one? How do you respond to these sorts of critiques?

I think it's very important that we start taking responsibility for what policies and changes will benefit the majority rather than looking at what an individual would do under current circumstances. If I were a subsistence farmer and I were offered VCRs and a nice standard of living in the city, I would certainly take it, and I don't blame any farmer for opting to do that. What I'm talking about, whether in Ladakh or here, is that we, as societies and concerned citizens, need to look at where these policies are taking us collectively. I do find that even subsistence farmers today respond when you provide information that shows that moving into the city in search of the VCR is not leading to prosperity for the vast majority.

The evidence is now so abundant—and frightening—because millions of farmers are being uprooted with the promise of having that lovely, consumer lifestyle, and we know that in many cases not even 10 percent achieve that goal. The remaining 90 percent, without any doubt, ultimately settle for a lower standard of living. When they leave the village, they are leaving a relatively secure source of food, water, and community. Conditions are not ideal in most rural areas of the so-called Third World (terrible poverty following generations of colonialism, monocropping, an exploding population, to give only a few indicators), but they are vastly better than in most urban slums.

I think it is very important that we keep in mind now that by offering the dream of a consumer lifestyle to people we are being fraudulent because we know that the numbers do *not* add up. We also know that the consumer lifestyle is one that requires that you use more than your fair share of resources. This is a formula that can never fulfill its promise, so we really owe it to ourselves and to other people to speak the truth: to say that if you choose to leave the village, you are leaving the security of being able to perhaps grow a few potatoes, have help from friends and family, and manage somehow. You are moving into a much more anonymous situation, a situation where even your food has to be imported. This means—for those of us who are concerned about the environment—that in slums, even the slum-dweller depends on imported food, which means that CO_2 emissions go up. With millions of people leaving their lands for the slums, CO_2 emissions are skyrocketing. We have to realize that the increase in CO_2 emissions in the South is the consequence of "slumification." By pursuing such policies, we are increasing the environmental burden and poverty at the same time.

Development policies today are fundamentally urbanizing. They are destroying the livelihoods of small farmers, fishermen, and small-scale producers and are responsible for centralizing them into these urban sprawls and slums. This is a consequence of *policy*, not a consequence of overpopulation. Overpopulation has nothing to do with urbanization because one has a better chance of building something that is workable in the village than in the city.

You have said elsewhere that "the most important reason for the breakdown of traditional cultures is the psychological pressure to modernize." Could you please elaborate on this?

The breakdown of local economies and cultures occurs at two levels, the structural and the psychological. I see them as equally important, and the problem is that they operate simultaneously so that together they are a tremendous force on people.

At the structural level, government policies offer jobs, education, benefits, health care, and energy resources in the urban centers, while in the villages most of these facilities are not offered, or if they are, they are of inferior quality. So this attracts people into urban areas. At the same time, economic policies that promote trade for the sake of trade destroy marketing opportunities for rural people, destroy their economies so they are economically forced out of their villages.

Simultaneously, at the psychological level, you have media, advertising, even schooling, promoting the notion that the future is urban, the future is, in effect, a Western consumer lifestyle. This lifestyle is associated with looking like a white European, eating European-style food, wearing European-style clothes, and, worst of all, having the skin color, eye color, manners, and language of a European. The end result is that young children are being made to feel that their own language, their own skin color, their own way of being is inferior. I have witnessed this very closely in Ladakh, and it is in no way an anomaly. We have ample evidence that millions of people around the world experience it in the same way. They have translated my book and video, *Ancient Futures*, into more than thirty-five languages; they use it regularly at the grassroots to raise awareness. Even though the book is about Ladakh, many people have responded by saying that the story of Ladakh is our story too.

This psychological pressure that I witnessed so closely in Ladakh literally led, in a very short time, to young people feeling that they, as individuals and as members of a culture, were inferior and inadequate. It was a tragedy to see that, particularly because it was so stark.

Ladakh again offers an opportunity to understand a process that in several parts of the world took many years, because in Ladakh they were shielded from the influence of the outside world and so it all happened very suddenly. When I first arrived and learned to speak the language, the level of self-respect and dignity was higher than in any other culture I had ever experienced. There were all sorts of indicators that make this indisputable, for instance, the complete absence or low incidence of suicide, aggression, and depression.

But then very quickly, after a whole barrage of changes (tourism, advertising, media), it became clear that young people got the impression that in Western modern society, people had almost infinite leisure, almost infinite wealth, and incredible power, and they found the culture their parents were offering them silly, useless and backward. Everything in education and in the media was reinforcing this. So they developed a shame for being who they are and their skin color (young women now use a dangerous skin-lightening cream called Fair & Lovely). The sale of contact lenses around the world is going up everyday. Often advertisements in Thailand, South America, India, carry the message: "Have the eye color you wish you had been born with." That is blue, of course.

It is a disaster, a tragedy, and we need to work together and support each other in our identities. We also need to recognize that what I witnessed in Ladakh in terms of loss of self-respect is just as serious in the heart of the Western world. In Sweden where I grew up, blonde, blue-eyed girls are developing terrible complexes, often around being slim. Eating disorders are increasing rapidly; six-year-old girls are saying they hate their bodies. So this is a universal problem, which is why we must work together to understand that a homogeneous, consumer culture is denying all of us the right to accept ourselves the way we are. Right now the typical Coca-Cola advertisement takes great pride in promoting multiculturalism; often they have people with black skin color or black hair and include Asian women, and white women, all together as one happy family. The imagery is still of a consumer lifestyle, and that is at the heart of the problem because human beings are looking at a standard of perfection they can't emulate. Children need to have real live role models because real live role models never have perfect eyes and perfect teeth and perfect bodies; they are just human beings.

You have also suggested that development policies as they are currently constituted cannot but amplify people's increasingly besieged sense of identity, thus creating the conditions for identity-based conflict (ethnic, sectarian, religious, etc.). Could you explain how and why this is the case? To cite only one example in support of your argument: the violence that occurred in central Kalimantan in Indonesia in early 2001, where the indigenous population of Dayaks were

killing Madurese migrants who moved to the area as a result of a government
program aimed, ostensibly, at reducing population pressure in Java.

Fundamentally there is a link between policies that promote trade for
the sake of trade and policies that promote a centralization of the demographic pattern, or urbanization. As I mentioned before, the entire infrastructure is set up to contribute to both urbanization and globalization in
terms of increased trade. If you have a completely decentralized population, it becomes, from the point of view of the traders, very hard to deliver
Coca-Cola and McDonalds everywhere. Structurally the dynamic is to
further this concentration of population.

Equally structural and endemic to the system is using more and more
technology instead of human labor—using fossil fuel and other forms of
finite energy and fueling more and more technologies to take the place
of human labor.

These three factors together—policies that favor trade for the sake of
trade, urbanization, and the use of technology instead of human labor—
create a system (and this is particularly evident in the South) where small-
scale producers, producing for a local economy, are being decimated economically and shoved into slums. Simultaneously, as I mentioned before,
their identities are threatened. In urban centers, jobs are very limited,
space is limited (the price of land shoots up), so suddenly, these people
find themselves in a highly difficult and competitive situation (people are
forced to fight for accommodation, for jobs, etc.). The entire process is one
of centralizing power and control.

In addition, what is happening everywhere around the world—I don't
think there are any exceptions—is that the people in power will tend
to favor their own kind. Now this still goes on in the West, but in the
West, the boundaries of my own kind and others are not so clear. In the
South people are often associated with community identity, either ethnic or religious. These ethnic and religious divisions mean that people in
power clearly favor their own group, and the other groups become more
and more disenfranchised and often more and more violent. I have seen
this as a pattern in many places, and I can report that whether it is the
Buddhist government in Bhutan vis-à-vis Hindus, or the Muslim-led
government in Kashmir, or the Hindu-dominated government in India,
it is the same pattern. So it is very important that we don't identify particular ethnic or religious groups as being the problem and that we look
instead at the structures and see what happens when power is centralized in this way.

Another factor is the centralization of jobs. This is true even in the West; if you want a job in America or in England or Sweden, the job centers are diminishing in number. In England, for instance, jobs are centralized in London, Bristol, and a few other cities. As a result, populations are being pulled in that direction, some of them traveling four hours a day in one direction because they can't afford to live near their jobs.

There is another aspect to this problem which is that poor labor is pulled in to do the dirty work; again a pattern that I have seen in Sweden, in America, and even in Ladakh, where the dirtiest jobs will be done by the most impoverished in the region, or from the periphery. In the case of Ladakh, there are Nepalis and Biharis coming to build the roads, clean the lavatories, etc. These are often people who have to leave their families, often young men, who come on their own, are often not very happy, will often drink more, and will often be those responsible for crime and violence. It is vital that we realize that this has *nothing* to do with racial or religious characteristics; it is simply a pattern among the marginalized in conditions of extreme structural inequality.

The systems of destruction must be understood so that we can find levers and points to change them, and it is quite evident to me that we need to decentralize rather than centralize, localize instead of globalize. The economic dynamic we have now is leading to an uprooting and to displacement of populations at an ever-escalating rate.

Once you threaten a local population's integrity with enough instability and enough pressure from the outside, it will lead to conflict and friction. We must also not forget that this pressure is combined with very intensified competition for scarce jobs. This is making it impossible for people to coexist. I believe that most of the violence we are seeing in the world today has to do with this structural problem. It does not have to do with any group's innate tendency for friction or intolerance.

How do you think IMF and World Bank policies fit into all this? What is the impact of these policies on the South?

IMF and World Bank policies have been fundamental to this whole process. They were established to further this process of so-called development, that is, furthering exactly the problems I've been talking about (centralizing jobs, particularly by subsidizing and encouraging centralized energy infrastructures; aiding a process whereby technology is made artificially cheap and human labor is driven up in price, and therefore human beings and their labor are marginalized; and encouraging urbanization and trade for the sake of trade). These are the structural features of their policies.

As fundamental to the process as the World Bank and the IMF was the General Agreement on Tariffs and Trade, the GATT, which was set up at the same time and was specifically intended to increase trade. What the World Bank was saying was helping to build up infrastructure, and the IMF was helping to provide the money to keep this going. There have also been export-import banks, or export credit agencies (ECAs), that have been helping this process.

At the same time, it is important to look at these policies without demonizing any individual institution or any individuals. The system we have inherited goes back so far that there are not very many people who have looked carefully at its dynamic; many people who have promoted this kind of development have sincerely believed that it was the only way to eradicate poverty. This remains true to this day.

However, after a while, one expects people in power to be willing to listen to the problems that these policies have created, and this is getting a bit frustrating now. The information gap is widening, and in a way we have less communication than we used to. I am hoping there will be more public debates between people who favor continuing in the same direction and those who oppose it. We have found that it is difficult to get the real powers-that-be to engage in serious debates about such issues.

Does development have to mean "destruction" (to use your words)? What would a more socially, ethically, and environmentally responsible development consist in?

I certainly think we can reserve the word "development" for positive change, for something we would like to see. I think it is not only possible, but absolutely necessary, that people experience positive change that we can call development (particularly those in the South, who have been ravaged for so many years by destructive policies in the name of "development").

There are a few points I would like to make. First, we must realize that institutions and elites in both North and South owe a debt to the poor. We need to move beyond this old analysis of North and South and understand that the peoples and structures that have furthered this development are now in both North and South.

Second, new policies need to look at reversing processes of centralization and urbanization (both prompted by an emphasis on trade for the sake of trade). We urgently need to be looking at a reduction in trade and emphasizing the building up of healthy local economies, particularly when it comes to food and farming. This will lead to food security and diversified production so that local populations can have an adequate and wide-ranging diet. I am convinced that investing in local economies will cost far less money than current policies. It will require less energy, but it will require energy that is decentralized, so we need to build up decentralized energy infrastructures.

Third, particularly in the South today, one of the most rapid transformations can be brought about if we help to build up a decentralized, renewable energy infrastructure. This must be done using renewable energy, emphasizing the fact that there cannot be one panacea, so we must look at the possibility of using water, wind, and solar energy together. We worked for twenty years with that in Ladakh, we know it costs less money, we know it is feasible, but there is almost no funding for it anywhere in the world today. This is an urgent priority for a healthier development.

Fourth, we also urgently need to realize that in order to build up such a decentralized development there needs to be more attention paid to the fact that every ecosystem, every village, every bit of soil is different from every other bit. So there needs to be a shift toward developing research, and science and technology, that is more related to place, that builds on diversity and strengthens diversity, while of course continuing international information exchange. The problem is that the information exchange we have today is essentially about exporting and imposing *one* standardized Western model. This model was based on having the whole world as a resource base, so it is a completely unreplicable model, which is why, everywhere it goes, it can only create a tiny wealthy elite and poverty for the rest. The model that could work is one that builds on diversity.

In Ladakh, for instance, just by introducing greenhouses, we managed to increase diversified production by a huge factor. They now have green vegetables in the winter, which they did not have before. So the potential for regions to produce a wide range of wonderful foods is enormous if we move away from this centralized, top-down model and help this more decentralized and diversified economic model to flourish.

THREE I Sanjay Reddy

In a widely publicized and rather controversial paper you coauthored with philosopher Thomas Pogge entitled "How Not to Count the Poor," you argued that the World Bank's global poverty estimates were based on methodology that is deeply flawed. Could you elaborate here what the main problems are with World Bank calculations?

Thomas Pogge and I identified in our paper a number of deficiencies in the approach to global poverty estimates of the World Bank, varying in their nature and importance. However, I think it is fair to say that there is a single, central flaw that is the underpinning of all, or almost all, of the diverse problems that beset the Bank's approach. This single underlying flaw is that the Bank does not start with a criterion for identifying the poor that is adequately related to whether a person has resources that are sufficient to achieve their basic requirements. In the language that I prefer, the Bank does not start with a criterion for identifying the poor that is related to elementary human capabilities: the ability to achieve certain basic forms of being and doing, as Amartya Sen would put it. Some of these forms of being and doing, for instance, the ability to be adequately nourished, are income-dependent, and others, such as the ability to breathe clean air, are not directly income-dependent. But certainly, even those latter achievements may be indirectly income-dependent in the sense that one's ability to breathe clean air may depend on one's ability to rent a home in an area that is free of aerial pollutants. The extent to which different elementary capabilities of human beings depend on possessing adequate income varies, but that income is an important means toward many of these ends is clear.

So even if we focus narrowly on income poverty, as the World Bank does in its global income poverty statistics, there is still a requirement to root that concept of income poverty in some understanding of what the real requirements of human beings are. The main problem with the World Bank's approach is that it starts with what we call a money-metric approach rather than an approach that is centered on basic human requirements. The money-metric approach of the World Bank begins with an arbitrarily delineated poverty line (of $1 and $2 per day) as defined in abstract purchasing power parity (PPP) units. There are at least two immediate problems that arise as a result of this approach. The first is that neither $1 nor $2 a day is sufficient to meet the basic requirements of human beings in many countries of the world, and certainly not in the currency of the base country in relation to which those poverty lines are defined, namely, the United States. Beyond that, the appropriate translation of these international poverty lines into local currency units is something that cannot be determined because there is no abstract equivalence between currency units. It is a conceptual error to think that there exists such an abstract equivalence. I can answer the question, "What does it cost to buy a bag of basmati rice in Karachi and what does it cost to buy an identical bag of basmati rice on Lexington Avenue in New York?" Or I can answer the question, "What does it cost to buy a certain brand and make of mobile phone in Karachi and what does it cost to buy that brand and make of mobile phone on Lexington Avenue in New York?" I can find out the relative number of currency units that I would require to purchase each of these different kinds of goods in the two places, but I cannot answer the question in general of what number of rupees in Pakistan should be deemed equivalent to a dollar. The answer to the question always depends on the identification of the end toward which the resources are meant to be put. Stating this a little more sharply, then, the number of rupees that ought to be deemed equivalent to a dollar from the standpoint of achieving adequate nourishment or buying the basic foodstuffs that are required to achieve adequate nourishment may be very different from the number of rupees that should be deemed equivalent to a dollar when they are put to the purpose of, for instance, maintaining the standard of living of an executive who may be posted in one city or another.

So the Bank's notion that there is an abstract rate of equivalence between currencies that can be applied in poverty analysis is simply a conceptual mistake. In fact the identification of what is the rate of equivalence that is appropriate to employ in the context of poverty assessment depends on having some underlying criterion for identifying the poor, and in particular, some idea as to what poverty is and what is needed to avoid it.

We think that there is really no escape from anchoring any kind of poverty assessment, whether at the national level or at the international level, in some conception of the basic requirements of human beings. We think that the abstract money-metric approach that the World Bank has applied is fundamentally misguided in that it does not do so, and it runs into diverse methodological and substantive problems as a result.

Your text has received some response from the World Bank. Could you tell me what you made of that?

We received an early response from Martin Ravallion, the staff member in the World Bank who is most directly responsible for the production of its global poverty estimates. He, in our view, although a very sincere person, failed to engage with most of our central criticisms in his response. Our view is also that in the intervening five years or so since we first articulated these criticisms, although there has been considerable worldwide interest in these criticisms, the World Bank has not made any serious effort to respond to them. Certainly it has not made any effort to involve us and other critics in an attempt to produce superior poverty estimates.

The Bank's approach has been very much one of trying to defend what it has already been doing. That is perhaps not entirely surprising in the context of the political economy and the politics of such institutions: once they commit themselves to a particular course of action, they invest a great deal of reputational capital in that, and of course a large part of their authority comes from the appearance that they possess technical expertise that is superior to that which is possessed by others. We therefore are not entirely surprised by the failure to confront our criticisms and to provide serious counterarguments or alternatively to revise the methodology that is applied in accordance with those criticisms. We do think that it is very unfortunate. Ultimately a subject of *this* importance—how many poor people there are in the world, where they live, whether their numbers are increasing or decreasing—is one that ought not to be hostage to the interests of any one institution or group of persons within that institution. The sanitizing and clarifying role of sunlight, of bringing public attention to the methodological details of an exercise of this kind, which is very often otherwise treated as if it is purely technical and ought to be the preserve of technical experts alone, is something that is very important to do. We strongly believe that an exercise of this kind is really of general interest to the world's people and ought to be treated as such. It ought to emerge from a much more transparent and consultative process in an ongoing way. It is a source of some disappointment to us in this and other areas that the World Bank and other important development institutions often seem to have the first reflex of closing ranks and trying to provide justification for the practices to which they are already committed, rather than investigating what would be necessary to do things better.

More specifically, what alternative criteria and methodology for identifying the poor do you propose? And what global institution would you like to see assuming this responsibility?

We have proposed an alternative to the money-metric approach that is currently applied to determine estimates of global income poverty by the World Bank that is well within the reach of countries and indeed of international institutions. This alternative is to adopt an approach to poverty measurement in all countries that is centered on, or anchored in, a common conception of the basic human requirements. What we propose in particular is that at the global level there should be agreement on some conception of what are the relevant elementary capabilities that ought to be achieved by human beings in order for them to be deemed non-poor, and what are the characteristics of goods needed to promote these capabilities. The question should then be asked, "What are the income requirements of achieving those elementary human requirements in each country in the world?" The first principle is one that must be agreed upon at the global level through some appropriately transparent and consultative global process. It must also, to an extent, be stated abstractly so as to accommodate national diversity in an appropriate way. But the second requirement, actually to estimate the cost of achieving these basic requirements as articulated at the global level, is one that must be undertaken at the national and subnational level. Our view is that both parts of this process should be done in a participatory and consultative manner to the extent feasible, while being appropriately informed by relevant expertise.

Poverty lines that are established in this way in each country will *automatically* have a common interpretation across countries because they will have been constructed on the basis of such a common interpretation. Moreover, this interpretation will be a meaningful one, and it will be one that will have been endorsed by the national and international public through an appropriate process. It may be objected that an approach of this kind, despite its conceptual simplicity, would be practically quite difficult to bring about because it requires that there be efforts in each country to establish poverty lines and to undertake poverty estimates that correspond to some common global understanding. Our response is that certainly it will require some period of time and some expenditure of resources to achieve this goal, but in our view this is not an inordinate obstacle. An example that we often offer and that we think is pertinent is that of the system of national accounts which the United Nations Statistics Division played a pioneering role in developing and which is used by almost every country in the world to produce national income and product accounts, and estimates of GDP. This achievement is an extraordinary one. When John Maynard Keynes wrote the *General Theory of Employment Interest and Money*, national income accounts of the kind we know today did not exist for any country. Today not only do national income accounts exist for many countries, indeed for almost every country in the world, but they have a common underlying conceptual basis for the most part. Moreover, they are the object of enormous attention, to the extent that the money markets quiver at small variations in the reported growth rate of GDP.

So the notion that coordination of poverty statistics (on the basis of a shared and meaningful conceptual foundation) is infeasible because it is too expensive or too logistically difficult or would be too time-consuming strikes us as false given the presence of this sort of historical example.

Another example we would offer to underline the idea that our approach is feasible is that there are today private consultancy firms and indeed nongovernmental entities such as the International Civil Service Commission that expend a modest quantity of resources every few years in doing surveys in various cities throughout the world to establish the cost of living in those cities. They do that in order to offer an appropriate basis for cost-of-living adjustments for executives of private, multinational corporations and for international civil servants. No one has ever complained that that exercise is too logistically difficult, time-consuming, or expensive to do. And indeed it has been done for a rather long period of time by more than one entity. One of the questions we would ask is why it is conceptually inappropriate or practically infeasible to do for poor people or for people who are potentially poor what we do every day for chief executives and international civil servants.

From your description it seems that such an initiative need not necessarily be coordinated by some global institution.

A degree of coordination is indispensable but coordination is not the same thing as top-down standards creation. Our conception of the process that would underpin the introduction of a more appropriate form of global poverty assessment is that it would be a dialectical one in which countries would bring to bear their respective perspectives on what constitute the relevant elementary capabilities as well as on what are the technical criteria that should be used to produce guidelines for national poverty assessments. We conceive of the process as being one in which there is a central coordinating body but there is also a great deal of input (certainly at the early stage) from national governments and in which there are degrees of freedom for national poverty assessment bodies or committees to interpret the guidelines in a manner that is appropriate to their individual case, while referring to the conception in order to maintain comparability and interpretability.

This central coordinating body you do not envision as being the World Bank since they would likely not be open to this kind of process?

From our perspective, we have no objection to any particular international institution providing the organizational or logistical support that this sort of a process would require. Our criticism of the $1 per day and $2 per day global poverty estimates is not fundamentally a criticism of the World Bank as an institution although the problems we point to certainly have origins in the flaws of that institution. It is a criticism of the way in which the Bank has gone about the task of global poverty assessment.

One important point I would make is that the International Comparison Program, which is the entity that has been constructing the purchasing power parity conversion factors that are used to characterize the rates of equivalence of currencies and which the World Bank uses in its poverty assessments, used to have its secretariat located in the United Nations. But that secretariat moved about a decade ago to the World Bank. One of the reasons that it moved is that the Bank had the financial resources that the United Nations lacked to support the secretariat. So the World Bank is already very actively involved in the production of global statistics of various kinds and has many more resources available for that purpose than the UN Statistics Division now does. That is not a reason for the World Bank to continue to have that privileged position necessarily, but it is certainly plausible that the Bank ought to have a role to play in the present environment.

What is indispensable is that the Bank should approach the problem with a greater degree of transparency and in a manner that does not allow a small number of people within that institution or any other institution effectively to decide how statistics will be produced. One of our recurrent themes has been that investment in the creation of statistics is systematically devalued but there is tremendous reliance on bad-quality statistics at the same time and that this has consequences. The cost of a program improving the quality of poverty statistics and other statistics related to human well-being is relatively small in relation to the potential harm that can be done by bad statistics or the potential benefit that could arise as a result of good statistics in forming assessments of national and world conditions and in guiding public discussions and choices.

One final point that I would make about our proposed alternative is that it does not constitute a substitute for what countries are already doing in the area of poverty assessment. On the contrary, our proposal offers a way for countries to improve the quality of their own national poverty statistics and at the same time make those poverty statistics internationally comparable. What we are proposing is simply that countries should construct poverty lines and should design their household surveys in a manner that permits international comparison of the income poverty statistics that are thus created. One could view our proposal as a proposal for the bolstering of the methodological and substantive basis of national poverty statistics with the bonus that the resulting national poverty statistics will be internationally comparable and will be susceptible to comparison and aggregation.

You have reviewed the most recent World Development Report *(2006) published by the World Bank and have pointed to a number of inadequacies from the point of view of developing countries. Did this report represent a significant departure from previous such reports? And could you elaborate what problems remain from the perspective of developing countries?*

As I commented in my review, the 2006 *World Development Report* (*WDR*), which was initially produced for the G-24 group of developing countries, was the product of what we might call the progressive face of the World Bank. In the last ten years or so, and certainly during the time that Jim Wolfensohn was the president of the World Bank, the Bank has shifted its substantive focus and its rhetoric toward many concerns that its critics have long emphasized, such as the importance of participation in development projects; the importance of attacking nontransparent and unaccountable government institutions; the importance of investing in human capabilities, in particular in the form of health and education; the importance of paying adequate heed to environmental concerns; and so on.

The subject of the 2006 *WDR* was equity and development. I was centrally concerned with the question of whether equity should be pursued as a means toward other development goals as well as an end in itself. The very asking of this question reflects the fact that the World Bank has very much evolved from the period in the 1980s when it was centrally dominated by economists, indeed by economists of a very particular stripe who would not generally have brooked a question of this kind let alone broached it. So from that standpoint I think this *World Development Report* ought to be commended. The report certainly contains many important points and some excellent proposals, which could be viewed as such by analysts outside of the bank including many of those who have criticized it for its past preoccupations and narrow concerns.

This having been said, the focus of the critical dimension of my review was that the *WDR* reads as if it was the product of an elaborate compromise between the orthodox and the more progressive elements within the Bank itself. For example, there is an extraordinary silence about many things that external observers would have thought it important to discuss, as well as very often rather simple-minded premises being exhibited. To give an example of the former, the *WDR* does not discuss at all the role of World Bank-sponsored policies in giving rise to increasing inequalities within countries and in some cases to increasing absolute deprivation. For example, the role of the World Bank in pushing for social sector reforms in many of the least developed countries (especially from the 1980s to the mid-1990s) was quite adverse. More specifically, the World Bank championed the introduction of user fees in the health and education sector, requiring that in some of the least developed countries in the world (for example in sub-Saharan Africa) users should be charged fees, which from their point of view were often prohibitive, for the use of primary health centers or for enrolment in primary schools. The Bank did an about-face on these issues in the late 1990s and now does not like to identify itself with its earlier positions, but the fact remains that many of the policy changes that were brought about in poor countries in the 1980s and the first half of the 1990s that could very plausibly be thought of as inequality-increasing or even deprivation-increasing were ones that the World Bank had a central hand in. Of course here I have referred to very specific sectoral policies, but there is also the broader question of the macroeconomic policies recommended by the Bretton Woods institutions and what role those policies were to play, especially in the early years when Structural Adjustment Programs were adopted in a relatively blind way without regard for the kind of protections and nuances that later came to be recognized as necessary to diminish their adverse impact on vulnerable persons. For the World Bank not even to mention this history in a report on equity seems to tell only half the truth. That is one example of the kind of blindnesses and errors in the report, and I do provide others in the review.

I also spoke of premises that are implicit. An example is that the report emphasizes the importance of private property rights protection throughout as a criterion for assessing the quality of national institutions but also calls for a more equitable distribution of assets as a way to provide for "starting gate equality"—which is to say for the ability of individuals to have adequate resources to enter the game of market competition and potentially to benefit from market opportunities. So on the one hand the Bank claims that to some degree adequate asset ownership is required in order to benefit from market competition, and on the other hand it views sound institutions as being those that protect private property rights in their present form and do relatively little to disturb them. Even if we agree that certain protections for private property rights may be very important from the standpoint of creating appropriate incentives for efficient resource use and resource accumulation, it is still plausible that egalitarian distributive policies are also required in order to create conditions where more individuals can have adequate resources to overcome the liquidity constraints, credit constraints, or other limitations that may prevent them from even becoming market participants in the first place. A concrete example of this schizophrenia is that the *WDR* praises China for having in place "initial conditions" that were relatively equitable and therefore created conditions for a large number of ordinary Chinese to participate in the market process once market-oriented liberalization began. On the other hand the *WDR* fails to recognize that these so-called initial conditions were the product of a national revolution that disturbed the preexisting regime of property rights. Without taking a view on the merits of that revolution, one can certainly recognize that there is some methodological inconsistency here.

I would not like to present a litany of the detailed respects in which I, as a particular external observer, might differ from the analysis presented by the authors of the *WDR*. It is well known that few people read the report, and it is certainly not a document that is especially lasting. There will be very little reason to read the 2006 *WDR* in 2010. So the important issue doesn't concern the details of the report's contents, although those do have an importance in the shaping of the global development discourse from year to year. The crucial issue concerns how the World Bank's resources, and global development resources more generally, are being spent. The question that I end my review of the *WDR* with is that of who the report actually serves. In my view, it doesn't very clearly serve the interests of the world's people, although it is fairly clear that it serves the interests of the World Bank and the World Bank staff. The World Bank has one of the largest research budgets—indeed, *the* largest research budget of any development institution. Its research budget in development studies dwarfs that of any academic institution and may be larger than the research expenditures of academic institutions considered collectively. However, almost all of the research that it does is constrained by the prevailing conceptions of what are important subjects of study and by the prevailing wisdom within the World Bank. There are internal politics that influence the kind of research that is deemed acceptable and that is supported and lauded. A very simple example that is widely known is that certain researchers who represent the most orthodox and conventional face of the World Bank have been rewarded repeatedly within the Bank. Whereas other researchers in the Bank, such as Branco Milanovic, who have been doing very interesting work that has brought about widespread attention outside of the Bank, have received few resources within the World Bank to conduct that work and certainly have not been internally lauded and promoted to the same degree. So there are systematic biases in the way in which the World Bank research establishment conducts itself.

The central question I would ask would be: Would these resources not be better expended if they were provided to independent development institutions undertaking independent development research in a decentralized manner? Why is competition in the production of development policy analyses not as good an elixir as competition in labor markets, credit markets, or goods markets is supposed to be, according to the wisdom of the World Bank? There is far too little competition in the production of development research, and, as we know, development research establishments in many developing countries have collapsed. I regret to say that to some extent they have collapsed precisely due to the visible hand of the World Bank. One example that I would provide is that many of the universities in sub-Saharan Africa that were once working relatively well and certainly were homes to a domestic intellectual class that was asking its own questions about development and producing very interesting research on development (for example Makerere University and the University of Dar-es-Salaam) have been gutted, in part because in the 1980s and the first half of the 1990s the prevailing wisdom in the World Bank was that expenditure on universities was regressive and that it supported the domestic elites rather than the poor of a country, and that it would thus be best to redirect expenditures within the education sector from universities to primary and secondary education. That point of view was superficially plausible, but it failed to recognize the many profound linkages between the existence of functioning universities, the existence of a domestically oriented and domestically rooted intellectual class, and the production of ideas and expertise within developing countries from which they could ultimately reap enormous benefit. Most importantly, the ability of countries to articulate a program of their own at both the abstract level and the level of detailed strategies depends on the existence of such a class. Indeed, many of these universities, which were once well functioning, have been reduced to consultancy mills because the faculty cannot afford to make a life for themselves without doing consultancies for bilateral development agencies or the World Bank. And that has in various respects impeded the ability to articulate a conception of national development with a domestic perspective and to do so in a self-confident, indigenously rooted and pertinent way.

I think the issues are very complex, but it is clear that there is insufficient funding for development research done within developing countries and from a developing country perspective. A very good thing that the World Bank could do would be to provide resources to such institutions in a manner that makes them structurally autonomous of the Bank (which existing initiatives such as the World Bank's Global Development Network fail fully to do). Ultimately what is needed are not individual contracts for specific research projects but the equivalent of endowments that enable high-quality research institutions in developing countries to exist as alternatives to research centers in the North. It is of the utmost importance for the future of these societies to secure the conditions for the independent production of ideas.

In an op-ed piece you submitted to the New York Times *when the World Bank president was being chosen in 2005, you wrote that "The U.S. nomination of Paul Wolfowitz to head the World Bank is an insult to the world's poor." Now that Wolfowitz has been in office for over a year, do you stand by your claim? How do you rate his performance more generally?*

It was my view at the time that the nomination of Paul Wolfowitz to the presidency of the World Bank showed a remarkable lack of concern for the Bank's ostensible mission. Paul Wolfowitz had limited experience in the area of economic policy or of development policy more generally. Indeed, in his immediately prior role in the U.S. government, he had, in the view of many, shown a remarkable lack of concern for evidence-based or fact-based policymaking. My view then was that the nomination exhibited a form of high-handedness on the part of the country that has traditionally nominated the president of the Bank, and a lack of seriousness about the Bank's supposed mission, emblazoned in its headquarters: "Our dream is a world free of poverty."

My view about that has not changed, and it could not change as a result of Wolfowitz's performance in the office. His performance is conceptually a separate issue. Even if he had been the best president that the Bank had ever had, my view as to the process that led to his being nominated for the position would not be a different one. I do think now, as many other people do, that the presidency of the World Bank and other similarly important positions in development institutions should not be the prerogative of any individual country or indeed of any individual group of countries. This aspect of the World Bank's governance, like many other aspects of governance of the Bretton Woods institutions in particular but international institutions more generally, must be greatly pried open and democratized if these institutions are to be made more legitimate.

With regard to how Paul Wolfowitz has performed in office, I cannot comment very much except to say that the single-minded focus on corruption that he has brought to bear has been criticized by others and is not entirely out of keeping with what one might have expected ex ante from someone who primarily had experience in the field of political affairs and had very little experience in the area of economic and social development. But I am not ultimately qualified to comment on that since I have not been watching his performance very closely. The fundamental need is to institutionalize governance norms securing accountability and transparency.

You have said that the Millennium Development Goals (MDGs) may not be likely to be met in many countries, indeed in entire regions. Could you explain why?

The Millennium Development Goals, as you know, are quite diverse and encompass a variety of concerns. So it is difficult to make any sweeping characterization that brings all of them under its ambit. But that having been said, it's quite clear that the Millennium Development Goals are not likely to be met in certain regions. Let us take, for example, the first goal, which is to halve world income poverty from its 1990 level by 2015, where world income poverty is interpreted in terms of the proportion of the developing world's population that is poor. Now there is some ambiguity as to how this goal should be interpreted, and in particular whether it should be interpreted on a worldwide aggregate level or at the level of individual countries. In practice in the United Nations it is being interpreted at the level of individual countries, and that seems quite an appropriate thing to do.

It is true that certain countries—for example, China—have enjoyed an apparent remarkable reduction in income poverty since 1990. In other major countries that possess a large number of the world's poor, such as India, there is some reason to think that a considerable reduction in poverty has also taken place, although there is great debate about that and the jury is very much out. However, in other regions of the world altogether, for example in Latin America and in sub-Saharan Africa, the rate of poverty reduction appears to be very low. It is indeed possible that poverty has been increasing in absolute terms in both of these regions. Of course, fundamental uncertainties about what internationally comparable criterion to use for identifying the poor create difficulties in making such judgments, as Thomas Pogge and I have argued elsewhere and as I have earlier discussed. That having been said, it seems clear that the dynamics of income growth and poverty reduction are different from region to region in the world, and that there may be a relatively poor prognosis for reduction in income poverty in Latin America and in sub-Saharan

Africa. Indeed, if one takes a disaggregated view even of the regions of the world where poverty reduction appears on the whole to be taking place (such as South Asia) one finds a very different perspective from country to country. Notably the rate of poverty reduction in Pakistan appears to have been very poor, and indeed there may have been very little poverty reduction in Sri Lanka and Nepal as well. This kind of disaggregated view gives a similarly mixed picture elsewhere in the world. If one questions whether development is taking place on a worldwide basis, one is forced to come to a decidedly mixed conclusion.

In an article that I did with a coauthor, entitled "Has World Poverty Really Fallen?" we asked whether the number of poor persons in the world as a whole fell between 1990 and 2000. To try to answer this question, we juxtaposed different plausible scenarios as to what may have happened in Latin America, sub-Saharan Africa, India, and China, taking note of the controversies that exist concerning the recent trends of poverty in each of those regions. What we found is that although under most of the scenarios considered there has been aggregate poverty reduction, driven primarily by the reductions in poverty in China, there are at least some more pessimistic scenarios, which we cannot rule out because of the fundamental uncertainties as to what is actually taking place, in which the total number of the poor increased in absolute terms or indeed as a proportion of the world's population.

Let me add one more thought here which is that although the United Nations system has been mobilized in favor of the Millennium Development Goals, it has not developed a coherent approach to promoting them. Professor Jeffrey Sachs, in his capacity as head of the UN Millennium Project, has presented a set of proposals as to how countries can best achieve the MDGs. Although these proposals are based on considerable evidence gathering and research, and are presented with the best of intentions, in my view and in that of my coauthor, Antoine Heuty, with whom I have written two papers on the issue, the proposals of the Millennium Project are unlikely to provide an ultimately successful basis for achieving the MDGs, or indeed broader development goals. Our fundamental concern about these proposals is their technocratic grounding and orientation. We believe that there has been insufficient recognition of the different means available potentially to achieve development goals generally. The technocratic perspective of the Millennium Project causes it to focus on a small number of physical interventions it views as especially important. For example, to reduce infant and child mortality, it has emphasized the role of certain technical interventions, such as the provision of insecticide-dipped bed nets that may diminish the prevalence of malaria in infected populations. We have no reason to doubt that such interventions are potentially quite valuable. However, the overwhelming focus on a small number of physical interventions of this kind with very little attention provided to the institutional arrangements that prevail at the national and world levels, and their conduciveness to promoting development, is, in our view, misguided. It is misguided both because those broader concerns are ultimately of considerable importance in determining development outcomes on the ground and because there are many potential interventions and potentially successful development policies that Professor Sachs and his team may have ignored. An example that we have given in the past in this connection concerns that of mid-day meal schemes for schoolchildren, which have proven effective at increasing school enrollment as well as improving child nutrition. The Millennium Project identifies such schemes as an example of what they refer to as a "quick win," which is a policy that, if implemented, is likely to provide very rapid gains. We point out, however, that when mid-day meal schemes were first pioneered on a mass scale in developing countries (in particular in India in the 1980s) they were criticized as a populist scheme that was likely to be ineffective. The legendary Indian economist (and then finance secretary of Tamil Nadu state, which had first introduced the largest such program) complained to me vociferously about them at the time along these lines, when I did research on the topic in 1989. Moreover, these programs were primarily viewed as a mechanism for improving child nutrition. It was only recognized subsequently that their primary benefit was in increasing school enrollment. Today very few development analysts are critical of such schemes, and most, like Professor Sachs, praise them.

This is an example, in our view, of the manner in which experimentation on the part of countries can potentially create substantial benefits over the longer term, both for the countries doing the experimentation and for other countries that can learn from their experiences. Rather than presenting a centralized menu of options and advocating that these be implemented a la carte or in toto in all countries, it would be better to create a learning environment within which countries could be supported in the construction of development plans and through which countries could learn from one another in that process. As a concrete mechanism for doing so, we have advocated what we call a mechanism of "peer and partner review" through which countries would periodically undergo a process of generating national development plans that they deem appropriate to achieving their development goals and would subject these plans to the friendly but critical perspective of peers and partners (namely, other countries at the same level of development as well as countries at a different level of development which are linked to them, for instance as donors or aid recipients). The peer and partner review process would serve as a basis for offering financial assistance for countries' national development programs.

The process of peer and partner review need not be confined to poor countries. We could imagine that certain developed countries would subject their programs of development assistance to the critical perspective offered by their peers and partners. A process of this kind would, in our view, be one example of a mechanism whereby countries could approach their development challenges in a more open-ended way, as well as in a manner that is participatory, consultative, and democratic, and which is ultimately learning-oriented. Such a proposal does not promise a magic bullet that will be guaranteed to achieve the MDG or indeed any other economic or social goals. However, it is our view that in the long run an institutionalized process that provides tangible support to countries in their development programs as well as creates opportunities and requirements for countries to experiment, and to learn from their own experience and from one another is much more likely to promote those ends over the longer term.

In an article entitled "Developing Just Monetary Arrangements," you argue that the details of international monetary arrangements must be taken into account in debates on international distributive justice. How so? And what kinds of monetary reforms do you advocate at the global level?

That article was really an effort to undertake an exercise that could probably be undertaken in various possible realms, which is to try to bring to bear normative reasoning as well as empirical reasoning to ask the question of whether the existing institutional arrangements in a particular area are really ones that could be rationalized on the basis of underlying moral principles, and whether, given what we know about human beings, about the workings of institutions and so forth, there are feasible reforms that we could imagine that would be desirable from a normative standpoint. So in that particular case, as you point out, my concern was with international financial and monetary arrangements. These, of course, encompass a variety of aspects.

To give you an example of what I meant by saying that monetary decisions have real effects of interest from the standpoint of international distributive justice, many of the developing countries went into debt crises in the 1980s in part as a result of the decision by the U.S. Federal Reserve to adopt a very contractionary monetary policy at the same time as there was an increase in government expenditures in the United States financed by borrowing (due to Ronald Reagan's heavy program of military expenditure, simultaneous tax cuts, and other factors). The consequence was a sharp increase in real interest rates, which made it very difficult for many of the large developing country borrowers to roll over their debt and to make timely repayments. The consequences of that debt crisis, which of course also had other causal roots, are still being felt in many of the developing countries. In some respects that debt crisis has never ended in at least some of the developing countries. This is an example of the manner in which decisions based on narrow considerations of the interests of particular groups in developed countries can have very large knock-on effects in the developing countries. Of course, often those knock-on effects are barely considered in the decision-making process to the best of our knowledge. Further, the knock-on effects in developing countries can have quite adverse distributional consequences within those countries, so it is not just a question of particular countries being unable to make debt payments, but of their being forced to undertake sharp limitations on government expenditure that can hurt the relatively poor within those countries.

The issue of distributive justice also arises in the context of inter- and intragenerational questions. In the case of countries, unlike individual persons, those who borrow and make promises to repay in the future are not necessarily those on whom the actual repayment burden will fall. In the case of countries, there are shifting populations, and often the very young will be forced to bear debt obligations contracted on their behalf by their predecessors. One issue, then, is whether the citizenry of a country ought to be made liable for the debts contracted by a particular government on their behalf. Obviously questions concerning whether the government is constituted in a manner that generates normatively binding obligations are important here. The debts contracted by Mobutu Sese Seko in the erstwhile Zaire (now the Democratic Republic of the Congo) may be thought not to create binding obligations upon the populace of that country, which cannot reasonably be held responsible for the decision to contract those debts or to have substantially benefited from the resources borrowed. In the recent academic literature as well as more broadly there has been a very lively discussion on this question of so-called odious debts and how to address them.

But quite apart from intergenerational issues of that kind, there are the intragenerational questions. What makes a child born today in the Democratic Republic of the Congo more responsible for the debts contracted ostensibly on that child's behalf by the prior government of Zaire than is a child born today in some other part of the world? What are the threads of interpersonal obligation that hold intergenerationally as well as intragenerationally is a very difficult question, which I think has never been adequately addressed in the literature on sovereign debt.

The existing institutional order doesn't seem to function in a way that adequately takes into account the interests of affected populations when particular decisions are made. The international economic order is difficult to rationalize even on the basis of uncontroversial moral principles. So there is, I think, a certain value to bringing critical scrutiny to bear on these issues.

You have pointed to the current debate regarding why poor countries are poor in an article in the Journal of Ethics. *You ask, "Did they come to be poor (or do they continue to be poor) because of choices that they have themselves made, or rather because of the features of the world order in which they find themselves, and because of the actions of other agents?" You then say that "The answer to this question will properly influence our judgments concerning the distribution of responsibilities for the alleviation of poverty." What do you think the correct response to this question is?*

It is fairly clear that if one looks at this problem on a world scale, the existence of mass poverty is evidently a phenomenon that cannot be understood simply in terms of the exercise or nonexercise of individual responsibility. There are clearly systematic factors that must be at play in the emergence and maintenance over time of mass poverty. It cannot then be sufficient to characterize individual disadvantage in terms of specific histories of individual responsibility, as some would like to do. I leave open the question of whether such a characterization is more plausible or more reasonable within the national setting in specific cases. There may be particular contexts, especially those in which it may be argued that individuals have been presented with adequate access to the means of pursuing individual advantage or adequate life chances, where one could plausibly make such an argument. However, it is not evident that that is wholly the case even in the most egalitarian of the developed societies, let alone on the world scale. This observation then opens up the question of whether there are systematic factors that account for individual disadvantage as a mass experience or mass phenomenon, and where the responsibility for those systematic factors can be placed. The answers to this question are complex, and in some instances, no definitive answer can be provided. Take, for instance, the question of the extent to which historical experiences of colonization are responsible at least in part for present-day distributions of advantage and disadvantage in the world. There are plausible arguments that can be made in various directions in regard to what the impact of colonization, and of European dominance in particular, on the prevailing patterns of advantage and disadvantage in the world has been. However, coming to a definitive conclusion in regard to this matter is difficult to conceive because it would require assessing a complex counterfactual, namely, identifying what *would* have happened if the entire history of the world had been different. Since we have had one world with one history and there are no alternative worlds or possible worlds that are directly observable through which this counterfactual can be identified, there are inherent inferential problems in coming to a definitive judgment on such a question.

The fact that there are always uncertainties in the ascription of responsibility, however, is fully compatible with there being reason to try to form judgments concerning whether particular actions by particular agents may have been responsible for present circumstances, or whether particular actions by particular agents could plausibly be beneficial now and in the future, whether or not those agents were causally responsible in the past. Our judgments concerning responsibilities for the alleviation of poverty will depend on diverse considerations: our understandings of whether particular past actions were important in determining the present distribution of advantages and disadvantages, nonconsequentialist considerations involving the nature of interpersonal obligations between human beings whether or not those human beings live in the same society or were tied by particular causal connections in the past, and whether particular agents at present have greater capacity than others to alleviate the disadvantages that exist. There is no single answer that can be given to this question other than to say that we must recognize that there are going to be a variety of considerations in different directions, and it is difficult for individuals to wash their hands of responsibility for the present situation in the world on the grounds that they were "not involved" in producing it.

You have shown that a very large number of developing countries have suffered extended periods of stagnation, understood as a sustained period of negligible or negative growth, and you say that it is very difficult to escape stagnation permanently. Why is this? And what changes in policy need to occur to alter this fact?

In this work, with Camelia Minoiu, we found that a very large number of countries in the world, as you say, have experienced long periods of sustained negligible or negative growth, and moreover, that whether they experienced stagnation, understood in this sense, in the 1960s was a very good predictor of whether they experienced stagnation in the 1990s. It appears, therefore, that certain countries are structurally disposed to experiencing bouts of stagnation because of their place in the world economy or their domestic institutional features or some other reasons that are longstanding and perhaps entrenched. Once countries experience lengthy periods of stagnation, they find themselves caught in poverty traps that make it difficult for them to avoid doing so subsequently, independently of whether or not there were any prior features of those countries that disposed them toward stagnation.

It is difficult to know what the causal pathways are that account for this finding. However, it does seem to be a finding that requires explanation. The idea that countries experience poverty traps is not implausible. Jeffrey Sachs, in a recent paper on sub-Saharan Africa in Brookings Papers on Economic Activity, has made some very good arguments as to why countries may find it difficult to escape poverty once they are in poverty for various reasons, including their being constrained from making certain kinds of investments that would be necessary to raise the productivity of labor and capital to a level that would enable them to escape their poverty traps. Of course, it has also long been noted in the development literature that there are features of the global economy that make countries that specialize in the production and export of primary commodities, for instance, especially prone to swings in economic conditions worldwide. At the present time, there is a commodity boom taking place that is benefiting many developing countries, but there was a very long period in the later half of the 1970s and the 1980s and even the 1990s in which many countries experienced a commodity bust and suffered very low prices for their primary exports, which were primary commodities. These structural features of countries may be of considerable significance in explaining why many countries have experienced stagnation since the 1960s and continue to do so. Certainly it is an important part of the explanation as to why particular regions of the world, for instance sub-Saharan Africa, have had very poor economic performance for lengthy periods of time.

As to what changes in policy need to occur to alter this fact, that is a complex question, and I think that there is a need to address various aspects of the world economic system as well as domestic political and · economic choices in order to do so.

You have also distinguished between developmental aid and geopolitical aid and argued that the former has a positive effect on growth while the latter has a negative effect on growth. Could you define the two types of aid and explain why this is the case? How much aid dispensed by the United States, for example, falls into the category of geopolitical aid? What are the policy implications of your findings?

In this work (jointly written with Camelia Minoiu) we define developmental aid as aid that could reasonably be expected to promote development, understood as the expansion of people's choices through various means, including economic growth. We define geopolitical aid as aid that could not reasonably be anticipated to promote development understood in this sense. Obviously the distinction between these two forms of aid depends on specifying an appropriate threshold of expected impact on development that differentiates the two.

The reason we make this distinction is that, in our view, it is evident that certain forms of investment—for instance, investment in rural roads, basic infrastructure, and human capabilities, such as improved health and education—are likely to have an impact on development, both intrinsically and instrumentally. For instance, investment in better health and education helps both to promote an end that is directly valuable as well as to enable what has sometimes been called the accumulation of human "capital," which may make workers more productive and contribute to the economic output of a country in the longer term. On the other hand, other forms of expenditure (for instance, one might think of highways between military bases) are likely to be of interest to particular groups within a country but less likely to have an impact on development understood as a process that expands peoples' choices. Much economic aid is of the latter kind rather than the former. For instance, the country you mentioned, the United States, happens to provide a great deal of aid to countries that are its strategic allies, and at least part of the purpose of that aid appears to be to shore up the governments that it supports in those countries rather than to protect from external threats. It would not be entirely inappropriate to judge that a small proportion of the aid provided to those countries was developmental in the sense that I have defined it here, and a large proportion was geopolitical.

We entered a debate that already exists. Of course, recently people like William Easterly of New York University (and formerly of the World Bank) have become very prominent in arguing that aid is ineffectual. David Dollar of the World Bank, Paul Collier, Craig Burnside, and others have also argued in this direction. One of the targets of their contrarian perspective on aid has been another prominent economist, Jeffrey Sachs, who has argued for a large expansion of aid to developing countries, especially the least developed countries. I think it is fair to say that Professor Sachs's perspective is the minority perspective in the debate, and that the aid "contrarians" have been quite influential. Most recently, the just departed chief economist of the IMF, Raghuram Rajan, has, with his coauthor Arvind Subramaniam, written a very carefully constructed paper arguing that aid has been largely ineffective. Our view on this entire literature is that it has failed to distinguish appropriately between developmental aid and geopolitical aid. The reason this literature finds that aid is ineffective is that it is measuring the average impact of aid. Our finding is rather commonsensical, and it depends on not doing this. We find that developmental aid, which one could reasonably anticipate to have a positive impact on economic growth, does in fact do so, and that other aid does not have such an impact. In fact, in our statistical work on cross-country experience, we find that geopolitical aid, which we, following the literature, identify as aid that is predicated on the existence of strategic relationships, linguistic ties, ex-colonial ties, and so forth, is actually sometimes associated with a negative impact on economic growth. Why this is is something of a mystery, although there are some plausible explanations. For example, it may be that geopolitical aid helps to sustain governments that are not development oriented and that systematically fail to use resources efficiently or to make investments that would benefit their people and improve the productivity of national economies.

In an article entitled "Safety Nets for the Poor: A Missing International Dimension?" you ask whether there are shocks whose appropriate level of reme-

diation is at least in part international, and if so what form the arrangements governing such remediation should take. You discuss the possibility of establishing a global reinsurance fund. Could you elaborate this proposal here?

The observation made in the article is that there are many countries, especially smaller countries, that appear to be quite seriously affected by economic shocks of international origin, for example, the variations in prices of export commodities that I mentioned earlier. So there are many factors accounting for the economic performance of countries over time that are external to them. Countries should be enabled to cope better with the shocks and the volatility that they experience through an appropriate international mechanism providing them with some degree of insurance. The form that such insurance could take are various; Robert Shiller, the financial economist, has, for instance, argued that futures markets or derivatives products tied to national income should be created so that countries can hedge against variations in their own national income. That is a very interesting but rather exotic proposal, and my own paper offered a fairly modest suggestion as to a means by which the relatively poor within countries could be protected from fluctuations in their incomes which threaten their basic interests. One way to avoid treating the poor as a "shock absorber" of the international economy would be to create what I refer to as a Global Reinsurance Fund or a similar mechanism through which individual countries would be able to make claims varying with the extent to which demands on their national social welfare system increase as a result of economic shocks. I had in mind here the Indian example of establishing welfare programs and social insurance schemes that reach the mass of the rural poor. The Maharastra Employment Guarantee Scheme is an important early example of such an initiative, which guaranteed rural able-bodied persons a certain number of days of work at a certain wage and thereby provided an institutional safeguard against extreme poverty and famine. More recently in India this idea has been generalized to the entire country in the form of the National Rural Employment Guarantee Programme. Many other developing countries could benefit from putting in place standing social safety nets of this kind, which would offer an automatic mechanism by which individual poor or potentially poor persons would be protected from adverse shocks. Such standing social safety nets would be activated automatically, rapidly, and at relatively low marginal cost in the event of stresses that affect the poor and cause a large increase in uptake from such programs. Of course many smaller countries are weary of establishing such a standing social protection mechanism because they do not wish to open themselves up to the potentially indefinite fiscal claims that such a program could generate, particularly if they are subject to very severe or long-lasting negative shocks that could create large demands for social assistance at the very time that a government is most fiscally constrained.

A way to counter this fear is to create a global reinsurance mechanism by which, through the provision of appropriate premiums, whether paid by the country or by donors on behalf of the country, the country would be guaranteed the means to finance any increase in expenditures that was necessitated by unanticipated adverse shocks. A mechanism of this sort could generalize the example that has recently been initiated in India (through the hard work of social and political activists) to the world scale. Of course, the particular mechanism or mechanisms appropriate in each country will depend on the specificities of that country. The underlying principle, however, of creating standing social safety nets that can provide for people who are most vulnerable without having to be created anew when the time comes and of creating the means for countries to pay the attendant bill through global risk sharing (and subsidy as appropriate) is what is most important. Here, as elsewhere, my intent has been to show that there are feasible means of creating a world order that serves the ends of justice (such as that the less advantaged must not bear the brunt of aggregate volatility linked to financial speculation). There may of course be other and better means of promoting these ends.

In your work, you have argued for policy changes that would address the large and often increasing inequalities both within and among states. How would you rate the success of the development paradigm as it has been implemented in the last sixty years, and the record of the global institutions entrusted with ensuring its success? What possibility do you see of reform under present conditions so that these inequalities might be diminished? Do you believe that structural change at the global level might be necessary given the highly unequal distribution of power and resources? And how do you think it might be achieved?

The best for last I see! Existing perspectives on whether the prevailing development paradigm has succeeded are very diverse. Amartya Sen and others who have been critical of elements of that paradigm would nevertheless point to the fact that there have been significant improvements, for example, in life expectancy, literacy, and indeed in real income in many countries around the world. Indeed, from a broader historical perspective it may even be argued that these improvements have been unprecedentedly rapid and large.

That having been said, there are evidently many reasons for deep concern. First, this progress has been extremely uneven across countries and populations. That which has been achieved has still been too slow and too unevenly achieved. Second, the criteria for success have perhaps been overly narrow. There are many respects in which it is reasonable to argue that conditions have become worse. We can think here, for instance, of the intensifying local as well as national and global depletion of the commons, which has affected (or threatens to affect) livelihoods and the quality of life—in some instances profoundly. The basis for trust and cooperation within and between societies is in some instances notably diminishing. The international economic order remains deeply unequal not only in its outcomes but in terms of its governance. We have already commented on the fact that the Bretton Woods institutions and other important global institutions that affect people throughout the world continue to be disproportionately shaped by specific countries and perhaps by specific interests within those countries. We can think also of the breakdown of social relations and the increasing anomie that is a part of everyday individual experience in large parts of the world; urbanization, the emergence of posttraditional attitudes, and the creation of mass society have been mixed blessings in this particular respect. The widespread prominence of chauvinistic politics and of simplistic understandings of the demands of authenticity may be related to the massification of society and increased social anomie, although these connections are obviously complex and ones that more sociological insight is required in order to understand.

For all of these reasons and still others, it is very difficult to assess whether the development paradigm as it has been implemented in the last sixty years has been a success or a failure. I think it is fair to say that it has been a disappointment for a great many people, and they are not wrong to feel a sense of disappointment. In saying so, however, one must still remain cognizant of the facts concerning improved health, improved access to basic education, and the progress of democratization and social equality in many societies around the world. For instance, despite the many aspects of India's record that are mixed, it is clear that an increasing atmosphere of social equality—although it has brought many political and social challenges—is an important and creditable aspect of India's postindependence history. I am firmly of the view that the development paradigm should ultimately be assessed in regard to all of these different outcomes. It would not be enough to focus simply on the economic impact that it has had, even though much of my recent work has focused on that impact.

Of course, we have not defined what the "development paradigm" is, and I have taken it as given that you are referring to a certain set of conventionally held notions—for instance, that economic growth is desirable, that it should be promoted through appropriate means such as national development plans (earlier) and through market-oriented liberalization (increasingly now). There is no doubt that such ideas have been vastly influential and are widely held. However, the concept of a development paradigm should also be put under the spotlight. There have been many critics of the very idea of development who have argued that by its very nature it entails an inappropriate valorization of particular institutions and norms, especially those associated with modern capitalism and the European cultural world. Notwithstanding the pertinence of such foundational criticisms, I think that it is difficult to do without a term such as development (although the term itself is dispensable) under contemporary conditions. Certainly we need some language within which to articulate our collective aspirations toward progress, even if we do not believe in what Ashis Nandy has referred to as the inclined plane of history, the idea that history necessarily tends or ought to tend in a certain direction (for example, toward a certain set of institutional and social norms) in order for it to constitute progress. I think that we should aim toward a pluralistic conception of the desirable worlds that we could inhabit as a world society, and indeed as nations and groups of nations, or as communities within nations overflowing across nations (which they increasingly do). That pluralization is an important task for development thought which is largely ignored by development economists. I personally have no attachment to the language of development, which is so improperly redolent of historical stagism and biological evolutionism, but do think that it is important to find some way in which to articulate the shared aspirations toward common betterment.

As to the possibilities for reform under present conditions, I am not especially sanguine, but I also believe that there is no need to be wholly pessimistic. I think that there are possibilities for transformation, though of course these possibilities depend very much on there being adequate collective action. To offer an example: the worldwide movement for debt relief in the last decade has been quite heartening. It has been very uplifting to see large numbers of people, especially in the rich countries, who have pushed for their governments to provide meaningful debt relief to poorer countries. Often without understanding the details of the issues, millions of people, in particular young people, have joined this movement, and they have made of debt relief an issue that could garner votes for the mainstream political parties, and as a result, they have made significant debt relief a reality, although of course with strings and under conditions that one might have wished did not exist that were inevitably appended by finance ministry technocrats. I am not one of those who believe that all actions of governments always redound into the interests of the dominant classes axiomatically. An example of this kind is to me heartening, although very modest and imperfect indeed.

In some recent work that I have been doing with my colleague, Christian Barry, we have jointly tried to articulate some ways in which the international trading system could be reformed so that it would be more worker-friendly. In our view there are prospects for reforming the rules of the world trading system so as to enable countries to realize potential gains from trade while also promoting the interests of people more than they can do at present without adversely affecting their international competitiveness. Of course, whether proposals of the kind we are making will ever be realized is a very open question. I do not necessarily expect that they will be realized, but to articulate what such reform could involve and how it could operate is at least to provide a necessary condition for the actions that could actually bring about such reforms. Ultimately structural transformation, whether of international institutions or of national or local institutions, requires not only ideas but imagination and collective will, which intellectuals are not in a position by themselves to provide. This is not to say that our task is simply to wait, but it is to say that we should strive better to recognize what we can do and what we cannot do. What we cannot do is less than is often thought, and what we can do is more than is often thought. We can only discover the limits of what we cannot do, and more importantly of what we can, by testing them.

FOUR I Joseph Stiglitz

You write in your book Globalization and Its Discontents, "*Even when not guilty of hypocrisy, the West has driven the globalization agenda, ensuring that it garners a disproportionate share of the benefits, at the expense of the developing world.*" *Could you explain how this is the case? How has the West continued to sustain, for example, its discriminatory and hypocritical stance on trade liberalization?*

In answer to your first question: it is not just that more advanced industrial countries have declined to open up their markets to the goods of the developing countries—for instance, keeping their quotas on a multitude of goods from textiles to sugar—while insisting that those countries open up their markets to the goods of the wealthier countries; it is not just that the more advanced industrial countries continue to subsidize agriculture, making it difficult for the developing countries to compete, while insisting that the developing countries eliminate their subsidies on industrial goods. Looking at the "terms of trade"—the prices that developed and less developed countries get for the products they produce—after the eighth trade agreement (in 1995),[1] the *net* effect was to lower the prices some of the poorest countries in the world received relative to what they paid for their imports. The result was that some of the poorest countries in the world were actually made worse off.[2]

How has the West managed to sustain this? The answer is fairly simple: the West has a disproportionate share of economic power, which it has used to maintain this power. The West been guided by its short-run interests. I have argued that it is actually not in the interest of the

West to maintain its position in this way, certainly not in the long run. It is a much more short-sighted and narrow vision since such a stance is only beneficial for *particular* interests in the short run.

One of the things that has allowed the West to maintain its power in this way is the absence of competition. That is to say, in the era before 1990, the ability to so badly take advantage of the developing countries was circumscribed by the fact that there was competition during the Cold War. With the end of the Cold War, there was no threat. I have said that this was a missed opportunity; it was a sad moment because the West had the option of allowing principle to guide economic behavior. During the Cold War, the only terms were the terms set by the competition between the Soviet bloc and the West. And that meant we wound up supporting Pinochet and other dictators, but we could have used the end of the Cold War to ensure that we no longer supported dictators and were trying to create a world based on principle. We chose not to do that. Instead we let our economic interests dictate everything.

The timing may have been particularly unfortunate because the United States was emerging from a recession. Periods of recession are not periods in which one has a high degree of generosity. So the focus of the Clinton administration was on jobs and growth. This was such a fixation that the administration tended not to look at the longer-run global implications.

Could you briefly outline the mandate of the three principal institutions determining the course of economic globalization: the World Bank, the International Monetary Fund (IMF), and the World Trade Organization (WTO)? From where do they receive their funding, and what are their governing structures?

The three mandates are as follows: the World Bank is fundamentally concerned with the alleviation of poverty; the IMF with global financial stability; and the WTO with opening up and regulating international trade. The WTO really has very little funding. It is basically a forum for discussion. It has a very small secretariat. As an organization, the WTO itself has little power. The power resides in the countries that are its members. The IMF basically receives capital contributions from various countries according to some formula, but essentially is like a bank: it lends money and gets paid back. In fact the IMF does not really spend money as long as it gets repaid; it is only a lending institution. There is one part of the institution that gives highly subsidized loans for developing countries, and that is done through an allocation process from the advanced industrial countries. The same thing is true of the World Bank: its funding comes from capital that was originally contributed. Unlike the IMF, though, it actually borrows huge amounts of money from international capital markets, uses its high credit rating and low interest rates, and lends that money with a margin to developing countries. One part of the World Bank can be viewed as a cooperative borrowing organization, like a co-op. By borrowing together, developing countries get lower interest rates. For very poor countries, they have what they call the International Development Association (IDA), which helps the poorest countries reduce poverty by providing interest-free loans and some grants for programs aimed at boosting economic growth and improving living conditions. IDA funds are very highly subsidized. These monies are again from grants that are given every three years from the developed countries.

As for governing structures: the most interesting aspect of the governing structure of the WTO has to do with certain procedural issues. In the past, much was discussed and decided behind closed doors. So much has happened in the infamous "Green Room", where a subset of countries get together, do a deal, and then arm-twist other countries to go along with that deal. There is more openness now, but still there is concern about whether the extent of the openness is adequate. And there is resistance to making it more open.

The IMF is at the other extreme where one country, the United States, has the veto power. All important measures require 85 percent for approval, and the United States alone represents 17 percent, so it effectively has veto power. There are additional concerns about the governing structure of the IMF: representation and who represents each country. The problem of representation is that it reflects economic power as it was distributed in 1944 when the IMF was founded, updated only marginally. The role of China, for instance, is probably much smaller than it ought to be. Equally problematic is the fact that at the IMF, it is only central banks and finance ministers who vote and who represent each country. So even though the actions of the IMF may have effects on education and health, these ministries have no say. The IMF programs in Thailand, for instance, resulted in less money for AIDS medicine. In Pakistan, education money was cut as a result of IMF programs, which resulted in children going to "alternative" schools—with enormous consequences. The finance ministers were focusing on the financial consequences. They did not have the broader societal consequences in mind. These consequences were therefore not reflected in the decisions that were taken, the way they are in democratic governments, where, for example, you can have somebody raising their hand and saying, "You can't do that! You can't ignore the effect of this decision on AIDS." No government would ever allow important decisions to be delegated just to the finance minister. But the IMF in effect makes those decisions without the concurrence of the other ministries. That, I think, is one of the real problems in its governance.

You argue that the problem with international economic institutions is that they are "dominated not just by the wealthiest industrial countries but by commercial and financial interests in those countries." What are the implications of this?

The intellectual property provision in the Uruguay Round of the WTO—Trade Related Intellectual Property Rights (TRIPS)—is a good example of the possible implications. Intellectual property is very important, but it is also very complicated. When this particular provision was discussed while I was at the Council of Economic Advisors at the White House, both the Council and the Office of Science and Technology Policy opposed TRIPS. But the U.S. Trade Representative reflected the interests of the pharmaceutical industry and the film industry. They wanted very tough measures. They were not reflecting the interests of the scientific community. They were not reflecting the interests of those who are concerned about poor people. Here in the United States, the Clinton administration had been elected with access to health as one of its main platforms. Yet we were taking action that would reduce access to health for millions of people around the world. We never would have done it if those special interests had not had such a play.

Another example is Chapter 11 under the North American Free Trade Agreement (NAFTA), where there is a provision called "Regulatory Takings," which says that if regulations adversely impact a firm, the firm needs to be compensated. The Clinton administration opposed that very strongly when it was raised in the United States. But it was buried in an international trade agreement. Special interests have always advocated that, but environmentalists and the Clinton administration were adamantly opposed to it. Yet we were never aware that it was buried in this agreement. So it went into effect. If we had been aware of it, we would have inserted a clause, a reservation of some kind. What was so remarkable was how hard we were fighting exactly that same kind of provision in the United States advocated by some conservative Republicans; yet we were approving it implicitly in NAFTA without ever being aware of it.

You often criticize the IMF for its political agenda. What is its political agenda, and what have been its effects? In how many countries does the IMF have a program, and how many people, would you say, have been affected by its policies across the world?

The general point is that it is often very difficult to separate economics from politics. We know that in the United States, for instance, we have heated political debates about taxation, social security, etc. The Clinton administration believed very strongly that it was important to increase the progressiveness of the income tax, and that the adverse incentive effects were far less important than the beneficial redistributive effects. Yet the IMF is pushing the value added tax (VAT), which is like a flat tax, around the world. We opposed it in the United States. That is a clear *political* position where the IMF is saying that good economics is the policy that many Republicans support in the United States. That is politics; economics does *not* support that. In fact, the economics in developing countries is even stronger against the IMF position because it is not even a uniform tax (that is, such a tax is not collected uniformly).

Another very telling example is that the IMF and World Bank have pushed privatization of social security around the world. Bush pushed it in the United States; the Democratic party, to a man (and woman), opposed it. And they won. We had a political debate in the United States, and as a result of that political debate, there was enormous consensus that we should not privatize social security, even *partially*. Yet countries like Argentina and Bolivia were forced to have privatization of social security, and were in fact told that this was "good economics." It is no such thing. This is politics. Now the consequences are enormous. Devastating. Almost all of Argentina's deficit at the time when it went into crisis was due to social security privatization. Arguably, they may not even have had a crisis had they not privatized social security. Certainly it played a very important role. Similarly, contractionary monetary and fiscal policies in East Asia exacerbated the crises there. Again that was not good economics. It was politics. They were trying to save the creditors. American creditors might have been saved. Of course it ultimately failed to work, but that was the intent. People in the East Asian countries were devastated. So literally one can say hundreds of millions of people have been adversely affected by IMF policies. Some have benefited, but enormous numbers have been hurt.

Could you briefly explain your critique of "trickle-down" economics?

Trickle-down economics is the notion that all you need to do is make sure that the economy grows, and if it grows, everybody benefits. Trickle down simply allows the rich to get richer, assuming that everyone will benefit (the logic is more or less that a rising tide lifts all boats). But the fact is that in the United States we have had growth in the last five years but the median—people in the middle—have actually gotten poorer. Real income has been declining. The number of people in poverty has been increasing. The simple point is that there is no theory that says that enhancing the well-being of the rich necessarily enhances the well-being of the middle or the poor. The evidence is quite the contrary. Particularly when you start mixing together economics and politics, if you get too much inequality, then the rich buy the political system and establish systems to maintain their economic power. So that is why it has not worked.

You refer often to the "Washington Consensus." Could you explain what this is and its significance for the way decisions are made regarding the global economy? On a related note, you write in your book that "The U.S. Treasury as the IMF's largest shareholder and the only one with veto power has a large role in determining IMF policies." What are the implications of this?

The Washington Consensus is used as a term to describe a consensus between the IMF, the World Bank, and the U.S. Treasury that evolved in the 1980s in the Thatcher-Reagan days. The Consensus is what you might call a conservative economic strategy for development that was conceived of particularly in relation to Latin America, with concepts extended to economies-in-transition as well as elsewhere. It had three main tenets: macro-stability, by which it meant mainly price stability, focused on inflation; privatization; and globalization, including liberalizing trade and capital markets, opening them up to short-term and speculative capital flows. This is sometimes described as just "getting government out of the way" or minimizing the role of the government. It was based on the doctrines of a free-market economy, on the assumption that private market economies solve all problems.

What is interesting is that these notions were being promulgated and promoted by the IMF, the World Bank, and the U.S. Treasury just at the time that economic science was casting doubt on them. That is to say, my own research in this period showed that whenever information is imperfect, capital markets are incomplete; wherever there are imperfect risk markets, that is, everywhere, markets are not in general efficient. The art of good economic policy is getting the right balance between government and the market. If you look historically at the success cases—the United States, East Asia—they have all involved a large role for government. So the real fact is that the countries that follow the Washington Consensus, the countries of Latin America, for instance, have for the most part not done very well. The countries that did *not* follow the Washington Consensus—East Asia, for instance—have done very well. In fact that was why—after an enormous amount of pressure from Japan—when the World Bank did a study called *The East Asia Miracle* in which they asked, "What did the East Asian countries do that generated their enormous success?" the results were quite clear. I do not want to say the answer was the *opposite* of the Washington Consensus, but it was very different from the Washington Consensus.

As far as the IMF and U.S. Treasury are concerned, to get to the last part of your question, one of the implications of the Washington Consensus is that it makes the IMF very much subject to the vagaries of U.S. politics. The IMF's policies are determined not by the U.S. government as a whole, but by the U.S. Treasury, and the U.S. Treasury is always linked to the financial markets, so even in Democratic administrations, it tends to be very conservative. There is less fluctuation in their position than one would have thought. So the IMF under the Clinton administration continued to push for privatization of social security, as I mentioned earlier, even though Clinton was adamantly opposed to the privatization of social security. They never discussed this with him. Had they asked him, he obviously would have raised questions. But in a large institution like the U.S. government, you simply cannot ask the president for his views on every question. More particularly, you want to make sure he does *not* get a chance to express his views on certain subjects because if he did in this case, for example, he would come out very much against what the Treasury was doing.

One of the conspiracy theories you talk about during the 1997 Asian Financial Crisis was that IMF policies were a deliberate attempt to "weaken East Asia—the region of the world that had shown the greatest growth over the previous forty years—or at least to enhance the incomes of those on Wall Street and other money centers." You say this is a theory you do not accept and argue instead that "the IMF was not participating in a conspiracy, but it was reflecting the interests and ideology of the Western financial community." Why are these two explanations mutually exclusive rather than possibly mutually reinforcing?

They could be mutually reinforcing. The ideology and the interest clearly could be used to reinforce an explicit conspiracy. The reason why I have doubts about conspiracies is that I just don't think that in a diverse market economy like the United States you can get everybody on board on a conspiracy. There are a lot of people in U.S. financial markets who believe that a strong East Asia is good for the global economy and good for the United States. They might wind up advocating similar policies to those who want a weak East Asia, but many people are working very hard to strengthen East Asia.

In Globalization and Its Discontents, *you write that some critics are so skeptical about the possibility of reform that they call for the abolition of the IMF. At the time, you thought this pointless, but have since said that the IMF does not even recognize its "own intellectual bankruptcy," that its credibility may have been so eroded that there is little possibility of reform and that "perhaps we ought to start from scratch." Could you explain what accounted for this change?*

You have read my writings too closely! I guess the bottom line is that I have a certain degree of ambivalence. In a way, the hard question is: To what extent is the position of the IMF the natural outcome of the political and economic position it occupies? If that is the case, then it is not an institutional problem, but a structural one. If you have an institution that is going to focus on finance, you are going to have to have it staffed by people who know finance and who are linked in one way or another with financial markets. They will begin to think like financial markets do, and they will therefore wind up with some of those positions.

At times, I have a sense of optimism. The fact that the IMF came out with a report where it admitted so clearly that capital market liberalization was not good for growth, and probably not good for stability, was a positive sign. It had actually shown that it was going forward, that it had begun to recognize that conditionality had not had positive values, that there might be some problems with its accounting frameworks. At moments like that, I feel a certain optimism. Then there are moments where such optimism is impossible: for instance, most recently, even after Argentina had done a deal with its creditors in restructuring its debt, and there was a group of creditors who had not signed on to the deal, the IMF was still trying to undermine the deal. At that point, one thinks this is an extremely creditor-friendly organization. It does not see its role as an *international* institution. There are clearly institutional problems of the kind that we talked about: the governance structure, the fact that Europe appoints the head, and so on, that leads one to think that maybe if one started from scratch, one could create an institutional structure that is not as vulnerable to the U.S. government or to a Wall Street takeover, or a combination of the two, and an institution that looks at financial markets from a *global* financial perspective. So it is that sort of vacillation in my own mind that accounts for what you quoted.

Most of your book is devoted to the mistakes and structural problems of the IMF. You suggest that the World Bank is less culpable because of the reforms the institution has undertaken under the leadership of James Wolfensohn. Could you outline what substantive reforms these have been and whether they can be reproduced at the IMF or the WTO?

Let me just list a number of the reforms that affected the way the institution operates, and therefore the outcomes. One thing is that it moved a very large fraction of its personnel into the countries concerned so it was no longer relying on these flying missions, where World Bank staff just showed up for a few days and came up with a country report. They became much more deeply embedded in the country. Second, the reality may not have been fully up to the rhetoric, but the rhetoric reflected a view that was important. It was about "putting the country in the driver's seat." It was saying that the country is really key, that the Bank has an advisory role, but they are the ones that determine things. There was a move—not all the way, but a move nonetheless—from conditionality to selectivity. We did studies that said conditionality did not work. The World Bank decided that it would select countries that perform well, that show they know how to manage money well, and that these countries would be recipients of more money from the Bank. And probably most important was the notion of going away from shock therapy, from a single magic recipe to a comprehensive development framework. Understanding that there are many aspects to society, including that of government—whereas the IMF and the old World Bank view emphasized minimizing the role of government; we talked about this in the context of the Washington Consensus—the Bank now said one of the main issues is *strengthening* government. The Bank began to place emphasis on how to make government more effective. This is when discussions of governance became important, and issues of corruption went to the top of the agenda. Before that, people said that such initiatives would go beyond the mandate of the World Bank, that this would be the realm of *politics*, not economics. Our research said that this affects development, and anything that affects development is the mandate of the World Bank. So these are examples of very big changes undertaken by the Bank.

Can they be reproduced at the IMF? Yes, they could be. But the fact is that right now, the mindset at the Fund would not allow such changes to be undertaken. The mindset would have to change so that the IMF could see itself as playing the role of an advisor from the outside, simply laying out what is known and what is not known, what is known with different degrees of certainty, what the debates are, and then letting the country decide itself. This would be a democratic process. The mindset of the IMF so far and to this point has been that it believes that it knows the truth, that it is capable of divine revelation. The view at the IMF is that if it even intimates that there are internal disagreements, it will be giving unclear advice. Well, my point is that if there are disagreements, then these disagreements are a reflection of the fact that the science is not clear. If that is the case, is it not essential that you inform the person or the country making the decision that the evidence on this issue is divided? The IMF should tell the country what all the evidence is, and then let the country hear why Person A thinks this, and Person B thinks something else. The IMF should also point out that, having provided all the information, the country will have to bear the consequences of whatever decision it takes with the information it was given. This would be a very different mindset from one that says that the IMF will simply tell the country what is good for the country.

The principal issue for the developing world at the WTO has to do with unfair trade practices, but there are also very important concerns surrounding intellectual property rights. Could you explain what the importance of this issue is for developing countries?

The Uruguay Round strengthened intellectual property rights. American and other Western drug companies could now stop drug companies in India and Brazil from "stealing" their intellectual property. But these drug companies in the developing world were making life-saving drugs available to their citizens at a fraction of the price at which the drugs were sold by the Western drug companies. There were thus two sides to the decisions made in the Uruguay Round: the first was that profits of the Western drug companies would go up, and second, that thousands were effectively condemned to death because governments and individuals in developing countries could no longer pay the high prices demanded. In the case of AIDS, the international outrage was so great that drug companies had to back down, eventually agreeing to lower their prices, to sell the drugs at cost in late 2001. But the underlying problems—the fact that the intellectual property regime established under the Uruguay Round was not balanced, that it overwhelmingly reflected the interests and perspectives of the producers, as opposed to the users, whether in developed or developing countries—remain.[3]

So the most important issue has to do with life and the access to medicines that TRIPS impedes. It is also important for a number of other reasons. Huge potential payments for intellectual property are transfer payments from developing countries to developed countries and will obviously make it more difficult for developing countries to grow. Everybody always points out that in the early days of U.S. development, in the nineteenth century, there were numerous allegations that the United States stole intellectual property in the production of steel. The real question is: What are the bounds of intellectual property rights? The WTO does not understand the role of intellectual property rights. This became clear to me in my discussions during the 1994 Uruguay Round because the U.S. trade representative did not know the issues around intellectual property. I had done a lot of research on the subject, but he was clearly ill-informed. Nobody at the WTO really understood intellectual property. The fact is that the most important ideas and innovations are not protected by intellectual property: mathematical theorems, basic research, and so on. We work very hard to disseminate our ideas, giving interviews like this, for instance. The model is not a closed model, it is a very open architecture. We see this right now, more recently, with the success of the Linux operating system, which is based on an open software architecture.

When Paul Wolfowitz was nominated for the post of president of the World Bank, you were quite critical, worrying that the World Bank may "now become an explicit instrument of U.S. foreign policy." Do you stand by this judgment since Wolfowitz has assumed this position? In an editorial in the Financial Times *("Everyone Must Do More for Doha to Succeed," October 24, 2005), Wolfowitz appeared to be advocating many of the same changes in global trade as you have. How do you explain this?*

No one knew at the time what Wolfowitz would do. Where you sit determines where you stand, so the hope was that when he assumed the position as president of the World Bank, he would become concerned with global poverty and development issues, even if he still saw them through a particular set of eyes, so that he would not become an instrument of American foreign policy per se but would still see the world with the same mindset that had supported shock therapy and Iraq beforehand. So there were actually two worries: one was whether he would be an instrument of U.S. policy, and the second was to what extent his worldview was one that was antithetical to a view of development that I thought was appropriate.

Since he has taken office, I think he has taken two extremely important decisions that are consistent with his acting in the best interest of the World Bank and the fighting of global poverty. The first is his strong position on global trade in favor of developing countries.[4] The second is his argument that the United States and other advanced industrial countries should assume responsibility for financing debt relief, rather than trying to finance debt relief out of World Bank money. Financing out of World Bank money, as I pointed out, would be like having the poor pay for the very poor. He did the right thing on both of these issues, and I think he should be commended for that. There are other instances where he has been presented with situations where he has taken the right decisions. There still is a worry, I think, about what the World Bank will be doing in Iraq, what the policies will be, whether he will go in before it is safe and secure, whether he will put at risk World Bank personnel, and so on. There are a large number of issues in Iraq that remain unresolved. And there are a lot of other issues too—the whole debate on the Washington Consensus versus the reforms that occurred in the last ten years in moving away from the Washington Consensus to some other perspectives, as I discussed earlier. So there is still some concern, but he has made the right decisions on a few of these key issues.

George Monbiot wrote in the Guardian *that Wolfowitz's appointment "demolishes the hopeless reformism of men like George Soros and Joseph Stiglitz who, blithely ignoring the fact that the U.S. can veto any attempt to challenge its veto, keep waving their wands in the expectation that a body designed to project U.S. power can magically be transformed into a body which works for the poor. Had Stiglitz's attempt to tinker with the World Bank's presidency succeeded, it would simply have lent credibility to an illegitimate institution, thus enhancing its powers. With Wolfowitz in charge, its credibility plummets." Could you comment on this?*

I think it underestimates the constraints that are imposed on the World Bank. My hope has always been that the World Bank would evolve into a truly multilateral institution. This is predicated on my belief that there is a need for global, collective action, that closer integration of the countries of the world makes collective action at a global level even more important. Doing something about poverty in the Third World is among the most important activities that need to be undertaken collectively. We need to have international institutions to help do this. In any such institution, any democratic such institution, the United States will, because of its economic and political power, play a large role. In any democracy, rich and powerful players have a role. Not only do they have a role, they have a *disproportionate* role. So the question is not whether we believe that we can change politics, but whether we can design institutions that are capable of undertaking collective, global action. In the context of the World Bank, the question is whether we can make the institution work in such a way that it broadly reflects the interests of the developing countries. The evidence is that there have been big changes. Not as big as one would have hoped, but big. Debt relief is a big thing. It involves billions of dollars. Aid is a big thing. It is not as much as we would like, but it is still billions of dollars. The debate on trade today is totally different from what it was a few years ago. Several years ago, in March 1999, when I first gave a speech on the need for a development round at the WTO, no one thought of that; it was the first call for a development round. I pointed out what was wrong with the Uruguay Round. Now everybody recognizes the inequity. We are not there all the way yet, but I think that the magnitude of concessions that will be made is much larger than it otherwise would have been.

What is important is to scrutinize every action of the World Bank and the IMF, recognizing that, as they are constituted today, they are not really fully democratic and they do disproportionately reflect certain financial interests. And therefore they lack legitimacy. In a way, we have succeeded in undermining the legitimacy of these institutions. Previously only the radical Left questioned the legitimacy of the IMF and the World Bank, whereas now I think that there is a broad acceptance that these institutions are not fully democratically legitimate. That recognition has really taken away a lot of their power.

Monbiot has also written that "The nationality of the bank's president, which has been causing so much fuss, is of only symbolic importance. Yes, it seems grossly unfair that all its presidents are Americans, while all IMF presidents are Europeans. But it doesn't matter where the technocrat implementing the U.S. Treasury's decisions comes from. What matters is that he's a technocrat implementing the U.S. Treasury's decisions." As someone who has also mentioned this problem, how would you respond to this?

It is clear that Wolfensohn moved the institution some degrees. I don't want to say he changed it completely, but he moved it some degrees. There is a symbiotic relationship between the technocracy and the head of an international financial institution. The head picks the technocrats that he likes and they get promoted. I don't think one should view the head of the World Bank or the IMF as being completely at the mercy of the technocrats. It was not, for instance, inevitable that huge bailouts of creditors would be arranged following the Asian financial crisis. The international financial institutions make political decisions so the president does not have a free rein, but at certain times, under certain conditions, he does shape things enormously.

Could you explain the magic whereby the United States is able to run trade and payments deficits amounting to hundreds of billions of dollars annually, without running the consequences that would follow for Third World countries with proportionate deficits, and do so with no audible protest from the rest of the world? Is this situation not repeated at the level of the middle-class U.S. citizenry?

The point about that is this: the difference between the United States and the rest of the world is that we have an enormous amount of wealth. That wealth provides confidence to many people in the world that we can repay that debt. But it is partially a confidence game. That is to say, if everybody started losing confidence and started pulling their money out of the country, then the country would be weaker and there would be very serious problems. So the issue is how bad do things get before people will have this response, before this becomes a significant risk? And many people think that we are nearing the point at which that could happen.

What do you think?

I think that it is beginning to get to a level that is worrying. Clearly anybody who has held their money in the form of dollars rather than euros has lost a considerable amount of money since 2003. If people extrapolate that this will continue to be the case in the future, and behave accordingly, then there will be an ongoing movement out of the dollar.

PART TWO I
POSTCOLONIALISM AND THE
NEW IMPERIALISM

FIVE I Partha Chatterjee

INTELLECTUAL TRAJECTORY

Could you tell us a little about your intellectual and academic trajectory? What impact did growing up in the immediate, postindependent period in India have on you? What relationship does this have to the fact that much of your work has focused on nationalism?

I did not actually begin my academic career studying nationalism. I completed my Ph.D. degree in political science at the University of Rochester where I studied international relations and nuclear war strategies. The political science department at Rochester was one of the earliest departments that focused on rational choice theory. I used to do game theoretic models of arms races and things like that. That is how I actually began, believe it or not! I suppose I did that kind of work because I was in a political science department at an American university and this was the kind of work being done there. Although even as I was doing it, I was quite certain that I was going to go back to India after I got my Ph.D.

Immediately after I finished my dissertation, I returned to Calcutta, where I was born and brought up. It was obvious that there was no way I could pursue the same kind of work in India because there was no one else doing it; nothing in the intellectual atmosphere would have made that kind of work meaningful. When I returned it was early 1972, in the immediate aftermath of the Maoist uprising that took place from about 1969 to 1971. That was the period I was away. Many of my friends in college were involved in the movement, and by the time I went back, some of them were still in jail and a few had been killed. So what I did was basically set a part of my training aside and retrain myself in areas in which other people were doing work.

In the early 1970s, a great deal of research was concerned with agrarian structures and peasant movements. The whole atmosphere was charged with questions regarding the nature of the Indian state. Even before the Emergency in India (1975–1977), as far as Calcutta and West Bengal were concerned, the face of the authoritarian state had become very clear in the period of the Maoist uprising and immediately afterward. So people were preoccupied with questions about the violence of the state and the possibilities of political movements based on the peasantry. Those were really the major questions posed by the Maoist movement.

So that is what I began to think about. The way of proceeding to answer those questions, given the methods then popular, was to examine the historical context. In other words, how had the independent Indian state emerged? The whole story of the movement against colonialism, and the question of how the Indian peasantry was involved with that movement and with the formation of that state, became the central questions. So that is how I entered into the field. It was not nationalism that was my immediate concern; it was much more the specific history of the emergence of the Congress party and the way in which Congress had included the peasantry within the national movement. This was the issue I ultimately took up: the emergence of, broadly speaking, movements of nationalism, but specifically, the kind of nationalism adopted by the Congress that found a base in rural areas by trying to organize peasants into the anticolonial struggle.

For the next three or four years, I lived in Calcutta, but for about fifteen to twenty days of the month I would go into various districts and just talk to people. There are now much better organized sources on the subject (that archive got organized precisely in that period, the 1970s), but at the time I began work there was no organized archive for this. Nothing like the Nehru Memorial Library in Delhi, which now has a very good collection of local literature from all parts of India in all Indian languages, existed at the time. The only way one could do this work then was to go into different rural districts and talk to people. At the time, there were still people around who were important leaders as well as middle-ranking, local leaders of these movements in the 1920s and 1930s. So that is what I did; I just talked to people like that. And this was when my interest in the larger subject of nationalism developed.

As you will notice, in a sense, even there, my early work was really concerned with the relationship between the national movement and the agrarian question.

You were trained in American political science, a rather narrow field as you have just suggested, and you have explained your intellectual trajectory upon your return to India, but you managed to develop a highly unusual and expansive range of interests. You are often characterized as a Renaissance man for this reason, given your work in theater, music, cultural studies, history, politics, and international relations. What made that possible?

I do not think this happened consciously at all. It is just that I became engaged in the activities and interests that were part of urban life in Calcutta. Theater, for instance, was not only part of academic and political life, but very much a part of urban life in Calcutta at the time. One of my interests—which many people in the academic world are not aware of—is sports. I was an avid soccer fan, which was, again, very much part of the urban life I am describing. Maybe someday I will write about football in Calcutta, a sport that I think is really a major part of urban India.

In the 1970s there was the film society movement, which was very much part of what people did in the city: watching classic European films that were never shown in regular theaters. There were about fifteen to twenty major film clubs in Calcutta, which acquired these films from various foreign embassies and consulates. Theater, in some ways, was part of the same kind of search: to become acquainted with modern European culture. Unlike the cinema, which was actually available—if you looked for them, you could find prints of Italian neorealist films, French films, and so on—there was no way you could actually see European productions of Brecht, Ibsen, Pirandello, or anything of the kind. The classics of twentieth-century European theater were produced sometimes as adaptations, sometimes as straightforward translations, for the urban theater enthusiast in India. Brecht was the greatest favorite. In the 1970s there were three hundred to four hundred theater groups in Calcutta (this is probably still true today). There were only about ten theaters. Nothing could run continuously for two to three weeks; auditoriums were booked per night. You could walk into any of these theaters on any night and one or the other of these groups would be doing a production of some European classic. This again was a very major part of the urban life I have been talking about.

It is rather curious now, thinking back on this period, that the same people who were concerned with political questions also seemed to look for certain forms of politics and certain forms of the state that were *not* simply copies of Western political formations. The differences seemed quite striking: the fact that India was very largely an agrarian-based, peasant-based country, so different indeed from the modern West—by which I mean the contemporary West. Yet, at the same time, there was such an urge to *know* about the modern West and, in a sense, to imbibe what seemed to be the best of modernity. The two went together. So I was, in a sense, completely a part of this. One did not think of this as consciously cultivating a Renaissance spirit or anything of the kind!

SUBALTERN STUDIES

Could you tell us about your work with the Subaltern Studies collective? What do you believe is the significance of the kind of history writing inaugurated by this school?

In some ways, I think that too has its source in precisely the sort of intellectual atmosphere that I was talking about. In a sense, the central question being posed by the Subaltern Studies group is the following: What is the relationship between peasants as the major demographic formation in India and the emergence of the modern state?

The background to that was partially, of course, the political failure of the answers that had been offered up to that point. The Emergency that Indira Gandhi declared from 1975 to 1977 was in effect seen as a symptom of a virtually terminal illness afflicting the Indian state. At that point, it seemed that all the liberal, constitutional foundations of the state had clearly failed to hold up. Even after 1977, when the Emergency regime came to an end, I don't think we seriously believed that Indian democracy in that particular form would last for very long. The signs of an essentially authoritarian core of the state had been revealed then, and it was very powerful.

So that was one failure. The other failure had to do with the peasant uprising attempted through the Maoist and other communist-led movements that had been beaten back by this time. It is in that context that the historical question once again was raised by Subaltern Studies. It tried to offer an answer to the question I mentioned earlier, namely: What was the relationship between the peasantry and the Indian state? The answer effectively was that when the peasants joined the elite-led national movement, it was not, as the nationalists believed, that the peasantry was prepolitical, was somehow completely unconscious of these sorts of political questions before, and was roused into political consciousness by the nationalist leadership. That was not the answer. The Subaltern Studies answer was that peasants always had their own reasons for joining or not joining this sort of politics. When they joined, they did not join for the same reasons as the elite nationalists who were launching the movement. Very often, they joined the movement on their own terms, and on many occasions they left the movement. On many other occasions they refused to join at all. Those became the instances that Subaltern Studies actually looked for.

In terms of the methods, I think those were in some ways innovative. As I said, there was no ready archive for this sort of work. What we tried to do was use the official archive in such a way that you could actually *read* peasant consciousness, that is, read the official reports and the official archive *against* the grain in order to try and find the voice of the subaltern, as it were.

Of course, we looked for other kinds of records, too. In fact, it was in the course of this work that we came across other evidence, the kinds of sources that conventional history would never have recognized as sources. We would look for things like rumors; we found, for instance, collections of rumors that were narrated in local newspapers at the time. Now, conventional history would dismiss this, saying it is a rumor and cannot be read as a *real* source. We tried to use this sort of evidence as a record of a *different* kind of consciousness. At that time, there was also a much greater appreciation for things like popular culture, religion in particular, and how these ideas and practices were important in trying to understand what peasants were doing when they joined movements or made certain demands from movements, what they were looking for. These were some of the methodological innovations made by Subaltern Studies.

One of the most productive formulations of the founding father, as it were, of the Subaltern Studies collective, Ranajit Guha, vis-à-vis the specificity of the modern colonial state, is that it is characterized by "dominance without hegemony." Could you explain what that phrase means and what it signifies? Also, in your book The Nation and Its Fragments, *you employ this term, calling it "the rule of colonial difference." Could you elaborate on your understanding of the nature of the colonial state and the consequences that follow from it for the nature of the modern experience of the colonies?*

One of the things that we tried to argue was the quite fundamental similarity between the colonial and the postcolonial states. The similarity was not so much in the actual bases of support for the two formations, because the sections of the Indian population on which the colonial state relied for support were not necessarily the same as those that supported the new nation-state. But many of the techniques of rule, the governing practices on which these regimes were based, were very similar. This was one of the strongest political arguments we were trying to make. Specifically, we would look again at the way in which state organs (courts of law, administrative agencies, etc.) would go about dealing with the large mass of the people, especially peasants. Our argument very often was that in a sense those techniques of rule had not fundamentally changed. The Indian Armed Forces were inherited fully intact from the British Indian Army. The body of civil and criminal law as well as the structure of the courts were inherited without any major change. The structure of the bureaucracy too, especially the famous district administration of British India, was adopted wholesale, only expanded several times after independence.

It was this state of affairs that we characterized essentially, as you just said, as dominance without hegemony. We defined hegemony as a form of rule where there is an active consent on the part of those being ruled. This active consent had to be produced through all sorts of institutions and practices in society. The contrast being made was with that of a fully developed, liberal, capitalist society where there was class rule—there is no question that some classes had greater power in society—and yet there was an overall structure of governance where you could say that even those classes that were not directly in power still consented to the way in which society was ruled. There was an *active* consent that was *produced*—it was not just based on sheer force. Whereas the phenomenon we were always concerned with was the fundamentally *authoritarian* character of the postcolonial state. Why did it have to be authoritarian in this way, if in fact the national movement was what it claimed to be, which was a movement of *the people* against an authoritarian, colonial state?

The argument was that, in effect, the postcolonial national state was *not* based on this sort of structure of consent, which again went back to the question of the relationship between the peasants and the new state. Clearly, there was a new state that was created, and this new state claimed to speak on behalf of the people as a whole and even granted formal rights of citizenship to people within its borders. This formal citizenship, however, did not mean *real* citizenship. So, for instance, in the classic case of Indian peasants, although they had been brought into the national movement and made members of a supposedly new *national* community, they actually did not have real rights of citizenship. The district administration still dealt with the rural population on the lines of the old colonial administration. Rural landlords claimed a privileged access to the local bureaucracy and the police because they were the real wielders of power in rural society. All sorts of progressive laws were made by parliament that could not be implemented because the old power groups in the countryside would not allow the agencies of government to subvert their power. Peasants now had the formal right to vote, but they could be coerced to vote as their landlords told them to vote, or even not allowed to vote at all. The necessity of force or coercion to keep peasants under control was always central, even in the new state.

I think I should add that a lot of this actually began to change—in terms of the fundamental understanding of the Indian state—through the 1980s. The 1980s were quite crucial in terms of a new understanding of how the different sections of the Indian peasantry actually learned to use the room for maneuver that was opened up through the process of electoral democracy. All of the things that we now associate with the day-to-day processes of Indian democracy were not clear to us *at all* in the 1970s, for instance, that one could pressurize elite representatives and so on. In fact, that is the most dramatic change that has taken place, and I think it has to do with what many people see as a change between the early Subaltern Studies and late Subaltern Studies. The background to this is essentially that the very real perception we had of the nature of the Indian state in the 1970s—and we saw it quite categorically as a fundamentally *authoritarian* state—changed quite drastically through the 1980s.

It was in the same period that many new kinds of social movements emerged in India, and these social movements tried to use a whole range of completely new forms of mobilization, using the power of the vote, using the kinds of new opportunities made available through the framework of broadly liberal rights. That is something that quite fundamentally changed our understanding of what the Indian state was like. We had to admit that the process of politics was far more complicated than what we had earlier thought it to be. But, as I said, that is a change that only began to be registered through the 1990s. So it is only in the last ten to fifteen years that these new kinds of social movements emerged, creating, in a sense, a new ethnography of politics in India. The emergence of the caste movement especially is a good example, alongside of course a whole range of movements of relatively marginalized groups, all of which are extremely vocal, are quite organized, and employ a combination of both legal, constitutional methods as well as some extralegal strategies—some degree of violence, for instance. All these movements, however, represent a kind of assertion of, broadly speaking, democratic rights of different kinds. So in trying to understand what Indian political life is all about, this has changed the picture. This was not the case in the 1970s largely because, I think, the processes of governance have changed quite fundamentally.

ANTICOLONIAL NATIONALISM

In Nationalist Thought and the Colonial World, *you suggest that nationalist thought operates "within a framework of knowledge whose representational structure corresponds to the very structure of power it seeks to repudiate." In other words, nationalism may succeed in liberating the nation from colonialism but not from the knowledge system of the post-Enlightenment West, which may continue to dominate maybe even more powerfully. Could you elaborate that argument?*

One of the things that is now quite widely recognized is how many of the postcolonial state forms—not just India—that emerged after decolonization in the 1940s and 1950s replicated quite consciously the forms of the modern state in the West. This prompted the obvious question: What, then, was the opposition to colonial rule all about? There were very strong strands within the anticolonial movement that in fact suggested that the real task of the anticolonial movement was not simply to replace the European ruler with local rulers, but to think of completely different *forms* of rule. Gandhi, for instance, often used to say that the point of the movement was not to have English rule without the Englishman. But this almost never happened. In most cases, the nationalist movement really sought to create a European-style or Western-style modern state, based on very similar constitutional principles, very similar technologies of administration, and simply to replace the personnel.

The question then was: Why was this so? One of the most general answers to this question, which is the one I offered in that book, is that the framework of ideas within which non-Western nationalism tried to answer the questions—of why these countries were subjected to European rule, why this rule was considered illegitimate, what would be a more legitimate form of rule—was completely derived from the whole body of modern, *Western* political thought and social theory. Within that framework, the question was, effectively, who was it that ruled? What is the structure within which people ought to be ruled? What were the most desirable forms of the state? I think all of those questions were effectively taken to have been answered *already* within the body of modern, Western political thought. In the case of many of these postcolonial debates within nationalism, there were liberals, Marxists, and socialists, but really all the debates were in effect the same debates that had taken place in the West. The interesting question then was: Were there possibilities that had been repressed in the course of these movements? That is where many of the new possibilities opened up: Were there alternative ways of thinking about a modern state?

In the Indian case, the whole Gandhian way of thinking was clearly very interesting. My answer, after having looked at what the body of Gandhian thought and practice meant, was: Yes, this was clearly an attempt to think of the state and forms of rule in very different terms. But it was effectively a failure. Having raised the question and having produced completely new conditions through which people could be mobilized for the anticolonial movement, the Gandhian intervention in effect completely failed to reach the sorts of objectives that it had placed before the nation. If you ask me why, I would say it was because of the way in which it tried to deal with the fundamental problem of violence in society. The original and distinctive contribution of Gandhian politics was to evolve amazingly effective techniques of nonviolent resistance by an unarmed people against the institutions of state violence. But it never managed to propose a theory, or even a set of techniques, by which a state could legitimately employ violence against wrongdoers. In the absence of such a theory, Gandhian thinking could only present itself as a nonmodern form of resistance, never as an alternative form of the modern state.

I think similar questions have been asked, for instance, about the place of religion in modern society, attempting to reformulate the question of religion in the light of modern conditions. Obviously, Islam is a very major field here in the Indian subcontinent and other parts of the non-Western world as well, and many things have been said about it. These discussions and debates continue even today. The questions that get opened up are essentially about whether a *different* modernity is possible.

My answer in the *Nationalist Thought* book was largely pessimistic. At the time, I would have said that, of course, there were many of these other possibilities that had been raised, and because they were raised

I think they allowed for many new forms of mobilization, which had never been seen in national movements or democratic movements in the West. These were completely new ways of mobilizing people. But if you think of the end results, they were largely imitations of the modern state in the West, which, I would have said then, would explain in some ways why many of these postcolonial states seemed to be deficient, like poor *copies*, second-rate modern states.

From the *Fragments* book onward, I have been more concerned with looking at practices rather than the big frame. In other words, I became aware that rather than asking the big questions—looking at the overall frame of modern politics and the modern state—if one were more sensitive to the local practices and the more localized innovations that have taken place, I think one would become more aware of where the differences lie. In terms of the overall frame (the constitution, the basic institutional structure), one could say that they are often quite good copies of the liberal constitutional state (India is a good example of this, I think). It is in the actual working practices, I think, that many of the innovations emerge. If one looks at the sources of these innovations and what these innovations actually try to achieve, in the local sense, one becomes far more appreciative of how even the so-called corruptions of the original are actually doing things that many of these constitutional or democratic forms of government in the West could never have achieved. These become much more interesting and important questions.

You have, for instance, rules of formal equality: the law applies equally to everyone. Everyone is aware that this is a major principle of the modern state in the West. If you move to the Indian context, it is a principle that is upheld by the courts and the constitution. Yet, if you look at the localized context, you will find that even state authorities make exceptions to that rule. The law does *not* apply equally to everybody. And the exceptions are often very interesting: Why exceptions are made, how and why they are justified, and what the exceptions actually achieve. Very often, one would find that if the exception had not been made, large sections of the people would probably have never been brought under this system of modern governance. They would have been excluded in ways that would have completely jeopardized the overall structure itself.

Some examples are common and actually quite obvious. For instance, in most Third World cities there are large populations that can only survive by breaking the law. They live on land that does not belong to them, they squat on public property, they travel on public transport without buying tickets, and very often they use electricity and water without paying for it. If the law applied equally for everybody, then those who were buying tickets to travel on trains should have refused to allow those who were not buying tickets to make the same journey.

But in actual administrative practice, that rarely happens. Administrators will tell you that they know that people are squatting on illegally occupied land, but it is best to let them stay. This is so because, for many reasons, this same population often has a very important role to play in the urban economy; in their absence, these urban economies might simply collapse. One could see this from another perspective as well: if these people had no livelihood *at all*, they would be even more of a threat to property, to the law, and to order. This is a way in which these people are actually controlled and governed, by precisely making them an *exceptional* case.

So if one looks at the local application of the principles of modern government, I think one will find extremely interesting innovations. Not all of them necessarily appear desirable, and many involve some degree of routine violence. Those are the more interesting areas in which one can actually see borrowed or copied models of the modern state being domesticated, often in new and innovative ways. They are actually producing different results and having different effects, which they do not have in Western contexts.

In the same book, Nationalist Thought in the Colonial World, *you say, "to the extent that nationalism opposed colonial rule it administered a check on a specific political form of metropolitan capitalist dominance. In the process it dealt a deathblow (or so at least one hopes) to such blatantly ethnic slogans of dominance as the civilizing mission of the West, the white man's burden, etc. That must be counted as one of the major achievements in world history of nationalist movements in colonial countries." Your parenthetical qualification ("one hopes") in this quote already indicates a doubt with regard to the historical finality of the postcolonial victory over Western racism. What was behind this apprehension?*

Well, you see it right now! Even today, I would put it in that slightly ambivalent way. I think, overall, the lessons of decolonization and what it means for world history are irreversible. I do not really believe that this call for a new empire, in spite of recent claims about how empire is actually good for everybody, carries any real conviction anywhere in the world. But it is true that in many ways, some of the slogans of the civilizing mission have returned, even if employing other phraseology.

I suppose even then there was some lurking suspicion that these things might come back. I really think it is impossible to return to any framework of colonial empires because, unlike in the eighteenth or nineteenth centuries when you could make a kind of moral argument about bringing modernity and civilization to uncivilized parts of the world, you cannot make the same claim today precisely because the main claims of European or Western modernity have actually become completely universal. You cannot claim that democracy is the exclusive preserve of the West, although in popular political discourse in the West these claims are often made, about democracy somehow just being part of Western *culture*. It is simply not true; whether they have it or not, the idea of democracy is actually available everywhere in the world. I think the same goes for many of the other claims on behalf of modernity, including the claims about science and technology and modern medicine and everything else. It is simply no longer credible to make the claim that modern medicine is somehow a "gift" of the West. People all over the world know that these are things that are available. There may be arguments and debates about whether they want them, at what cost, on what terms, etc., but everyone is aware of their existence. Many of these may well be real questions, but it is no longer a question of a Western "gift" to the rest of the world.

In that sense, what is generally described as the period of decolonization after the Second World War did deliver a complete deathblow to any kind of traditional colonial structure in the world. I do not think that form is ever going to return.

How do you explain the resurgence now of precisely the same kind of rhetoric?

There are a lot of people who are trying to make sense of the structure of dominance in the world, what it means and how it is to be exercised—and of course we are talking now of the dominance of the United States. They are making sense of it in terms of an older rhetoric, an older language, which is why there is suddenly a spate of books about the British empire of the nineteenth century and how that historical lesson might be relevant for American rulers today. This rhetoric has become so fashionable simply because that historical moment offers a certain justification for worldwide dominance by one power. It offers a set of rhetorical languages by which that power can be justified.

I do not believe that the effective structure of dominance of the United States today is anything like the British dominance of the world in the nineteenth century. U.S. dominance is not simply a dominance over the so-called less-developed parts of the world; it is dominance over Europe, over Japan, over China. These formations over which the United States is seeking dominance are completely within the structure of a global modernity, in the standard conception of what "modernity" entails. This is a new kind of dominance. I do not think there is a good language to describe it. For this reason, there is so much apprehension over what this form of dominance might mean for the rest of the world. The real apprehension is that those that wield this power do *not* actually understand what this power is all about and how they are going to use it. After all, this power is almost entirely the power to use violence; it is *fundamentally* military power. There is such an enormous concentration of the means of violence in one country and so *little* ethical justification for using that absolute military power. We are living today in a very dangerous situation. But for the reasons I have given, I do not think this is the same as the nineteenth-century British empire.

Also in Nationalist Thought and the Colonial World *you indicate that the emergence of both separatist movements and the fundamentalist cultural revival in the third or postcolonial world has to be seen in terms of the structural tensions in the history of nationalist thought in the colonial world. What do you mean by that?*

Well we should return to some of the things we were talking about earlier. The innovations in nationalist thinking and nationalist mobilizations that have occurred in the postcolonial world have tended to get repressed by the emergence of fairly standardized forms of governance. Many of these innovations were actually repressed because they were *not* seen to be consistent with the *known* forms of the modern state. For instance, if you had movements or parties that were largely based on religion, this was seen to be somehow *inconsistent* with the idea of a modern constitutional state. Therefore, there was always this problem of what to do with such movements. Yet, those movements have been very influential and powerful in terms of mobilizing people against colonial rule.

So, once the objective of decolonization and transfer of power to a new nationalist elite had been met, the question was how to contain or manage these forces that had been released in the course of the national movement. That is where many of these tensions remained unresolved. If you look at the case of postindependence India, this whole debate about the "secular" state and what the secular state must do and what it means, in a sense, reflected this unresolved tension. In the historical process of the emergence of that state, a great deal of the mobilization had used religion, had depended on extremely powerful religious reform movements, of actually shaping what were seen to be religious beliefs and religious practices but changing them, reformulating them, in order to conform to what were seen to be the new challenges of the modern world.

So these religious reform movements were often completely part of the broader set of social changes that brought about nationalism, that brought about the new state, that brought about new political formations. They were integrally tied with many of those movements, and yet the requirements of the secular state presumably forbade religion in public places or public life, or forbade political parties based on religion, because these were somehow inconsistent with a *modern* nation-state. Very often there were all kinds of shortcuts or repressive ways of keeping those things under cover, as it were. Many of the tensions around secularism, for instance, and the kinds of challenges that emerged later on, in the case of India's Hindu right wing in the 1980s, for instance, were very much part of these unresolved questions from within the national movement. What the Hindu Right then appealed to was not to say that nationalism was all wrong; they said, in fact, that they were the "true" nationalists. That could be said persuasively because of a great deal of religious-based rhetoric and the presence, as I said, of these powerful religious reform movements, which were always part and parcel of nationalism.

So these remained unresolved problems. The overall frames remained derivative, almost imitations of forms of the state as developed in the West, but in actual practice what had to be done was to find completely innovative practices at the localized level. The real problem occurred when many of these local adaptations and innovations required a new translation into the larger frame. If you look back on the many kinds of tensions that were brought out later on, such as complaints about minorities being given all sorts of privileges—one standard complaint against the secular state—you will find that many of these so-called concessions or privileges were completely justified but entirely *localized* arrangements. There were certain locally acceptable forms of public display, for instance, that clearly reflected a certain majoritarian understanding of what a public ceremony meant. But these required certain local adjustments. Through the postindependence period, for instance, there have been public celebrations of religion where state functionaries and officials have participated because they were seen to be *local* festivals that large numbers of people attended. Many of these forms also meant that at the local level there were celebrations by minority communities that also had their place. So people knew that on a particular day, during a particular celebration, there would be music on the streets and so on, but on another day, because it was the local minority community that was celebrating something, this would not be done. It is a *local* understanding, a local consensual arrangement. In many of these cases, these local understandings evolved and the arrangements often varied from one place to another. But once you had these local arrangements being compared and translated in terms of the overall framework of the character of the state, then it posed problems. Is it *truly* a secular state? If it is a secular state, then why is the minority community treated one way in this place and another way in the other place? It is then that the autonomy of the local arrangement is called into question. The criticism would always be that if India is a secular, democratic state, then these local arrangements cannot hold because all citizens are supposed to be equal, and supposed to be treated equally, so there can be no such special concessions made to minority communities. This became the new problem because many of the issues that appeared to have been resolved were resolved *purely* in the local context. But once the autonomy of the *local* is called into question, what begins to appear is the inadequacy of the *overall* arrangement. This is when the whole thing became exposed and began to unravel, as it were.

POSTCOLONIAL MODERNITY

You have also written a lot about how modernity ought to be understood in the postcolonial context. You say, for instance, "Ours is the modernity of the once colonized. The same historical process that has taught us the value of modernity has also made us the victims of modernity." Could you explain what the term modernity encompasses in this view, and what it means in the context of the postcolonial world?

In some ways, it means precisely the sorts of difficulties encountered in actually resolving the different demands of the *overall* framework. The way I put this in *Nationalist Thought* is the distinction between what I call the "thematic" and the "problematic." The thematic was the overall frame, and I think we failed in finding a thematic for *our* modernity. In other words, we did not succeed in formulating a *different* thematic. The thematic description of modernity was exactly the same as in the West; we always wanted to be exactly the same *kind* of moderns. In terms of more specific answers, especially in terms of actual practices, I have always emphasized that many of these practices, in terms of their innovations and elaborations of so-called modern ideas, are applied only locally. Those local elaborations of the modern—and an incredibly large number of innovations have been made—allowed for the great themes of modernity to become *domesticated*. These specific situations, however, remained very different from the situations of Western modernity.

The number of different things that non-Western modernity has produced in terms of actual practices in localized situations never really managed to find a larger language that could give them the identity or the character of a *different* modernity. That is what I meant when I said that we also became the *victims* of modernity. The overall *constraints* of a given framework have always bound us to merely innovating at a localized level but without ever succeeding in claiming that this is in fact a more general framework of modernity that can be universally used by others.

So, in terms of intellectual claims, we still remain victims of Western modernity, despite the fact that places like China might well become the *real* powerhouses of modernity in the twenty-first century. China is in fact the perfect example: in spite of all this amazing transformation, intellectually there are almost no claims that emerge from there that suggest that they are changing faster than any other part of the world. The language in which this change is being described is the *old* language of modernization, growth, technology, and so on. It is *exactly* the same language. That is why, even for places like China, in this respect, they remain *victims* of modernity.

Here in the West, as I am sure you're aware, it is often thought that postcolonial studies represent a tendency in the Third World to disavow responsibility for the problems that are endemic to that world. Why, it is argued, do they keep on talking about colonialism when colonialism ended half a century ago? How do you respond to such allegations?

It is not to disavow responsibility at all, it is actually to *claim* a certain responsibility that has been denied. In a sense, what is often seen as the *inability* of postcolonial states to resolve many of these new problems of modernity is not because the people have not often managed to find innovative solutions; the problem lies with the larger formation of ideas invented in the West. I think that is where the colonial legacy is so strong. That China can grow at such a pace, and grow in forms that can only be described as "modern," and yet have no larger frame of political discourse within which this experience can be described as anything other than simply a replication, indeed a poor replication, of what had happened in the West, I think, summarizes the problem. That is clearly a misdescription of what is happening in China; yet, there is no other language to describe it. *That*, I think, is the colonial legacy. The only way one can assume authority over what one is doing, the only way one could claim responsibility for what one is doing, would be, in a sense, to finally get *rid* of that colonial legacy.

This is to declare that Western modernity is, in fact, an incomplete and probably imperfect modernity; there are better ways of doing things. Those better ways can emerge in other parts of the world that are becoming modern. That is the claim that needs to be made. As I keep saying, there are numerous examples of actual localized practices where this kind of innovative thinking and innovative functioning has actually taken place. It is a question of finding a larger discursive frame, which is different and new and innovative. That is where I think the colonial legacy is the constraint; it actually has not allowed for that larger representation to be made.

My answer is that perhaps the field of postcolonial studies has not actually managed to provide that discursive frame. It is not that it tried to disavow responsibility or said that all the travails of the postcolonial world are because of what colonialism did to those places. That is not true at all. The origin of Subaltern Studies, as a specific postcolonial project, was in fact to understand the failures of the Indian nationalist elite. No argument was ever made that, for instance, what Indira Gandhi did was because of British colonialism. Not at all. The problem is actually very often misrepresented by those who feel uncomfortable with the findings of postcolonial studies. They say: "Let bygones be bygones; forget about colonialism because that's history—let's get on with the present." Well, people in the postcolonial world are all trying to get on with *their* present. What is happening is that people all over the world are desperately trying to forget the legacies of colonialism and trying to get ahead with the project at hand. Effectively, in terms of actual practices, that is what people have been trying to do, successfully or unsuccessfully. The real constraint, however, has been of trying to develop a larger or universal language within which those efforts can be understood and described. The weight of the claim that Western modernity is a complete and finished project keeps imposing these enormous shackles on other attempts elsewhere in the world.

You conclude the article "Beyond the Nation? Or Within?" by suggesting that the framework of global modernity will "inevitably structure the world according to a pattern that is profoundly colonial." What did you mean by this?

Again, I think I probably meant more or less the same thing as I said before. By the framework of global modernity, I meant this overall discursive frame claims to be universal and complete. But it is not actually universal, nor is it complete. All of the things that have been described as globalization in the last decade or so are good examples of this. Globalization is often claimed as a *new* thing that has emerged. Yet a lot of what has happened with globalization has happened for the last 100–150 years.

This is the weight of a language that can *claim* a certain *universality*, an applicability to almost everything that happens anywhere in the world. That is really the *discursive* power of Western modernity, which can encompass and bring under its wings almost anything that happens anywhere in the world. So, a lot of the local innovations simply never get recognized for the specific differences that they represent; the differences are simply erased. The only time the differences get recognized is when they are seen or argued to be inconsistent with the larger pattern. That is the profoundly colonial pattern of the structure of theoretical discourse; what is recognized as different is *necessarily* excluded, whereas everything else that can be made consistent is not recognized as different. If you go back to what I said earlier about the rule of colonial difference, it is exactly that.

POLITICAL SOCIETY

At a time where civil society is almost universally thought to be the panacea for the Third World and its ills, you have been criticizing the concept for a while and have instead developed the concept of "political society." Could you tell us what you see as the problems with the concept of civil society and the meaning of "political society" that you have been developing in The Politics of the Governed?

It is interesting that even though there is an eighteenth-century genealogy of the concept "civil society," it had been completely forgotten. It was only revived in the last twenty years or so, largely in the context of the collapse of the socialist regimes in Eastern Europe. It was revived largely to make the practices of modernity, in this case largely *political* practices of modernity, understandable and effective precisely in these localized, everyday situations.

The idea of civil society and the way it has been used in the last twenty years is not simply to describe the overall, large constitutional structures of the state; it is used largely to try and understand how politics operates on the ground, at the community and local levels. It is really at the local-ized level—if one is to use the concept of civil society meaningfully, as I've been saying in answer to your previous questions—where most of the innovations have been done. In fact, even if the overall structures of the state and the overall governing principles remain the same, the real differ-ences are at the level of localized practices. It is fundamentally misleading to claim that the same concept of civil society can describe the everyday, localized practices of governance in Western democracies *and* what hap-pens in non-Western situations today. Localized practice is where the differences lie, which is why I have tried to show numerous examples of how communities actually cope with questions of illegality, of violence, of different people not being treated equally. These are the contexts that demonstrate the inapplicability of the large structures of modern forms of governance. The reason these large structures fail is that they are made effective precisely by *not* following the same idea of civil society.

Civil society is typically about a kind of free associative, modern bourgeois life. It is quintessentially *bourgeois* politics. The challenge that the modern state faces in most of the non-Western world is that most people are *not* bourgeois. What sense does it make to use the forms of modern law and modern administrative procedures on populations that cannot *survive* if you simply insist on protection of private property, equality of law, freedom of contract, and these kinds of things? Most of these people would simply die or would rise in revolt and break down the whole structure.

The reason why many of the forms of modern government actually manage to work is because they make adjustments and negotiate with many of these contrary forms. They do so at the localized level, very often by recognizing themselves as merely exceptional cases. But, of course, exceptions pile upon exceptions, and very often there are localized norms that are quite contrary to what the larger principles would dictate. Very often, at the local level, people have an understanding that the norm is actually quite different. It is only by recognizing that norm at the local level that the larger structure will survive.

I have deliberately called this *political* society to suggest that the civil does not necessarily translate easily into the political; there is in fact a rift there. Yes, there is a zone of civil society in many of these countries. Yes, there is a zone where people rely on a modern contractual system, where there is free association, and I think many of those ideas—of free association, of modern, bourgeois life—actually have very powerful, often pedagogical, uses. Certainly many people lay great store by these ideas, which still continue to be effective as a way of thinking about what society *ought* to be like. It is recognized, however, that all of society is *not* like this and will not become like this overnight.

On the one hand, there is the modernizing project, which insists that at its completion, everybody will be properly respectful of the law and so on. But, in the meantime, how does society operate? There is a clear recognition that you have to make exceptions and that you have to negotiate very different claims. And these negotiations, I think, are fundamentally *political*.

GOVERNMENTALITIES

Also in The Politics of the Governed, *you argue that the increasing proliferation of what you call "governmental technologies" has made liberalism irrelevant. Could you tell us a little bit about the nature of these technologies and what they reflect about liberalism?*

These technologies have emerged largely through the twentieth century and are now available all over the world. Even in the West, it is in the last century that mass democracies emerged; prior to that, everybody did *not* have the vote at all. In the United States, for instance, universal adult franchise was granted only as recently as the 1960s, after the civil rights movement.

The emergence of these mass democracies produced new challenges, new problems of governance. A crucial development through the twentieth century was the emergence of an idea of governance where it was understood that you could not have one or two very simple, straightforward policies that would apply equally to all citizens. There was an increasing differentiation of sections of the population. It was understood that different sections of the population required different things, that different policies needed to be targeted at specific population groups.

For instance, you could say at a very simple level that men and women required different kinds of benefits from the government; even among women, different age groups would have different requirements. All of this was elaborated in Western countries in terms of what was called the "welfare state." Even in that welfare state, it was understood that in order to be properly responsive to the needs of different groups of people, the state must be flexible in its policies; you could not have one simple blanket policy for everybody.

These techniques were then transferred and adapted to postcolonial countries, where for these policies to be effective—in health and education, in the basic needs sector, for instance—you needed similarly flexible policies. Even in terms of delivering food, it was understood that urban populations and rural populations would have to be treated differently. Among rural populations, children must be treated differently from adults, and so on. There are numerous ways in which specific policies began to be formulated for very specific groups of people.

So these are the new governmental technologies that I say were developed and made available. The idea behind this, which I think is a late-twentieth-century development, was that no matter what the form of government, all governments needed to perform certain basic services and provide certain basic goods. At the global level, for instance, the United Nations is an international institution that provides certain services to anyone if the local government fails. If there is a famine in Ethiopia, one cannot simply say that the government in Ethiopia has failed, therefore nothing can be done. The idea is that certain basic services have to be provided to the people of Ethiopia, and if the local government cannot do it, then other people must. And how does one provide these services? That is where I am suggesting that certain technologies have now been developed to ensure that particular services and resources are allocated to particular population groups, no matter where they are.

What this means is that there are certain expectations that are now more or less universal; everybody, everywhere in the world, expects that a government *ought* to provide *certain* kinds of services at the very minimum. The interesting question now is how this technology of governance and the forms through which these services are provided will be combined with or related to *political* mobilization and ideology. This is where some interesting and perhaps quite basic changes have in fact emerged, starting with different forms of political mobilization. Specifically, I mean the ways in which population groups get classified and divided in the context of precisely these governmental services. Governmental classification could take numerous forms, for instance rural-urban, or could employ cultural or religious or ethnic categories, or some combination of the above. The point is that there is a whole range of ways in which populations might be classified for purposes of providing these services.

Very often, one would see that mobilizations would then occur around those governmental classifications. In other words, mobilization would take place precisely to make demands of the government on the basis of the category of which one was a part. The argument is roughly that the government has categorized people in this way and has guaranteed the provision of certain services to those belonging to that category. What you then get is a form of organization of political groups around classifications that are determined by the government. This can easily result in forms of mobilization that have nothing to do with the older ways in which people conceived of their identities. A lot of the identity politics that seems to have exploded in the last twenty years or so is probably conditioned by the ways in which people expect governments to provide them with certain kinds of basic services—welfare of different kinds, particular claims on things like education or employment, and so on.

The interesting question is how many of these categories—which have no moral foundation or any kind of ethical claim at all but are completely empirical descriptions of particular population groups—have actually managed to acquire a certain moral content *through* these political mobilizations. The claim is made that a group formed by a government classification is actually a *community*, there is a kind of solidarity, there is some *moral* identity of these people. This is the really interesting aspect of many of these political mobilizations: how do they manage to give themselves the form of a community when in fact there is no necessarily primordial or any other basis for this?

There are very interesting examples: in India, for instance, there is a category called BPL, which means "Below the Poverty Line." This is obviously an administrative demarcation. But there are policies of the government that say that if you belong to the BPL category, you are entitled to certain things and you actually carry a BPL card. In many places, there are organizations or associations of BPL people. People below the poverty line could be from many different communities, many different caste groups, but suddenly the fact that all these people are classified as a group, as the target of a particular kind of policy, produces the ground on which these people can mobilize as a community. I think the interesting questions would be: What is the moral character of this group? How is this local contextual community invented?

This is how the question of governmental technologies is connected with new forms of political mobilization, much of which is simply described as identity politics or sometimes as *ethnic* politics. Unlike the old anthropological understanding that most of this ethnic or identity politics has some kind of basis in primordial loyalties, a lot of it is probably simply a product of the way in which the new governmental technologies actually categorize people for purposes of administering policy.

SIX ❙ Mahmood Mamdani

In your previous work—both in Citizen and Subject *and in* When Victims Become Killers—*you have emphasized the need to understand the form of the postcolonial state. Since decolonization occurred several decades ago in much of Asia and Africa, why do you think it is important to continue talking about the legacy of the colonial state? What might such an understanding illuminate about the present political configuration in much of the Third World?*

There is a big debate on this issue in the study of Africa, more or less along the lines in which you frame your question. The two sides of the debate are represented by the Nigerian historian Ajayi and the Congolese philosopher Mudimbe. Ajayi is an older historian who started writing in the late colonial period and got better known in the early postcolonial period. He wrote several articles arguing that colonialism was a short interlude in the tapestry of African history that stretches over millennia, and sooner or later, we will see colonialism as nothing but a beep against this massive backdrop. In fact, he suggested, the quicker we begin to move away from thinking about colonialism, the freer we will be of the colonial hold.

Mudimbe's book, *The Invention of Africa*, does not respond directly to Ajayi, does not even mention him, but his position is completely different, indeed contrary, to Ajayi's. Mudimbe's argument is that it is not the duration of colonial influence that is relevant, but its depth and its texture. Mudimbe speaks of its ideological texture, but I would add also its *institutional* texture. So long as we keep on living our institutional lives within the institutions crafted in the colonial period, our lives will continue to be shaped by the colonial legacy even a thousand years from now.

Probably the best examples of this are the radical political revolutions in colonial Africa, like the Hutu Revolution of 1959 in Rwanda, which were determined to redress the grievances of the colonial period in a radical way. In doing so—in the particular instance of Rwanda, redressing the history of Tutsi privilege and Hutu servitude—they ended up *entrenching* the colonially crafted identities of Hutu as native and Tutsi as civilizing Hamites coming from outside. Even though the history of Tutsi privilege had long predated Belgian colonialism, the notion that this privilege could be *justified* as the prerogative of civilizing foreign Hamites was a colonial invention that the Tutsi elite swallowed along with colonial petty privilege. Ironically, the Hutu elite in the Rwandan revolution of 1959 also confirmed Hutu as "native" and Tutsi as "alien." It turned the pursuit of justice into a vendetta. In doing so, it turned the world of Hutu and Tutsi upside down, but without changing it. The ironic result was to further entrench political identities crafted under colonial rule by embedding these in the political legacy of the postcolonial revolution.

You have said elsewhere that "[P]ostcolonial studies brings home the fact that intellectual decolonization will require no less than an intellectual movement to achieve this objective." What does "intellectual decolonization" mean? How does this differ from formal, political decolonization, and what is its import?

We have learned through experience that political decolonization cannot be complete without an intellectual paradigm shift, which is what I mean by intellectual decolonization. In other words, by "intellectual decolonization" what I have in mind is thinking the present in the context of a past. Unlike radical political economy, though, the past needs to be thought through deeper than simply the colonial period. One unfortunate tendency of radical political economy was that it tended to reduce the usable past to the colonial period. We should recognize that the various forms of nativism around the postcolonial world—from racialized Black nationalism to ethnicized nationalisms to religious Muslim and Hindu nationalism, what we tend to call "fundamentalisms" these days—have been the first to raise this question. They are the ones who have accused self-declared modernist intellectuals of being nothing but a pale reflection of their colonial masters. They have emphasized the necessity to link up with the historicity of their respective societies. The only problem is that they rule out the colonial period as an artificial imposition, as a departure from an authentic history. Preoccupied with a search for and a return to origins, they tend to freeze the past in the pre-colonial period. This search also determines their notion of the colonial period: the Hutu nationalists think of the colonial period as the period prior to Tutsi migration, and the Hindu nationalists tend to think of it as the period prior to the Turkish invasions and the Islamic conversions. As a result, they underestimate—or sometimes fail to understand fully—the present by ignoring how the institutional and intellectual legacy of colonialism tends to be reproduced in the present.

I do acknowledge the importance of the nativist critique that calls for a fuller grasp of historicity, but one also needs to understand its weakness, because its sense of historicity is compromised by its search for authenticity. The point is not just to sidestep the nativist critique but to sublate it, in the manner in which Engels understood sublating Hegel in his critique of Ludwig Feuerbach; to take into consideration that which is relevant, effective, and forceful in the critique but at the same time to break away from its preoccupation with origins and authenticity.

You begin your book, Good Muslim, Bad Muslim: America, the Cold War, and the Roots of Terror, *with a discussion of Fanon and his insistence that the proof of the native's humanity consisted not in the willingness to kill settlers in a colonial context, but in the willingness to risk his or her own life. Are you suggesting that we should read contemporary acts of terrorism in a colonial frame, or at the very least as the violence of yesterday's victims, of victims who have become killers?*

To understand terrorism, we need to go beyond self-defense, beyond the violence of liberation movements, beyond the violence of anticolonial struggles and liberation movements. To understand nonstate terror today, we need to understand the historical relationship between state terrorism and nonstate terrorism. There is a clear and discernible historical dynamic: during the Cold War, state terror was parent to nonstate terror, and, having given rise to nonstate terror, it has then proceeded to mimic it—as, for instance, in the "War against Terror."

Fanon of course was not talking just about terror. Fanon was primarily talking about the relation between political violence and political modernity, between violence and freedom, so that those convinced that freedom was a value *higher* than life were willing to sacrifice life for freedom. Fanon went beyond Hegel. Modern man—and woman—is not simply willing to die for a cause higher than life, as Hegel said. He and she, for Fanon, are also willing to kill for that cause.

These two aspects of our political modernity seem to come together in the suicide bomber. The suicide bomber, however, has been widely understood in the Western media as a throwback to premodernity, either as adult irrationality or as a response of adolescents coerced by patriarchal authority. I think this explanation may be too easy and too self-serving. The reality is more likely the opposite: the suicide bomber is more likely born of a youth revolt than of patriarchal authority. The suicide bomber comes out of the history of the Intifadah. The first Intifadah in Palestine was coterminous with the Soweto uprising in South Africa. Both were testimony to youth revolts on two fronts: against both external authority—such as apartheid or the Zionist order—and the internal authority of the generation of their parents, a generation they saw as having capitulated to external authority by accepting the conditions of apartheid and occupation as normal. It is not very different from American youth during the civil rights and the antiwar movements of the 1960s. This is how I recall Bob Dylan's ode to the youth of the 1960s:

> Come O Mothers and Fathers of the land
> Get out of the way if you can't lend a hand
> Your sons and daughters are beyond your command
> For the times they are a-changing.

The point about the Vietnam War is that it ended, and so did apartheid with the end of the Cold War. The only thing that has not ended is the occupation in Palestine. Instead, it has turned into what George W. Bush called "facts on the ground," a brutal reality. The failure of the older generation to find a humane alternative in Palestine in part explains the desperation of the younger generation, resorting to violence in politics. Even then, we need to recognize that the term suicide bomber is a misnomer. The suicide bomber is a category of *soldier* whose objective is to kill—even if he or she must die to kill.

You repeatedly emphasize the importance of distinguishing between cultural (or religious) identity—what you call Culture Talk—and political identity. Why is this distinction necessary to understanding present debates regarding terrorism? To what extent does Culture Talk enable violence against particular peoples?

It is essential to make this distinction in an era of nationalism and the nation-state; in other words, in an era where the claim that cultural communities should be self-determining—meaning they should have their own state (with the "self" in self-determination a cultural self)—is considered obvious and normal, something that does not require an explanation. It is important to recognize that the raw material of political identities may be taken from the cultural sphere—common language, common religion, and so on—but once these identities are crafted into *political* identities, enforced within a territorial state, and reproduced through the mechanism of the law, which in turn recognizes its bearers as particular subjects, then identity becomes rather more complicated. It becomes extremely important to distinguish between political and cultural identity because political identity, unlike cultural identity, as enforced by the state through law, is singular, it is unidimensional: "You are this and nothing else." Whereas cultural identity is not only multiple but also cumulative, and it is not really territorial—something now widely acknowledged. It may have a territorial resonance, but it is not reducible to a territorial dimension, nor is it reducible to power. Political identity, on the contrary, is enforced through law and is an effect of power. I would even go further and say that, even in the case of resistance, its starting point is none other than political identities reproduced through the legal regime. This is notwithstanding the fact that there is a world of difference between resistance that reproduces political identities, whether in the name of reform or revenge, and resistance that sublates the political order by forging new political identities.

Could you explain the origins of the title, Good Muslim, Bad Muslim? *Is it not the case that the United States—or the West generally—should be supporting moderate, secular forces within the Muslim world to counteract extremist, fundamentalist currents?*

Even when Bush speaks of "good" Muslims and "bad" Muslims, what he means by "good" Muslims is really *pro-American* Muslims, and by "bad" Muslims he means *anti-American* Muslims. Once you recognize that, then it is no longer puzzling why *good* Muslims are becoming *bad* Muslims at such a rapid rate. You can actually begin to think through that development. If, however, you think of "good" and "bad" Muslims in cultural terms, it is mind-boggling that in one week, you can have a whole crop of "bad" Muslims—cultural changes do not usually happen with such rapidity! But if you have the aerial bombing of Falluja and the targeting of civilian populations accused of hosting "bad" Muslims, then you harvest an entire yield of bad Muslims at the end of the day, and the whole phenomenon becomes slightly less puzzling.

This is connected to my claim that political identities are not reducible to cultural identities. Political Islam, especially radical political Islam, and even more so, the terrorist wing in radical political Islam, did not emerge from conservative, religious currents, but on the contrary, from a *secular* intelligentsia. In other words, its preoccupation is *this*-worldly, it is about power in this world. To take only the most obvious example: I am not aware of anyone who thinks of Osama bin Laden as a theologian; he is a political strategist and is conceived of in precisely such terms. Of course, part of his strategy is employing a particular language through which he addresses specific audiences.

Why do you insist on using the term "political Islam" rather than the more common "Islamic fundamentalism"? Do the two not gesture at the same phenomenon?

I have doubts about the use of the term "fundamentalism" outside of the context in which it arises, which is the Christian context. My real discomfort with using the two interchangeably—political Islam and Islamic fundamentalism—is that "fundamentalism" is a *cultural* phenomenon and I want to zero-in on a *political* phenomenon.

Even in the history of American Christianity, Christian fundamentalism is a turn-of-the-century movement that was the result of battles fought out in all kinds of institutions, including schools and courts. But the decision by a group of Christian fundamentalist intellectuals to cross the boundary between the religious and the secular and to move into the political domain, to organize with an eye on political power, is only a post–Second World War phenomenon. I distinguish between Christian fundamentalism, an end-of-nineteenth-century countercultural movement, and political Christianity, a post–Second World War political movement.

I also do not identify the mixing of religion and politics as necessarily retrogressive. One only needs to understand the many forms of postwar political Christianity, from the involvement of black churches in the civil rights movement to that of Jerry Falwell's Christian Right, to get to a more nuanced understanding of religiously informed politics.

One also needs to recognize that the history of Christianity is very unlike the history of mainstream Islam, which simply does not have an institutionally organized church. The Catholic Church is organized as an institutionalized hierarchy, as a prototype of the empire-state, and the Protestant Church hierarchy is organized as a prototype of the nation-state. Until Ayatollah Khomeini created a statewide clerical authority in Iran, there was no such institutionalized religious hierarchy in Islam, and it still does not exist elsewhere. Without the existence of an institutionalized religious hierarchy parallel to a state hierarchy, the question of the proper relation between two domains of power, that of the organized church and the organized state, a central question in Western secularism, has been a nonquestion in Islam—at least until Ayatollah Khomeini created a constitutional theocracy in Iran as *vilayat-i-faqih*.

Now with Iraq very much in the throes of resistance, there is an entirely different notion of Iraqi Shi'ism articulated by Sistani. His is a critique of Khomeini; Sistani's is a secular, religious perspective. His view is that Shi'a clerics are scholars; they should be the conscience of society, not the wielders of state power.

So when political Islam develops—unlike political Christianity—it is not the result of the movement of religious intellectuals into a secular domain but rather the reverse move, that of secular intellectuals into the religious domain. Extremist political Islam, by which I mean Islamist thought that puts political violence at the center of political action, came into its own with Mawdudi and Syed Qutb. Neither was an alim or a mullah. Both had *this*-worldly pursuits. Mawdudi says, "*Mere* preaching will not do, it is not enough." Now which religious person is going to say *mere* preaching is not enough?

You argue in the book that "The shift from a reformist to a radical agenda in political Islam is best understood in the context of the transition from colonialism to postcolonialism." Can you explain what you mean by this?

I tried to understand the movement away from Jamaluddin al-Afghani, Jinnah, Mohammad Iqbal, from a time when the project of political Islam was to bring more and more Muslim peoples into the political arena, to increase political participation through mass mobilization. I tried to understand the shift from the politics of mass mobilization to its radical opposite whereby a form of political Islam emerges that is allergic to mass movements, that is modeled on the notion of creating small, conspiratorial groups, almost as if it were a caricature of the Leninist idea, "better fewer but better": evoking the picture of tiny groups in smoke-filled rooms, strategizing in the late hours of the night, not accountable to anybody. After all, does not the use of a religious idiom in politics, whether by bin Laden or by Bush, make heaven the arbiter, so there is no accountability in this world? President Bush said recently that freedom is God's gift to human beings, and that it is America's responsibility to spread it!

The shift from creating a state in a Muslim-majority society to creating an ideologically Islamic state began in Pakistan under Zia. Similarly, the construction of an ideologically Jewish state in Israel began under Begin. Coincidentally, both projects unfolded as part of a larger, global American Cold War project. We should not underestimate the importance of the shift from an Islamic state as a state of actually existing Muslims to an *Islamist* state as one whose mission is to enforce an agenda on the population so as to make of them true believers.

Whereas the quest for an Islamic state in a Muslim-majority society began in the colonial period, that for an ideologically Islamist state was more of a postcolonial phenomenon. It was born of a critique of political Islam as a societal project that yielded no more than a banal nation-state in a Muslim-majority society. Mawdudi could turn to Jinnah's Pakistan and say this was "Na-Pakistan" (literally, not Pakistan, or the Land of the Impure) as though to say, "What is this? We did not mean a banal nation-state, we meant something else."

The term "collateral damage" has become ubiquitous in the American media as a euphemism for the unintended victims of U.S. military operations. In your book, you make a connection between collateral damage and the spread of terrorism. Could you outline here the contours of that argument?

Collateral damage makes a distinction between victim and target. Victims are not necessarily the target. If you need to drain the entire tank to target the fish, so be it. The damage is regrettable but it is collateral. It is the language of power, it is the language of an *exclusive* focus on power, of a premeditated, wholly preoccupied focus on power, and it is not surprising that this language emerges in the late Cold War. Terror emerges as a strategy of the United States after defeat in Vietnam, when it is on the verge of losing the Cold War. The strategy comes to a head with the Reagan administration, which throws overboard the language of "peaceful coexistence," now demanding an agenda to "roll back" the Soviet Union.

You argue in the book that it was U.S. policy in the Reagan years to support terrorist movements across the Third World, from Mozambique and Angola to Nicaragua and Afghanistan, in an attempt to quash militant national-ism—then equated with Soviet expansionism—with no American loss of life. You point especially to the transition from counterinsurgency to low-intensity conflict and the shift in the locus of the Cold War from Europe to the Third World during the 1980s, both as significant reorientations of U.S. war strategy. What was the significance of these changes for the global spread of terrorism?

I focus on what I call the late Cold War, which I date from the Ameri-can defeat in Vietnam to the most recent invasion of Iraq. After defeat in Vietnam, the United States was faced with opposition to overseas military intervention, both at home and abroad. Kissinger was the first to respond to this changed international context. The year the Vietnam War ended, 1975, was the year the Portuguese empire collapsed. The cen-ter of gravity of the Cold War shifted from Southeast Asia to south-ern Africa, where the former Portuguese colonies of Mozambique and Angola became independent. Kissinger looked for a pragmatic solution. Unable to intervene directly, the United States looked for proxies. If the United States could not intervene itself, it would have to find others to intervene on its behalf. Kissinger first tried this in Angola with South African intervention, but it did not work. The day it became known, that very day it was discredited.

Ronald Reagan ideologized proxy war in a religious idiom. Rea-gan ideologized the Cold War as a war against "evil," against the "Evil Empire." His speech about the Evil Empire was first made to an annual gathering of American evangelicals. I think it is very important that we be clear about the political uses of "evil": you cannot coexist with evil, you cannot convert evil, you have to *eliminate* evil. In that titanic battle, any alliance is justified.

The first alliance, which lasted throughout Reagan's two administra-tions, was with apartheid South Africa, what was called "constructive engagement." It was under the American protective umbrella that apart-heid South Africa created Africa's first genuine terrorist movement: Ren-amo in Mozambique, which was genuinely terrorist in the sense that it was not interested in fighting the military, its focus was on targeting civil-ians as a way of demonstrating that an independent African government was incapable of protecting its citizens, spreading fear. America's responsi-bility in Mozambique was not direct but indirect. It did not provide direct assistance to Renamo, but it did provide a political cover to apartheid South Africa for over a decade as South Africa nurtured, from scratch, a genuinely terrorist movement in an independent African country.

Whereas the United States was an understudy in Mozambique, its embrace of terror became direct and brazen after the Sandinista Revolution of 1979. In Nicaragua, the United States created a terrorist movement called Contras, more or less as apartheid South Africa had created Renamo in Mozambique, also from scratch. The lessons the United States learned from southern Africa and Central America were put into practice in Afghanistan in the concluding phase of the Cold War.

You say that "The Reagan administration took two initiatives that were to have lasting impacts on U.S. foreign policy. The first was to turn to the drug trade for an illicit source of funds; the second was to turn to the religious right to implement those foreign policy objectives that Congress had ruled against, thus beginning a trend toward privatizing war." What were the lasting effects of these developments?

As I traced the history of proxy war, I was struck by how it tended to run alongside another underground development, that of drug trade, whether in Laos, Nicaragua, or Afghanistan. The reason was simple: if you don't declare war, you don't have access to public funds to wage it. The search for funds to wage an undeclared war time and again led the CIA into an embrace of the underworld, particularly the drug lords.

The Afghan war exemplified the extreme development of two tendencies: one, the *ideologization* of war in a religious idiom, and two, its *privatization*. War no longer had national boundaries; the United States was no longer interested in any Islamist group with a national orientation, which it considered too narrow. It wanted internationalist groups, groups committed to an international jihad, groups that could be relied on to join a fight to the finish. In fact, the United States wanted the war to be expanded to include the Muslim populations of the Soviet Union from the outset but backed down because the Soviets threatened to retaliate with an invasion of Pakistan.

With its ideologization, war ceased to be a necessary evil; rather, it became a way of *removing* evil. It became a praiseworthy thing. The ideologization of war was done in heavily religious terms. By the time Afghanistan happened, war was not even conceived as a national project, as with Renamo in Mozambique or the Contras in Nicaragua. The war in Afghanistan was justified as a *global* jihad. To wage it, the CIA recruited volunteers globally; Muslims everywhere, in the United States, in Britain, all over the world, were invited to participate in this global war. The CIA was busy creating cells everywhere, the nuclei of the same cells they are busy trying to smash today as a network of terror.

The ideologization of war also led to its privatization. The Islamist network was both global and private. What we are reaping today is the whirlwind.

At the time of the Soviet invasion of Afghanistan, you suggest that the Reagan administration "rescued right-wing Islamism from [a] historical cul-de-sac." How so?

Right-wing Islamism was preoccupied with the question of power and yet was allergic to mass movements. So it had either to embrace existing forms of power—like the Saudi monarchy or the Zia regime in Pakistan—or it would remain a fringe group. It is this cul-de-sac from which the late Cold War and the American strategy rescued it.

What we need to keep in mind is that without the American project it is difficult to see how this group of intellectuals could have translated an ideological tendency into a political project. How, indeed, it could have developed the numbers, the organization, the training, the self-consciousness, the sense of mission, strategy, tactics, and so on, and come out of it with the notion that they, the Islamists, destroyed the Soviet Union, and now it was time to destroy the other superpower. None of this would have been thinkable within the short span of a decade had it not been for American policy after Vietnam and in Afghanistan.

America's relations with Iraq have gone through several phases, all of which you outline in the book, and you argue that the penultimate phase involving the sanctions regime and continual aerial bombardment—before the 2003 military invasion and present occupation of the country—was "nothing short of an officially conducted and officially sanctioned genocide." Is that not too strong a statement?

Well, if you target an entire generation of children, and if studies confirm the fact that indeed the principal victims of sanctions are those below the age of five, and if you choose to continue and in fact *intensify* the sanctions because you have no eyes for the victim, but only for the target, then it is hard to find a more suitable word than genocide to describe this state of affairs.

I should also say that in my view, it is really hard to imagine the sanctions continuing for as long as they did without the complicity of Western media. If mainstream Western media had made it their business to inform their audience about the effects of these sanctions, I cannot imagine the sanctions continuing for as long as they did.

In some sense, the question that pervades much of your argument is: At what cost was the Cold War won? Are you suggesting that the cost of winning the Cold War—definitively with the defeat of the Soviet Union in Afghanistan—was ultimately September 11, 2001?

I do not think the cost was ultimately September 11, 2001, I think the cost is more, much more, and goes well beyond September 11, 2001.

We are sometimes unaware of the ways in which we are shaped by the enemies we choose to fight to the finish. We need to think of the ways in which the United States became like the Soviet Union. We need to remember that America in the 1980s was no longer a classical imperial power, interested in exporting just commodities or capital; America developed aspirations like the Soviet Union: that is, it was interested in exporting entire social systems. America developed an ideologically empowered self-righteousness as it mimicked Marxism-Leninism. America began using multilateral institutions like the World Bank and the IMF to export entire social systems around the world. I know this because Africa was the first place they did it.

When President Bush talks about exporting freedom and not commodities or capital, he is mobilizing his constituency behind the export of a *way of life*. An entire way of life. The America of Bush seems to have no patience with any other way of thinking through the good life. The good life is necessarily American. And if it is not American, then it cannot possibly be good.

So the pluralist project is in danger if the consequences of the Cold War are not clearly understood. September 11 is just the beginning, a blowback from a small, dedicated network. America has been preoccupied with a self-satisfied celebration of victory in the Cold War. There has been an almost total absence of self-criticism with regard to what happened to its own polity as a result. There has been no reflection on the extent to which American society, the economy, the state, were militarized; the extent to which a strong, detached executive power was built up, which has made a mockery of any meaningful democracy; the extent to which the press has come to be intimidated and harnessed internationally as part of the Cold War. All of these issues cry out to be thought through and addressed. In my view, the possible implications of these are likely to be far more serious than September 11.

Your book also seems to suggest that there is some continuity in American for-eign policy from at least the end of the Second World War to the present, and that is a sustained attempt on the part of the United States to subvert militant nationalism wherever in the Third World it appears. During the Cold War, since militant nationalism was synonymous with the possibility of Soviet expansion, the threat to American interests was clear. What potential threat does militant nationalism—as allegedly evinced by Iran or North Korea, for instance—pose to the United States?

You have to ask this question of the American president!

Bush said recently that there is an opportunity to change the world that should be seized, and that Iraq was a threat to the region and there-fore was a threat to the United States! So that anything, anywhere, in any part of the world, that moves without American consent presumably turns into a potential threat to the United States that must be removed preemptively before it grows into a real threat. But is it a threat? From which point of view is it a threat? Which is why I said, half in jest only, that you have to ask this question of President Bush. This is the point of view that is America's legacy from the Cold War. This is America mimicking the Soviet Union: there is a correct line, anything that devi-ates from it is a potential danger, and if it is not squashed early enough it will actually become a *real* danger. Which is of course the logic of preemptive war.

Preemptive war is now part of official American policy, and you suggest toward the end of the book that there is a direct link between the logic of pre-emptive war and genocide. Could you elaborate this link here?

My last book was on the genocide in Rwanda. When I was writing that book, I was struck by the fact that most genocides happen at the time of war. This, I think, is no mere coincidence. Genocide requires the complic-ity of significant sections of the population. The emotion most amenable to harnessing such popular complicity is fear. It takes war for the govern-ment to convince the population that if you do not kill them, they will kill you. Those who commit genocide think they are doing to others what others will do to them if given half a chance. They have reached the zero-sum point where it is either them or us. And genocide is the logical con-clusion of preemptive strikes. War no longer becomes self-defense, or the category of self-defense is stretched so out of recognition that all violence is rationalized as self-defense.

You suggest in your book that democratic empires are "potentially self-correcting" and warn that one of the effects of U.S. foreign policy since the start of the Cold War has been the systematic erosion of democratic rights at home. What hope do you see of a change in the course of U.S. policy given this fact?

It will have to be a combination of democracy coming to life in the United States and resistance coming to life in the places official America occupies overseas. Without resistance overseas, it is going to be difficult to have an oppositional movement that goes beyond the intelligentsia within the United States.

How do you respond to criticisms that your attempt to explain terrorism perpetrated by Muslims exclusively in terms of politics risks the same mistake as the "cultural" approach because it refuses to acknowledge that one cannot understand such violence discretely, that is, either only in political terms or only in religious terms, that one must take the two together?

I do not claim that one must explain the phenomenon of terrorism exclusively in political terms. Mine is a critique first of all of those who try to explain it exclusively or predominantly in cultural terms because I think it is too convenient to explain political terror by the culture of its perpetrators.

Culture Talk involves a double claim. The first is that premodern peoples possess an ahistorical and unchanging culture, like a badge they wear or a collective twitch from which they suffer. The second is that their politics can be decoded as a necessary and direct effect of this unchanging culture. How convenient and self-serving for official America to explain political terror as an outcome of a terrorist culture without taking into account the changing political contexts and relations to which political terror is a response!

I do not claim in the book that political Islam or the terrorist tendency in political Islam was an American invention. Rather, I argue that as an ideological tendency, political Islam had its own autonomous history, but it was not a linear history that has emerged as a natural outgrowth of Islamic thought. It developed both through debates internal to Islam and through engagement with competing modes of thought. During the late Cold War, that engagement was in particular with Marxism-Leninism, another mode of thought that put political violence at the center of political action. I was intrigued, indeed struck, by Marxist-Leninist echoes in the thought of Mawdudi, and even more so in that of Syed Qutb, as when Qutb said that he wrote *Signposts* for a vanguard, or when he wrote that we must distinguish between friends and enemies and use reason and persuasion with friends and force against enemies.

It is when I tried to understand how extremist political Islam, particularly its terrorist variant, turned from thought to action, from an ideological tendency to a political movement, that I found it necessary to turn to political analysis. The question that intrigued me was: How did an extreme ideological tendency, the preserve of small groups of intellectuals in the 1970s, turn into political movements that came to occupy the political mainstream in just two decades? To answer that question I had to turn to the late Cold War, to the period after defeat in Vietnam, when America had almost lost the Cold War. The point of the book is that terror is a strategy to which the United States turned to win the Cold War, that nonstate terror was born of state terror, and that Islamist terror represents only the final and concluding outcome in this relationship, that its earlier outcomes, whether with Renamo in Mozambique or the Contras in Nicaragua, have little if anything to do with Islamist terror.

Having said that, I am aware that extremist groups must ideologically justify the centrality of political violence in their tactics. The extreme Islamists must find something in the history of Islam and Islamic thought itself in which to anchor political violence and consequently to develop it. They find it in the notion of jihad, and to do so, they also give that notion a very particular interpretation. So, first of all, jihad ceases to be a broad notion, which is intellectual, social, personal, and political—it becomes exclusively political. Even in the political, it becomes militarized, driven by political violence. Finally, political violence ceases to be about self-defense. Even when it is proclaimed as self-defense, it is no longer different from Bush's notion of self-defense as preemptive: if you are defending yourself in Afghanistan by attacking New York, how is it different from defending yourself in New York by attacking Afghanistan?

The politicization of culture no doubt has important consequences for both culture and politics. To understand these consequences, we need to give up the idea that there is something called premodern culture with an unchanging essence and accept that any living body of thought is driven by debates, internal and external, and that these debates are informed by changing contexts, relations, and issues.

SEVEN I Anatol Lieven

You argue in your book, America Right or Wrong: An Anatomy of American Nationalism, *that American policies following the terrorist attacks on September 11, 2001, "divided the West, further alienated the Muslim world and exposed America itself to greatly increased danger." You suggest that this response must be understood in the context of the particular character of American nationalism. What are the features of American nationalism that are important in this respect?*

In the book I suggested that there are two principal features of American nationalism, both of which were evident in the response to 9/11. These are, in spirit, to a great extent contradictory, but they often run together in American public life. The first is a certain element of American messianism: the belief in America as a "city on the hill," a light to the nations, which usually takes the form of a belief in the force of America's example. But at particular moments, and especially when America is attacked, it moves from a passive to an active form: the desire to go out and actually turn the world into America, as it were, to convert other countries to democracy, to the American way of life.

In principle, the desire to spread democracy in the world is of course not a bad thing. But there are two huge problems with it. One is that because this element of American messianism is so deeply rooted in American civic nationalism, in what has been called the "American Creed," and in fundamental aspects of America's national identity, it can produce—and after 9/11 *did* produce—an atmosphere of debate in America that is much more dominated by myth than by any serious look at the reality of the outside world: myths about American benevolence, myths about America spreading freedom, myths about the rest of the world wanting America to spread freedom, as opposed to listening to what the rest of the world really has to say about American policies.

The second feature that cuts across this American messianism, how-ever, is what I have called the "American antithesis," that is, those ele-ments in the American nationalist tradition that actually contradict both American civic nationalism and the American Creed. These elements, which are very strong in parts of America, include national chauvinism, hatred of outsiders, and fear and contempt of the outside world. This is particularly true in the case of the Muslim world, both because America has been under attack from Muslim terrorists for almost two genera-tions now, but also because of the relationship with Israel, and the way in which pro-Israeli influences here have contributed to demonizing the Muslim world in general.

This results in an incredible situation: on the one hand—and I am speaking here particularly of the neocons—the Bush administration wants to democratize the Muslim world, while on the other hand, neo-conservatives do not even bother to hide their contempt for Muslims and Arabs. Sometimes you hear, and even read, phrases like, "The only language that Arabs understand is force," "Let them hate us so long as they fear us," and so on. This is utterly contradictory: people saying they want to democratize the Arab world but displaying utter contempt for Arab public opinion. Of course this is not just a moral failing, or a pro-paganda failing. It also leads to practical disasters, like the extraordinary belief that you could pretend at least to be introducing democracy, and on the other hand, you could somehow *impose* Ahmed Chalabi on Iraqis as a pro-American strongman, and that somehow the local population would line up to salute you and happily accept this.

So these are very dangerous aspects of American nationalism. And these aspects by the way used to be very sharply and profoundly ana-lyzed by great figures in the American intellectual tradition, conservative as well as liberal: figures like Reinhold Niebuhr, Richard Hoffstadter, Louis Hartz, George Kennan, and William Fulbright. Though most of these figures were strong anticommunists, they directed their critique at the reasons for the particular anticommunist hysteria of the early 1950s, and at the reasons that led America to become involved in the war in Vietnam. And their arguments and insights are of tremendous impor-tance to America today in understanding American behavior after 9/11.

But one of the striking and tragic things about the debate leading up to the Iraq War—although one can hardly call it a "debate"—was that the vast majority of it, outside certain relatively small left-wing journals, was conducted with almost no reference to the genesis of the Vietnam War, the debates that took place then, and the insights that were generated about aspects of the American tradition. Instead of analyzing what it was about their *own* system that was pulling them in the direction of war with Iraq, too many members of the American elite, including leading Democrats as well as Republicans, talked only about the *Iraqi* side.

Even that, of course, they got completely wrong, but they did not even once ask the obvious question: What is it about *our* system that may make this a disaster? After all, is this not a general pattern of American behavior in the whole world by now? This business of a Green Zone in Baghdad, American officials bunkered down behind high protective walls, with no contact with Iraqis, is this not part of a larger trend? Yet somehow it was assumed that in the case of Iraq it would be different, that America would go in, be welcomed with open arms, quickly reshape Iraq in accordance with American norms, and then quickly leave again.

You have said that "Belief in the spread of democracy through American power is not usually consciously insincere. On the contrary, it is inseparable from American national messianism and the wider 'American Creed.'" You have just talked about some of this, but could you elaborate your definition of American national messianism? And what do you think enables such naiveté—or perhaps cynicism?

As the American historian Richard Hofstadter said, "It has been our fate as a nation not to have ideologies but to be one." What really marks out America from the other Western democracies is not the content of America's democratic creed—because the basic principles are commonly held in all the democracies. Rather, it is the intensity and conformity with which these beliefs are held. This is because, precisely as Hofstadter said, these principles are or are *felt to be* essential to holding America together; that is, they are an essential part of the American national identity in a way that they are not to the British or the French or the German national identities.

This difference between the United States and Europe may change, of course, because of the huge immigrant populations in Western Europe now. Western European countries too are having to rethink their identities and emphasize common values rather than common heritage or ancestry. But certainly up to now, America has stood out because of the extent of its commitment to this so-called American Creed. I should say here that the word "creed" was chosen for this advisedly by a series of American thinkers (though the original phrase was G.. K.Chesterton's) as suggesting an almost religious form of belief.

The extent to which this is fundamental to the American national identity and is widely believed to keep Americans together means that it is very difficult in this country to challenge these myths. They are also remarkably impervious to experience. Vietnam did not fundamentally change them, it only battered them for a while. Endless lessons in the Middle East have failed to change them. Now, despite the lesson of Iraq, there are still leading Democrats writing about the need to create alliances of democracies and spread democracy in the region. Not to ask what the people of the region actually want, not to ask about a sensible diplomatic strategy, but to use democratization as a *substitute* for any real strategy. This comes again from a central part of the American national and nationalist heritage.

There is some continuity in American foreign policy, as you suggest, from the Bush Sr. administration through Clinton to the present Bush administration. Although you argue that Clinton's multilateralism was more befitting of a stable hegemonic state, is it not the case that as far as policy is concerned, this was only a change in form rather than substance? And if so, what accounts for this extraordinary unanimity in foreign policy between the only two serious political parties in this country (further evidence of which was the Kerry campaign's inability to offer any policy alternatives to the most pressing foreign policy issues then confronting the United States: Iraq and Israel–Palestine)?

On the Middle East, both of the American parties are, frankly, crippled above all by their inability to confront the question of America's relationship with Israel. Indeed, not just to confront it, but even to *mention* it, as we saw in the presidential debate.

On a range of other issues, though, Bush has not actually been as bad as many people think, or at least he has been much closer to Clinton—whatever that means. In the case of China, for example, the Bush administration came in with a very un-Clintonesque policy of confronting China, of containing China—and this could have led to some extremely dangerous results. But then 9/11 came along and ever since, the Bush administration has been pursuing an extremely Clintonesque policy of engaging China, of putting pressure on Taiwan not to declare independence, and so on. There was that moment in the presidential debates when it was Bush who was saying that the United States needs a multilateral policy toward the threat of North Korea with a key role for China; a curious irony given the Bush administration's frequent celebration of its own unilateralism, but not actually wrong. Similarly with Russia, while I would not necessarily describe the Bush administration's policy as multilateralist, they have certainly been pursuing a very traditional, pragmatic, realist policy, and not an aggressive one.

The area where the Clinton and Bush administrations are farthest apart is in relations with Europe. Clearly the Bush administration is not nearly as interested in Europe as Clinton was, and it is not nearly as interested in NATO. I should emphasize here that it was not interested even in the eight months *before* 9/11, let alone afterwards. If Gore had won in 2000, there would have been a very real difference: he would have made a much greater effort to engage NATO and to consult with European governments after 9/11.

That does bring out certain key differences between Bush and the Clinton tradition. Of course they are both interested in expanding America's power in the world; they are both imperialists, in a certain sense. They both profess at least their belief in spreading democracy. But Clinton, I think, was much more of a genuine Wilsonian. Bush in many ways is a fake Wilsonian because while he professes this messianic, democratization line, he has completely ignored the other key aspect of Wilson's strategy: international cooperation, international institutions, creating a web of alliances, and so forth. Clinton talked about this a great deal and was savagely attacked by the right wing in this country for doing so. Clinton's idea was to place "America at the center of every world network"—a position that implies influence, leadership, and even hegemony, but also consultation and negotiation.

So when it comes to the differences between Bush and Clinton, and the similarities, one requires a rather nuanced picture in which in some ways they are closer than it appears, but in other ways, they are genuinely quite different.

In several articles and in your book, you point out that unlike in previous empires, the vast majority of ordinary Americans do not think of themselves as imperialist, or as possessing an empire. At the same time, you mention repeatedly the extent to which the American population is unaware of the policies pursued in its name, is indeed alarmingly ignorant of world affairs. Given this, how could they conceive of the United States as an imperial power? And why is the perception of "ordinary" Americans relevant to understanding the place of America in the world today?

If I remember rightly, according to a poll in Britain in the 1930s, a very small proportion of the British population could remember the name of more than two British colonies. They could remember maybe India and Australia, or probably they remembered the white colonies, but most of them could not remember the name of a single African colony. No one would ever have used that as an argument that the British people did not believe in empire; they were just ignorant.

In the book, I quote C. Vann Woodward on this subject, another great American critic of the past, whose insights I wanted to try to revive for contemporary Americans. Woodward talked about the American people as being bellicose but not militarist, and I think it is also true that they are bellicose but not imperialist. That said, this kind of bellicosity, this instinctive reaction to lash out if attacked or even if insulted, has been repeatedly, and by the way quite explicitly on the part of the neocons, used as a way of whipping up nationalist anger, and nationalist commitment to what are in fact *imperialist* projects.

This is a very old tradition in imperialism. In my book, I cite many examples from history to show that in general even at the height of the Western empires, ordinary Western people were not really very interested in great imperial projects if they were going to be expensive. They liked the idea of power and glory, but they were very dubious about losing lives and spending large amounts of money to go out and conquer bits of Africa and so forth. If they could be convinced that this was not simply an imperialist project, but rather part of national rivalry with France or Germany, then it was possible to generate much more support.

In some ways, the American people do fit into this tradition. It is quite clear, for example, that even most of the ones who do consider themselves imperialist would be dead against the reintroduction of conscription in America. Even if it were proved to them that conscription was absolutely necessary to maintain America's imperial power in the world, they would not be persuaded. Equally the assorted jackasses who bray in the media about the American empire and the need for great sacrifices in its cause have shown no very ardent desire to go themselves and serve in Afghanistan or Iraq or anywhere else.

There is therefore a good deal of lack of underlying commitment to American power on the part of Americans themselves—more commitment certainly than exists almost anywhere else in the world by now, but still not enough to generate a really full-scale imperial project. This also explains in part the relative pragmatism of the Bush administration in some areas of the world. After all, even this administration recognizes that it cannot simultaneously run its present program in the Middle East *and* risk war with China *and* radically alienate Russia. If there were war with China or with North Korea, then America would have to reintroduce conscription. Then the end of the American imperial project would be very close indeed.

Another differentiating feature of nineteenth-century empires and the American empire is that the former were characterized by the so-called civilizing mission, whereas the latter, in its self-conception, is motivated by the purely benevolent aspiration of spreading democracy and freedom. Are these two imperial strategies not more similar than they at first appear?

Well in some ways, yes, of course. The nineteenth-century liberal-imperialist strategy was also enormously benevolent in its own esteem. The European powers conquered most of Africa while assuring their own populations and everybody else who would listen that this was all part of the process of ending slavery, expanding progress, bringing peace, spreading Christianity, and so forth. Even the most ghastly European colonial project of all, King Leopold of Belgium's conquest of the Congo, professed benevolent goals: Belgian propaganda was all about bringing progress, railways, and peace, and of course, ending slavery. In other words, hypocrisy is completely common to both, as it was to the Soviet or communist imperial project. So in that way they are very close.

But there is a critical difference. There was no absolutely intrinsic or self-evident clash between what the nineteenth-century liberal imperialists said they were going to do—leave aside what they actually did in terms of massacres, land theft, etc.—in terms of bringing progress and the inherent nature of their project; these were not radically incompatible because the nineteenth-century liberal imperialists *never* talked about quickly bringing democracy to the countries they conquered. To have done so would have been logically completely counter to the assumptions of Western superiority and "native" cultural inferiority and incapacity for self-rule upon which the entire ideology of the "civilizing mission" was based.

When they did talk of bringing democracy, they only did so in the context of the far future, something that might come about after several generations; in Africa, they talked about a thousand years of British or French rule eventually leading to self-government and democracy. In other words, they were absolutely clear and logical. These countries would need a long period, centuries literally, of Western authoritarian, imperial rule before they would be capable of self-government, constitutional rule, democracy, and so forth. Indeed to an extent this was the way that it actually worked out: the British had ruled India or parts of India for 150 years before they introduced the first *very* limited local, district elections with fairly circumscribed powers and a franchise of less than 0.5 per cent of the population. They started doing that only from the 1880s on. They and the other liberal imperialists had a policy of what one might call authoritarian progress, not of democratization.

Now, of course, it is completely different. The liberal imperialists of today, because of the completely different ideological era in which we are living, have to say that what they are bringing is *democracy*. So they conquer a place and then, within a year or two, they have to hold elections, they have to claim to be introducing free government, and so forth. That is just, once again, absolutely, *manifestly* contradictory. There would have been nothing contradictory in the nineteenth century about imposing Ahmed Chalabi on Iraq; the British and French did that kind of thing again and again. They had some client ruler, some dissident prince, or whatever, whom they wanted to make emir of Afghanistan or of somewhere in Africa, and they just marched in and imposed him. People may have criticized it, but there was no suggestion that this was incompatible with what they were setting out to do. Of course, if you say that you are bringing democracy, if you preach about democracy, if you say your whole moral position is *based* on democracy, and then you *impose* a puppet leader, then frankly you look not just hypocritical but *ridiculous*, which is essentially how the United States appears in much of the Muslim world.

In the wake of nationalist movements in the colonial world, imperial powers—in particular Britain—slowly ceded a variety of powers to local elites, in effect developing sophisticated ways of ruling through them (what Marxists called a "comprador elite"). Is it possible to say that the U.S. empire runs the Third World—of which the Muslim world is an important part—through such a model of what has been called "indirect rule"?

Yes, to a considerable extent this is the case. Of course the comprador model, in the strict Latin American sense, never quite fits because very few governments elsewhere in the world have been so completely subservient as some of the Latin American elites in the past. After all, Egypt still tries to take a different line on Israel; Jordan supported Saddam Hussein in 1991; Saudi Arabia could be seen as a comprador state in that it exists to produce and export oil, but clearly in its internal arrangements it is not at all responsive to what America would like.

Perhaps it may be more difficult these days to run such manifestly comprador systems given that, as I suggested earlier, there does tend to be more democratic pressure from below than in the nineteenth century. A good example is Russia, although admittedly Russia also has its tradition of Great Power status and so forth, which prevents it from becoming completely subservient to America. As I wrote in a previous book on the reasons for Russia's defeat in Chechnya between 1994 and 1996, there was a real attempt by America in the 1990s, with tremendous help from the Russian elites themselves, to turn Russia into a kind of comprador state, whose elites would be subservient to America in foreign policy and would exist to export raw materials to the West and transfer money to Western bank accounts. In the end, neither the Russian state nor the Russian people would accept that. The Yeltsin order was replaced by a kind of authoritarian, nationalist backlash under Putin. One sees the same thing in a rather different form in Venezuela, for example.

So I think there are strong elements of this comprador tradition in the present American-dominated international system, but at the same time it is a troubled and contested setup.

You have said that the era inaugurated by the attacks of September 11, 2001, brought out into the open "the complete absence of democratic modernization, or indeed any modernization, in all too much of the Muslim world." What do you mean by modernization, and how is its absence related to the professed motivations for earlier imperial conquests?

How many hours do I have! Modernization is after all such a tricky concept. If we take our canonical attitudes to modernization from Max Weber, as most of us do, unconsciously at least, then of course, as I wrote in the book, America itself today does not conform to Eurocentric patterns of modernization!

Certainly much of the Muslim world—not all by any means, there are exceptions, but certainly large parts of the Middle East—does not conform to many of the criteria laid down by Weber for successful modern states. These countries have clearly not been able to imitate some of the East Asian countries in bringing about radical economic growth and reform. Many of these countries remain ruled by what are essentially clans. The famous unkind phrase of Charles Glass of Arab states being "tribes with flags" is, I am afraid, rather accurate. Syria is a monarchy of the Alawite clan. The Ba'ath started very much as a modernizing fascistic movement, like fascists in Italy, but broke down into a kind of monarchical oligarchy. Then there are the formal autocratic monarchies in Jordan, Saudi Arabia, and Morocco. As East Asia has demonstrated, authoritarian rule as such is not necessarily an obstacle to economic modernization and progress. But then again, this has not worked in the Middle East either.

One of the tragedies is precisely that so many different models have been tried in the region and all in a sense have failed, if not absolutely then certainly to bring the countries concerned up to the economic level of the West or East Asia. The failure to compete successfully with the West has been horribly demoralizing in view of the Muslim world's past cultural and economic superiority, now followed by several hundred years of relative decline. Just as for several centuries Muslim states exploited the relative weakness of the Christian world to expand their power, so later Western states took advantage of Muslim weakness to conquer most of the Muslim world. This was followed by the establishment, in the heart of the Muslim world, of Israel, a tremendously militarily and economically successful Western surrogate power. Israel's successes, and Israel's oppression of the Palestinians, have underlined various aspects of Arab failure. Israel is in no sense the originator of these historical feelings of resentment and humiliation, but in recent decades it has acted as a catalyst and focus for these older and deeper feelings.

If you take the example of Pakistan, the part of the Muslim world that I know best, that country of course is in some ways a vastly more modern society than it was fifty years ago, but then again in some ways it is not. In this context, it is interesting to ask what constitutes "modernity" in the case of political religion. Radical Islam in Pakistan and elsewhere is after all in many ways a modern force. It is not just a reaction to modernity, but also uses modern methods so one certainly cannot say that it is purely reactionary or regressive.

But certainly so far there has been in Pakistan a failure of political modernization in the form of democracy. Pakistan has essentially remained a state that is run by the military and the civil service. The political elites, with the exception of the MQM and to some extent the

Islamists, cannot really be described as modern political parties with a serious mass base. The PPP is a cult of personality party presiding over an alliance of big landowners and urban bosses. And while the military and civil service have held the country together, they have obviously failed to develop Pakistan as a successful modern state.

The weakness of political culture, when added to economic and military weakness, lays the Muslim world open to the threat of physical intervention by the new world imperialist power, and it also weakens Muslim states morally and ideologically in terms of resisting such intervention.

You have pointed out several times the authoritarian character of most states in the Arab and Muslim worlds but do not mention the fact that a majority of these regimes depend for their existence on continued American patronage. Is it not the case that a number of these states are viewed as client regimes of the United States, and that this is one of the major sources of Muslim resentment against the United States? This is particularly true of your comments about Pakistan, where the United States supported the Zia regime for over a decade and now supports the military government of General Musharraf.

As I have often said with regard to American and British professed support for democratization, we can all believe in a human capacity for redemption even if we are not born-again Christians, but most of us, not being saints, do not ask reformed burglars to guard our houses! We should not therefore ask Arabs and Muslims, given the British-American record on democracy in the Muslim world, to trust our professions today that we are sincere in our wish to bring democracy.

By contrast, I have always believed and continue to believe in the force of the United States and Western example when it comes to spreading democracy. If we can go on demonstrating to the world that our societies are more peaceful, more stable, less oppressive, and more economically successful than authoritarian or theocratic states, then there will be a strong tendency for democracy to spread without our having to intervene in other places to bring this about. In this sense, I am a strong believer in the American tradition stretching from President Adams to George Kennan that takes immense and justifiable pride in the American political system, but believes that America spreads democracy best when it maintains the health and strength of its own system. By the way, President Eisenhower said much the same thing at the end of his second term, so this is hardly a radical position, let alone an anti-American one.

As to United States (and British) support for dictatorships, and the resentment this has caused, this is true. On the other hand, I think it cuts both ways. Does one believe that if these authoritarian regimes fell then viable democracies would follow? In Pakistan, unfortunately, this did not happen. Of course it is true that the army always stepped in eventually, but then again look at the PPP government under Bhutto in the 1970s—certainly not a regime that was strongly supported by Washington—and its extremely brutal treatment of dissent. Look at the fact that when Musharraf took power he was supported by the great majority of the population because of the outrageous corruption of governments in the 1990s.

I think that is a rather misleading claim. How do we know what proportion of Pakistan's population supported Musharraf's coup?

Quite right. Opinion polls are not necessarily reliable in a country like Pakistan. Let me put it another way: a great majority of the people certainly did not protest against it. If there had been true faith in democracy and its record in Pakistan, they presumably would have done so. My point is that when Musharraf assumed power, he was certainly not acting on behalf of America. Clearly, several of these authoritarian regimes do not stand because of American support but because of local tradition and domestic support: Iran, which is directly opposed to America; Libya; and the House of Saud, which is in some sense America's tool but also has its own tradition and legitimacy that has nothing to do with American support.

Well, the argument could be made that the Americans are only interested in Saudi Arabia's domestic political setup to the extent that it continues to serve their interests: oil, and in the case of the first Gulf War, the provision of military bases. Therefore the present arrangement works rather better for them than any subsequent setup might.

Until 9/11, this was true. But since then, there has been a strong and widespread belief in the United States that the Saudi system is incubating terrorism, which of course is a somewhat belated realization. I met Saudi-backed extremists in Afghanistan while I was based in Peshawar in the late 1980s, and it was already apparent that we were building up a monster for ourselves. Since 9/11 this has been recognized.

I do not believe that America will improve its image in the Muslim world just by abandoning its present allies and preaching democracy, because I do not believe that given its geopolitical and other interests America will ever be truly sincere in this regard. America's professed ideals of democracy and freedom are always likely to come to a screeching halt at Israel's occupation of the Palestinian territories, but also whenever American ideals seem likely to lead to a result that will be really harmful for American geopolitical interests. One of the images that has been seared into American elite consciousness is what happened to Carter. When Carter tried to pursue a more moral policy, by putting pressure on the Shah over Savak atrocities, by putting pressure on Central American governments, was he thanked for it by the American establishment? No, he was pilloried as naïve, weak, as supporting communism, as giving opportunities to America's enemies, and so forth.

If a U.S. president were to push Saudi Arabia really hard, for example, over democratic reform, and the Saudi regime collapsed and there was an Islamist takeover, that American president would simply *fall* in the next election, as Carter did. Ditto with Pakistan. So America is trapped in this.

Looking beyond the publicly stated goals for the American invasion of Iraq, you said that the neoconservative nationalists were all more or less unanimous in their agreement on one basic plan: "unilateral world domination through absolute military superiority." To what extent did the Iraq invasion have the intended results, and what is the likelihood that such policies will continue to be pursued in the second term of the Bush presidency?

Iraq has been a disaster for their aims. They have gotten away with it, of course, in that they have been reelected, but it is perfectly obvious that they cannot launch another war of choice, an invasion of Iran, say. They simply do not have the troops. With almost 150,000 men pinned down in Iraq, they could not launch another war on that scale without introducing conscription. That would tear American society apart and for the first time since Vietnam lead to a significant anti-imperialist movement in this country. It would also, for the first time, lead to really serious questions about what America is doing in the Middle East at all.

From that point of view, Iraq really has not worked out as they had anticipated and has greatly reduced their plans. After all, in the immediate aftermath of the overthrow of Saddam Hussein, all the neocons were going around saying: "Next stop: Iran." Or Syria. This kind of rhetoric has not disappeared completely—they are still refusing to talk to the

Iranians—but the agenda on Iran has really narrowed just to the issue of nuclear weapons. So Iraq has had a major effect in this respect .

You suggest that various practices and institutions put into place during the Cold War make the constant threat of war a virtual necessity for the American foreign policymaking and security establishment. This may account in part for why Islam came very quickly to replace communism as the great ideological enemy of the United States. Given that Islam has no locus, that there are a billion Muslims spread out across the world, how is the U.S. security establishment likely to continue to deal with this kind of enemy?

I say in the book that what seems essential is not the *imminent* threat of war, but rather constant belief in the possibility of war. There are all these institutions and economic interests that were put in place by the Second World War and still more by the Cold War. Eisenhower's original phrase apparently was "military-industrial-*academic*-complex." There are so many people in my world of think tanks in American universities with a deep stake in all these foreign policy agendas. In the book I also point out that—and this has been mentioned in other forms by people like James Mann, Richard Clarke, Paul O'Neill, and others—one of the reasons why 9/11 was able to happen was that the security elites under Clinton, and very much under Bush, were not looking seriously at the terrorist threat because, due to their Cold War backgrounds, they were obsessed with the very much lesser threat from major rival states.

When the Bush administration came to power, they had radical anti-Chinese agendas of containing China, of rolling back China, of creating a new Cold War with China. On the other hand, now there is this tremendous effort, certainly among the neocons, to present Islam or the Muslim world as the new Cold War enemy. You see all this nonsense by people like Norman Podhoretz about the Fourth World War. The interesting thing is precisely that, as you say, Islam is not a superpower like the Soviet Union, nor does it represent a relatively clear set of social, economic, and political principles like communism. One is dealing with an *extremely* diverse world with different cultures and societies and multiple motivations.

Even if you narrow the war on terror down to al-Qaeda and its allies, which of course the Bush administration and Israeli lobby have deliberately and manifestly failed to do, even then one is speaking of a web, a network of many different groups and nodes in this web that sometimes cooperate, sometimes act independently, with varying degrees of relative importance. Zarqawi's group in Iraq, like the international forces fighting in Chechnya, are in no sense subordinate to al-Qaeda.

To combat these groups requires a really detailed and acute knowledge of the societies concerned. Something once again that America failed to generate in the case of Vietnam before going to war there, failed to generate about Iraq before going to war there, and is indeed failing to generate in the case of large parts of the Muslim world. It does seem that there is a natural pull toward concentration on alleged threats from states. This was especially clear after 9/11: the astonishing speed with which the Bush administration turned its attention from the actual terrorist perpetrators of the 9/11 attacks to confront the "axis of evil" states and draw up plans for war with Iraq.

It is clearly much easier to threaten and invade Iraq than to think seriously about how to combat the appeal of groups like al-Qaeda and its allies in the Muslim world. Similarly, it is much easier to concentrate on preventing Iran from acquiring nuclear weapons than to think seriously about the Shia–Sunni relationship, or what to do about Hezbollah in Lebanon. This is part of the built-in bias of military bureaucracies but also owes much to the effects of the Cold War and the present intellectual configuration of American academia.

You explain in your book why the Cold War legacy has made it difficult for U.S. policymakers, trained for the most part in the so-called Realist tradition, to conceive of a security threat as emanating from somewhere other than a nation-state, an assumption that is rather inadequate for addressing the threat of terrorism, as you just pointed out (and may account in part for why, as you say, quoting Bob Woodward, the Bush administration seemed incapable of staying focused on a terrorist threat, before and after the attacks on the United States, and started planning for war on Iraq on November 21, 2001; that is, seventy-two days after 9/11). Yet you supported the American invasion of Afghanistan when it seemed clear that al-Qaeda was a diffuse, dynamic network, with no state to claim as its own. Why was Afghanistan, then, a legitimate—morally, but also pragmatically—target for military strike?

The invasion of Afghanistan was justified by absolutely traditional and universally accepted traditions of self-defense. Al-Qaeda had launched this attack; this was generally accepted by every rational person in the world. Al-Qaeda were quickly and clearly identified as the perpetrators, and indeed subsequently made no real attempt to deny it. When it comes to the responsibility of the Taliban, al-Qaeda after all was functioning very much as part of the Afghan state under the Taliban and provided the Taliban's praetorian guard.

It is true that, had I been in a position of authority, I would have made a greater effort to get the Taliban to extradite the al-Qaeda leadership, if not directly to America then to somewhere else in the Muslim world from where they could be passed on to America. This was partly because I was afraid of what to some extent has in fact happened, which is that by going into Afghanistan with the Northern Alliance, America would alienate the Pashtuns.

Nonetheless, I thought the invasion of Afghanistan was covered by self-defense. Al-Qaeda launched this attack, al-Qaeda was functioning as part of the Taliban and was being protected by the Taliban. Al-Qaeda had, after all, also launched a series of attacks previously on American targets, which one should not forget: they were responsible for the massacre of very large numbers of Africans and others. I also regarded their Taliban protectors as a genuine "rogue" regime in a way that Iran certainly is not. They really were in the business of spreading instability, radicalism, and terrorism (especially of course anti-Shi'a terrorism) in their area.

On a personal note, I detested what the Taliban stood for, and the damage that they and their allies were doing to Pakistan. Above all, I supported the U.S. invasion of Afghanistan as legitimate self-defense and because of genuine shock at 9/11, shock at the idea that this could happen to a great modern city, and the belief that forces like al-Qaeda are a real threat to modern civilization—Muslim as well as Western. America did also enjoy a general international consensus behind its invasion of Afghanistan. To some extent the United States even managed to gain some support in the Muslim world for the invasion, at least as far as states and elites are concerned. This is largely because the Sunni revolutionary element represented by al-Qaeda and the Taliban is of course a threat to every organized Muslim state as well.

So I felt that both on what Kerry called the "global test" and on the traditional test of self-defense, Afghanistan passed. Iraq did not.

You have suggested that radical American nationalists—many of whom will continue in the present Bush administration—either wish to "contain" China by overwhelming military force and the creation of a ring of American allies, or "in the case of the real radicals, to destroy the Chinese Communist state as the Soviet Union was destroyed." Have these radical elements in the present administration been sufficiently chastened by their experience in Iraq to relinquish such aspirations?

Yes, I believe so. Not to permanently relinquish their aspirations in principle: obviously they would still very much like to destroy China if they could, or at least destroy China as a potential future threat to American hegemony. But as long as they are tied down in the Middle East in the way they are, they will not have the military forces to do so.

Therefore, I believe that the Bush administration and future Democrat administrations will continue the existing line. That said, of course there is always room for mistakes on the part of either Washington or Beijing or Taipei or most likely all three simultaneously. The Taiwanese can go too far, and the Chinese can overreact, not because the Chinese want war, but because they would trap themselves into a position where they would have to do something. If they were sensible, of course, the Chinese leadership would not react militarily, they would just tell any power that recognized Taiwan that China would break off diplomatic and trade relations the next day. Nobody would in fact recognize Taiwanese independence, and then the Chinese could simply declare that these people have declared independence but no one recognizes them so why does it matter. This is by the way what Russia should have done in the case of Chechnya before 1994. But the Chinese could of course miscalculate and use force, and then the United States, and particularly the American Congress, would have put themselves in such a position that they would be forced to fight as well.

So I certainly do not rule out some kind of stumbling toward conflict. If that happens, of course, then all the old agendas would come back. Then the anti-Chinese hardliners in the bureaucracy, the think tanks, and Congress would start roaring again about communist aggression; they would gain greater influence and the Cold War agenda vis-à-vis China would be reestablished. But I do not believe that any really powerful forces in Washington today actually want that.

In a recent article, you say that "The Bush administration may be stumbling toward an attack on Iran's nuclear program that could have the most disastrous consequences for Iraq, Afghanistan, and the entire American position in the Middle East." What is the likelihood of such an attack being carried out in the near future by either the Americans or the Israelis?

It is still a possibility. Not I believe such a strong possibility now, because apart from everything else the Iranians do seem very anxious to play along with Europe and are willing at least to suspend their nuclear weapons plans in response to a mixture of European pressure and incentives with American threats. But if America were to attack Iran, it would be a catastrophe. Poor old Tony Blair has accepted so many shattering blows already maybe nothing will finish him, but having invested so much in this process with Iran, if it were to end in an American attack, it seems likely that there would be a serious revolt within his government and party and he would have to resign. There are leading members of the British government briefing in private that whatever Tony Blair says, if America attacks Iran, that is the end. They will resign. This would almost certainly be the end of Blair's tenure as prime minister. It would also create a massive crisis with the Europeans. Moreover, given the fact that Iran's nuclear sites are dispersed and buried, America would very likely *miss*, at which point we will have the worst of all possible worlds. As the American military know very well, Iran in these circumstances would have numerous means of retaliation against American forces and plans in Iraq—whereas an American invasion of Iran looks impossible because of America's lack of troops.

So I am less worried on that score than I have been in the past. There is, however, a wild card involved: this is that the Israeli government appears implacably determined to prevent Iran from acquiring nuclear weapons, without themselves offering any concessions in return, and may itself either attack or exert irresistible pressure on the United States to reject a deal with the Iranians. The present deal between Iran and the West Europeans could also break down for a number of other reasons. It is not inconceivable that there could emerge some disastrous quid pro quo whereby Israel will make certain concessions toward the Palestinians and in return America will go after Iran's nuclear weapons. But of course the consequences might be frightful because of course Iran would then have every incentive to try to really destabilize Iraq. Hezbollah could be reactivated as an international terrorist force. Iran would set out to destabilize Afghanistan, and so forth and so on.

All this is known to the American security elites. The uniformed military is certainly extremely opposed to anything like this. Of course they were also opposed to Iraq, but it still happened.

Could you elaborate on your argument regarding what accounts for the special relationship between Israel and America: namely, the parallel between the situation of Palestinians and Native Americans?

This is not the core either of my argument or of the relationship itself, but only a subsidiary factor. At the core of the relationship lie completely legitimate sympathies and identifications between a majority of Americans and the state of Israel. These are rooted in old features of religion and culture, and more recent admiration for the achievements of the Israeli state. I should say by the way that I believe strongly in U.S. support for Israel within the borders of 1967. In my book I express a number of positions that are certainly extremely unpopular in the Muslim world, and on the Left in Europe: support for the Jewish character of the Israeli state, opposition to all but the most limited Palestinian refugee return, and opposition to ideas of a binational state. I also accept that given the tragic circumstances of 1948, and the imperatives created by the Holocaust, a measure of ethnic cleansing was probably inevitable and would also undoubtedly have been carried out in the other direction if the Arab side had won.

So I am not arguing against sympathy for Israel as such, but only against certain forms of this identification. Sympathy rooted in comparisons between the American and Israeli settlement processes are generally confined to the American Right. Leo Strauss made land theft the founding principle of every state, which, it must be said, if you go back far enough historically, is actually true to a considerable extent. Admittedly you have to go back in Britain fifteen hundred years. Certainly in the United States there is a very interesting contrast in attitudes toward this issue between Americans on the East Coast and in the south or the west of the country. East Coast Americans are either embarrassed about the dispossession of the Indians or have simply forgotten it. For most it is totally irrelevant, since they never encounter any Native Americans and since their ancestors in many or even most cases arrived in the United States long after the East Coast Indians were dispossessed. In the southern and western United States, however, the frontier tradition is so much stronger. There is no real embarrassment over the dispossession; there is basically a celebration of the fact that their ancestors conquered this land and turned it, as the phrase used to be, into a "white man's country."

It does seem to me—and I am not original in pointing this out; there have been leading Israelis like Amos Elon who have done so—that this began by creating a certain community of sentiment between sections of the conservative Christian heartland in America and the right wing in Israel, or Israel in general. In other words, it is a mistake when looking at this community of sentiment just to look at the apocalyptic element: millenarian religion. This is present, but it would not have nearly the resonance that it does if it were not set in a wider context.

Here I am talking about the conservative tradition in the American heartland, the Christian tradition, but of course sympathy with Israel is much broader: it has a great deal to do with the Holocaust; it has to do with the perception of Israel as a modern, democratic society, as a very successful society. This goes together, obviously, with tremendous support from the Jewish community for Israel on the whole. So all these factors work in concert.

There is nothing at all in principle wrong with people here supporting Israel as such, or admiring Israel for its tremendous success as a society. But on the American Right there are very much darker elements to this affinity, one of which is precisely the radical religious one, but the other is a kind of sublimated racism.

You have also argued that American nationalism has become increasingly entwined with the nationalism of the Israeli Right. What are the historical reasons for the alliance between Christian fundamentalists in this country and Zionists? In other words, how should we understand the words of Jerry Falwell when he says, "The Bible belt of the United States is the security belt of Israel"?

If one just looks at the Christian fundamentalist issue, leaving the millenarian question aside, American evangelical Protestantism is Old Testament Protestantism—just as its forebearers in English radical Protestantism and Scottish radical Protestantism were in the sixteenth and seventeenth centuries. This creates a natural affinity with the Jewish religious tradition. When evangelical Christian Lieutenant-General William Boykin was quoted last year as saying, "My God is bigger than his," in reference to a Muslim, he was directly citing from Isaiah, and this is obviously a man who spends a lot of his time in the Old Testament.

It is fascinating the degree to which the Old Testament eclipses the New Testament in the thought of evangelical Christians, and this automatically leads one to a sympathy with Israel. Cromwell was the first ruler of England who allowed Jews to settle again in England after the Middle Ages. He was very much influenced in this by his Old Testament-based Christianity. But also it seems, from the time of Cromwell on, there has been this millenarian idea as well: the restoration of Israel is essential to bringing about the Apocalypse. Given the influence of millenarian thought on a minority of evangelicals, but a very significant minority, one cannot deny this influence. Look at the immense popularity of the "Left Behind" series, for example.

Finally, there is also a considerable element of straight political opportunism. The Republicans are already well on their way to putting the Democrats in a very difficult position from the point of view of political demographics. The Republicans have this tremendously solid base—mostly white, not just Protestant anymore but Protestant and Catholic conservative, including many Latinos. Unlike the deeply fractured Democrat base, the Republican base agrees on a majority of important issues. The Democrats, by contrast, are trying to tie together the remnants of the white working classes in the northern cities, the blacks, the Latinos, more progressive women, and the various cultural liberals—groups that often detest each other.

If on top of this advantage the Republicans can take away a majority of the Jewish vote and campaign financing from the Democrats, they stand a chance of actually destroying the Democratic party's chances of power for a generation to come. This hope is not a secret. It has been written about quite openly by conservative commentator Robert Novak and others. If the Republicans can conclusively seize the issue of support for Israel from the Democrats, then they can rule for the foreseeable future. Rightly or wrongly, that at least is the calculation the Republicans are making.

You point out the complicity of the American media in both supporting the government in various foreign policy adventures—you say in fact that the "propaganda program" in the wake of the Iraq War has few parallels in peacetime democracies for the systematic mendacity of its reportage—and, for the most part, keeping silent on the excesses of the Israeli state. What accounts for this blindness in the context of a free press in a democratic country?

This is a little stronger than what I actually said. What I said was that the Bush administration's propaganda program had few parallels in peacetime democracies and that the American media had not criticized this. I did not mean to suggest that the American media as a whole were all part of the same propaganda machine. Even in some of the papers that supported the war, dissenting voices appeared.

When it comes to keeping silent on the excesses of the Israeli state, the reporting as such has not been very unfair or inaccurate—certainly if you look at the respectable media: the serious newspapers and some of the serious television channels. Israeli bombing raids are reported, shooting of Palestinian civilians is reported, and the issue of settlements too is reported to an extent. There are two things that are completely missing, as Michael Lind pointed out in *Prospect* magazine in England last year. The first is historical context and the second is the almost complete absence of analysis or critique. One of the questions I raise in my book has to do with why Palestinians were expected to have peacefully acquiesced to what was being done to them in the 1940s. According to any historical precedent, this would have been absurd. No other people would have ever accepted this. Are we suggesting that the Palestinians should have been insane? This is ridiculous. So that is the context. Second, as Michael also pointed out, in terms of analysis, the violence and its causes are always presented as Palestinian "terrorism," not Israeli *occupation*. Finally the opinion pieces seriously criticizing Israeli policies are simply heavily outnumbered, even in the mainstream and liberal media, by expressions of support.

On Iraq, why did the media not stand out against the war? It was partly because of the role of the Israel lobby. It is very difficult to conduct a truly searching analysis of the underlying reasons for American policy in the Middle East, and very difficult to draw up really serious alternatives to existing policies, if you are not prepared to address the question of Israeli policies and the part they play in damaging American interests in the Middle East. This does not mean that Israel must be at the heart of the argument, but its influence cannot be denied: it is there not just in the form of the effects of the struggle with the Palestinians but in relations with Iran, Syria, and the Muslim world in general. If this is to be swept aside, as it so often is by the accusation of anti-Semitism, it just makes the entire debate here much more difficult. You could as well ask why there was no really serious debate in the presidential campaign over the "war on terror" as a concept. The Israel factor is a part of that too.

I should say, by the way, that I never wrote about this issue before 9/11. I have no history whatsoever of attacking Israel. But after the terrorist attacks on America, the Carnegie Endowment asked me to concentrate on the war on terror and on aspects of the situation in the Muslim world. After that, it would have been intellectually dishonest and morally cowardly not to discuss this critical issue. I may add, as a British citizen, that it would have been unpatriotic, since my country is fighting in Iraq and Afghanistan alongside America and is running the same risks of terrorist attack. British citizens therefore have both a right and a duty to speak out against policies and attitudes that are undermining the war on terror and endangering British security.

Concerning the behavior of the media and intelligentsia in the United States, the second point is that after 9/11 people were clearly running scared. There was this tremendous militant nationalist wave sweeping the country. This is not unique to America—the same would have been true in most countries that suffered an attack of this kind. However, in the United States the response took certain forms that have precedents in U.S. history. The silencing effects of such a wave have been seen before: McCarthyism most recently, and the anti-German, then the anticommunist hysteria in the First World War and the 1920s. People were to a considerable degree intimidated into silence.

There was a very good piece by Russell Baker about A. J. Liebling in the November 18, 2004, issue of the *New York Review of Books* in which Baker was talking about how journalists used to regard themselves as just hacks. I used to be a journalist myself, essentially writing for money, trying to be accurate in my reporting and as amusing and intelligent as possible. Now there is this ghastly tendency of journalists, particularly those who get to the top of the U.S. media, to regard themselves not as hacks but as pillars of the state. So they begin to behave almost as if they were senior officials, not hacks like the rest of us; and not just that, but as if they had occupied a great office of state during some great crisis in American affairs, as if they had been Acheson during the Second World War or the Korean War. So many of these columnists and television journalists are like that now.

One last point, and this may appear at first sight contradictory: the figure of Bob Woodward bridges these two things. After Watergate, on the one hand journalists got an exaggerated sense of their own importance as the Fourth Estate, a political force that makes and breaks administrations. On the other hand, they became more and more addicted to being given enormous dollops of constructed information and "spin" on a plate—instead of doing real fieldwork and investigative reporting like Woodward did. So Woodward is turned from an investigative reporter into a court chronicler. He has fascinating information and very good insights but is nonetheless essentially a praise-singer of the American system. I think a lot of American journalists are like that now. When they depend for leaks and for information on either the government in power or the opposition, they are clearly not going to say anything that will wreck their chances of getting what they regard as scoops.

You have said that "The younger intelligentsia [in the United States] has also been stripped of any real knowledge of the outside world by academic neglect of history and regional studies in favour of disciplines which are often no more than a crass projection of American assumptions and prejudices.... This has reduced still further their capacity for serious analysis of their own country and its actions." In addition, you point out the very close links that exist between relevant university departments and government institutions. What are the implications of this?

Well, it contributes enormously to conformism when it comes to debates like that about the Iraq War or about Israel. As Henry Kissinger pointed out almost thirty years ago, too many people in the academic world are either defending previous records when in government or aiming to be in the next administration. This is not a situation likely to produce radical critiques or really strong alternative policies. These people are not at all anxious to say something that will lead either to them not being selected or to their being vetoed by a Senate committee.

I used to think that it is wonderful that the American state can recruit from people in academia, but I have come to find it deeply corrupting. I almost prefer the British system now, of career civil servants who serve one administration after another. But one needs a strong ethos of the independence of the civil service and a very strong ethos that people cannot be sacked or penalized for political views as long as they maintain the discipline of their service. This actually leaves the public debate in the UK freer than in the United States, particularly in the strange, solipsistic world of Washington, DC. It is amazing in a republic with a strong tradition of individualism and cultural egalitarianism that in DC the sense of hierarchy, of sometimes obsequious deference, of the court game, who is in, who out, dominates everything just as much as it did in an early medieval court. It does contribute to this lack of debate in America.

This is compounded by the tremendously strong power of American national myths. As previous American authors like Loren Baritz pointed out, Vietnam knocked these myths off their pedestal, but many Americans spent a whole generation resuscitating them. Reagan was elected very much to do just that, to restore America's image of itself. It would seem that these myths are so important to America's national identity and image of itself that the American political and intellectual establishment is simply incapable in the end of seriously examining them and asking what flaws they may embody. Of course, there are dissidents—

even some very senior ones like Senator Fulbright; but it is striking how little influence they seem to have had in the long run.

In consequence, there are all these people running around Washington—very much among the Democratic intellectual elites as well as the Republicans—who really believe that all America has to do is try harder to generate and display a sense of *will*. If only America *wants* something badly enough, anything can be achieved. Any society in the world can be transformed, irrespective of the wishes and traditions of its people. Any country can become not just a democracy, but a *pro-American* democracy, irrespective of its own national interests or ideals.

This is part of a deep inability to see America as others see it. It is incredible, but again and again I have found myself at meetings discussing Russia and China in Washington at which I have been the *only* person to point out that America does after all have its own sphere of influence in Central America and the Caribbean. Not just that, but a sphere of influence that is not doing very well either economically or, to a great extent, in terms of real democracy. The rest of the world sees this perfectly well and, as a result, develops a belief in American hypocrisy that is itself very bad for American prestige and influence.

After all, how much did Haiti get after floods that killed thousands of people and devastated the country? Peanuts. A mere fifty million dollars or so from America. And Haiti is only a few hundred miles from America's own shores. Haiti also has a very large population here in the United States, and they got virtually nothing. Yet when I point this out to people in DC, and suggest that pouring money into the Middle East when countries close to America's shores and within America's old sphere of influence are suffering so badly, they often become furious. There is this strange moral bubble, it seems, and of course it is particularly bad in Washington, but then again, outside Washington and the universities, nobody thinks about these issues at all!

You end your recent article in The Nation *with the following quote from Arnold Toynbee: "Great empires do not die by murder, but suicide." Is that the present trajectory of the United States?*

I must state very strongly that in principle, and when thinking of the historical alternatives, I do not want the American empire to end. I have never been against a moderate, civilized, and rational version of American hegemony. I certainly would not want to replace it with Chinese hegemony!

But it is easy to see how a combination of different events could bring American hegemony down over the next generation. America at present has no serious strategy for the Middle East. It has a series of ad hoc strategies for dealing with bits of the terrorist threat, and for trying to contain Iran, and manage Pakistan and Saudi Arabia. It does not, however, have anything approaching a general strategy. If America continues to infuriate more and more Muslims, if then there is either a revolution elsewhere in the Middle East or a terrorist attack on the American mainland again, then it is very easy to see America lashing out in a way that not only will spread chaos and instability still further, but will lead to a complete breakdown of the alliance with Europe.

If America gets involved in another major war of occupation, then conscription will be back. When conscription comes back, Americans will come out onto the streets and start demanding answers: maybe even about energy saving and about the relationship with Israel.

Even given the profound weaknesses of America's strategy and position in the Middle East, however, the American empire has immense underlying strengths. In the Far East, for example, as long as the United States does not grossly overplay its hand, most of the East Asian states actually want America to stay there as a balancer against China. In Europe, East Europeans in particular are anxious for the United States to remain strongly present, whether out of continued fear of Russia or resentment at French and German domination. In Central America and the Caribbean, the United States will always be predominant through sheer force of economic and military might.

But if the Bush administration were feeling suicidal, and were actually in the mood to throw itself over a cliff, like the Hapsburgs in 1914, there are a number of ways it could do that. It could invade Iran—that would do it very quickly. Or it could invade Saudi Arabia. Or it could support Taiwanese independence. I don't believe it will actually do any of those things. Unfortunately, one can much more easily imagine the Bush administration doing something like bombing Iran, which would not lead to immediate disaster but could begin a spiral of retaliation leading ultimately to catastrophic conflict.

It has become increasingly clear that world oil reserves are depleting and their exhaustion is within sight. In addition, global oil and energy resources have formally been a "national security" concern of the United States since Carter. How, and to what extent, will the geopolitics of oil determine U.S. foreign policy in the coming decade?

To a great extent, they already do. One has seen the tremendous attempt to build up the Caspian as an alternative to the Persian Gulf as a source of oil. But the striking thing is that this has to a great extent failed. It has failed both because there is not enough oil in the Caspian really to compete with the Persian Gulf, but also because there are other buyers: a great deal of that oil will go east to China and even to Japan. If the Chinese economy continues to grow, it is likely that oil prices will rise and rise—until, perhaps, environmental disaster destroys the present world economy and forces the world to limit oil consumption.

So America's presence in the Middle East is of course not just about Israel. A tremendous amount of it is about oil—and not just the interests of the oil companies, but genuinely, in the view of many Americans, the preservation of the American *way of life*. It will be interesting if one sees serious instability in several of the major oil producers simultaneously. If there were major instability in the Persian Gulf *and* some kind of meltdown in Nigeria, which is entirely possible, *and* in a very different way of course serious instability in Venezuela, then there is the possibility that somewhere at least America would intervene with its own troops on the ground to guarantee its oil supplies. Then once again we will be confronted with the whole question of whether America has enough troops, what this will lead to, etc. In some places in Africa, American intervention could be presented as a peacekeeping operation, and indeed could even have genuine elements of that.

I am not saying that any of this will happen, but the geopolitics of oil will be absolutely central to America's global strategy in the years to come. Of course, what I would like to see would be an approach to the same issue from the other end, which is simply to reduce America's dependence on oil. This has been one of the very worst things that Bush has done, or rather *not* done: his complete failure to use 9/11 to make an argument for decreasing America's reliance on oil. Instead we have just seen American consumption going up and up. There is a strong possibility in the future that just as in Iraq, America could again be drawn into occupying a country (or countries) in a way that would be perceived by the rest of the world as just about keeping its grip on oil supplies. The thing that might discourage a U.S. administration from this, however, is that, as Iraq has demonstrated, there is nothing easier to blow up than an oil pipeline.

Such a contingency has been widely discussed in the case of Saudi Arabia. If the United States were to occupy other countries in order to secure its oil supplies, then every suspicion of the rest of the world concerning the United States and its motives for the invasion of Iraq would essentially be confirmed. The United States would begin to shed its last elements of true international idealism. It would become much more like a classical empire preoccupied with seizing raw materials and controlling them, irrespective of the wishes or the well-being of the populations concerned. In this case, America's ancient and very positive role as a beacon of democracy and progress for humankind would be destroyed. We should all pray, therefore, that this does not happen.

PART THREE I FEMINISM AND HUMAN RIGHTS

EIGHT | Shirin Ebadi

How did you become interested in the field of human rights?

Everyone is born with certain characteristics. I always had a feeling during childhood, almost like a calling, which I could not name then but I later found was about seeking justice, a certain commitment to justice. When I was a child, whenever I would see children fighting, I would naturally try to defend the underdog, the weakest. I even got beaten up myself a couple of times doing that!

This natural tendency led me to choose law as my field of study. In addition, my own father was a professor of law. And it was this natural tendency to seek justice that also led me to choose to become a judge after getting my law degree. I thought that by being a judge I could practice justice even better.

After the revolution, we were told that women, according to Islam, could not be magistrates or judges. So as soon as it became possible for me to do so, I decided to retire prematurely. Following which I requested a license from the Iranian Bar Association to practice law. I was turned down for seven years, although in that same time period others were given the same license. The reason was that I have always had a sharp tongue! Once I did get the license to practice, I knew exactly where I was headed, and that was toward the defense of human rights as a means to getting justice.

I am extremely grateful to Banafsheh Keynoush, the interpreter for Shirin Ebadi, who made this conversation possible.

What kind of human rights work have you principally been involved in?

I have been active in both the theory and practice of human rights. I have published eleven books, mostly focused on human rights: the rights of women, the rights of the child, comparative law on the rights of the child, underage laborers, the history and documentation of human rights in Iran, the rights of refugees, and rights within the framework of arts and literature insofar as they pertain to freedom of speech.

In practice too I have been active. Along with a couple of others, I set up an association for the defense of the rights of the child aimed at disseminating and promoting the International Convention on the Rights of the Child in Iran. Fortunately, this NGO has been quite successful. I was also able to set up another NGO with the help of a number of lawyers. In this NGO, we offer pro bono legal services to political defendants and those who are sent to prison for ideological reasons. We also provide support to the relatives of political prisoners. We raise awareness or at times publish declarations in areas where human rights have been violated.

Following the Nobel, I have also set up another NGO for demining.

Why do you think that in contemporary debates, Islam is frequently viewed as incompatible with human rights?

Unfortunately the human rights situation is not very good in most Islamic countries. When people object to cases of human rights violations, they are told that Islam and human rights are, in essence, incompatible. It is claimed that governments are observing Islamic rules and regulations. By doing so, that is, by invoking religion, these governments are clearly attempting to silence those who object. But this is absolutely incorrect. Islamic studies show us that Islam has no incompatibility with human rights.

On the other hand, the advocates of the so-called clash of civilizations thesis are also interested in making the case that Islam and human rights are incompatible. In making this argument, they are suggesting that Islam and democracy are incompatible, and that the clash between Western and Eastern civilizations is inevitable. To make their task easier, they resort to phrases such as "Islamic" terrorism. A single, terrible deed carried out by a Muslim, according to them, is a result of the fact that the person is *Muslim*. Whereas, obviously, *anyone* can engage in wrongful acts. To take one example: in Bosnia there were those who did terrible things, but we did not say that those acts were committed

SHIRIN EBADI | 141

in the name of Christianity, or that Christianity was responsible. Or in Palestine for that matter: the Israeli government has not implemented *any* UN resolution that has been issued so far, but we do not blame Judaism for this inaction. So it is not clear to us why when *one* Islamic group is responsible for an act of violence, everyone in the world starts talking about it as *Islamic* terrorism.

So those who believe that democracy and Islam are incompatible fall in the following categories: first, Westerners who are advocates of war; and second, some Islamic governments that are also dictatorial regimes that violate the rights of their people (and seek legitimacy for doing so).

You have said elsewhere that "The discriminatory plight of women in Islamic states, too, whether in the sphere of civil law or in the realm of social, political and cultural justice, has its roots in the patriarchal and male-dominated culture prevailing in these societies, not in Islam." How do you understand the difference between culture and religion?

Culture is more deep-rooted than religion. Several factors combine to constitute the culture of a nation, one of which is religion. Like any other ideology, religion is open to interpretation. It is the culture of a society that offers its own interpretation of what religion should constitute. For instance, there have been various interpretations of socialism: Was the former Soviet Union administered in the same manner as China considering they both followed a similar ideology? Is Cuba administered the same way as Albania was under socialism?

Therefore interpretations of an ideology or religion (including Islam) are not specific to any one society. Any ideology is open to various interpretations.

In the present global dispensation, there seems to be greater emphasis placed on civil and political rights rather than on economic and social rights. Why is this the case and how, if at all, would you like to see this change?

Human rights are indivisible. Mankind needs all these rights. Freedom without social justice is useless, and social justice is useless in the absence of individual freedoms. Human rights in its entirety is required for an individual.

In the context of large—and in some cases, increasing—inequalities between and within states, how can human rights be guaranteed? In other words, do you think structural change at the global or national level may be necessary before every human being can be granted some measure of dignity and freedom?

Yes, organizations like the United Nations and the World Bank need restructuring. For example, when the right to veto is granted in the Security Council, is it possible to talk of democracy at a global level? This means that if all the countries of the world are on one side and only one of the five permanent members of the Security Council is on the other side and chooses to exercise its veto power, it can override the will of the rest of the world.

To take another example, when the World Bank offers loans to undemocratic countries, it is an injustice to the people of those countries. Look at how much, in terms of loans, Saddam Hussein may have received during his time in power. Now, with Saddam Hussein overthrown, it is the people of Iraq who have to repay these debts. I deem it necessary to stress that for the majority of the time that Saddam Hussein was in power, Iraq was favored by the United States, and it was through the support of the United States that Iraq was able to receive loans from the World Bank. And now the people of Iraq are left with millions of dollars in debt. Saddam Hussein is not the only dictator who received such loans. This has unfortunately happened in many parts of the world. Therefore it is very important not to offer any form of support to countries that are undemocratic and violate human rights.

What impact do you think the war on terrorism has had on human rights globally?

The war on terrorism is a legitimate fight and must be carried out. However, it should not become an excuse for violating human rights. Fighting for human rights should be within the framework of the United Nations. At the same time, terrorists should be arrested and prosecuted. But given the large number of terrorists that have already been arrested and prosecuted, have we been able to mitigate terrorism or its impacts?

Obviously not. The reason is that prosecuting terrorists alone is not sufficient. One must approach terrorism by addressing its root causes. Terrorism emanates from two basic sources: one is prejudice. Prejudice results from ignorance and the lack of education. If we seek to eradicate illiteracy globally, we are in fact taking steps to control and fight terrorism. The second root of terrorism is injustice. We must seek to reduce the sources of injustice in the world. If these two root causes are taken away, we will surely be able to get rid of terrorism as well.

NINE I Lila Abu-Lughod

Following the events of September 11, the American public sphere has been saturated with discussions of what is unique about "Muslim" societies. To what extent is the character of Muslim societies determined by Islam? How can we begin to think about these societies, and what distinguishes them from our own?

Many aspects of societies around the world cannot be understood without reference to the history and influences of the major religions in terms of which people live their lives. This is just as true for people living in the Middle East, Africa, Southeast Asia, and other Muslim regions as it is for those living in Europe and the United States, where Christianity has historically dominated. The point to stress is that despite this, it is just as unhelpful to reduce the complex politics, social dynamics, and diversity of lives in the United States to Christianity as it is to reduce these things to Islam in other regions. We should ask not how Muslim societies are distinguished from "our own" but how intertwined they are, historically and in the present, economically, politically, and culturally.

Muslim women have of course figured prominently in this public discussion. You have suggested recently that "understanding Muslim women" will not serve to explain anything. Could you elaborate on this claim?

The arguments presented in this interview have been elaborated in Lila Abu-Lughod, "Do Muslim Women Really Need Saving? Anthropological Reflections on Cultural Relativism and Its Others," American Anbthropologist 104 (3): 783–90.

Many of us have noticed that suddenly, after 9/11 and the American response of war in Afghanistan, the hunger for information about Muslim women seems insatiable. My own experience of this was in the form of an avalanche of invitations to appear on news programs and at universities and colleges. On the one hand, I was pleased that my expertise was appreciated and that so many people wanted to know more about a subject I had spent twenty years studying. On the other hand, I was suspicious because it seemed that this desire to know about "women and Islam" was leading people away from the very issues one needed to examine in order to understand what had happened.

Those issues include the history of Afghanistan—with Soviet, U.S., Pakistani, and Saudi involvements; the dynamics of Islamist movements in the Middle East; the politics and economics of American support for repressive governments. Plastering neat cultural icons like "the Muslim woman" over messier historical and political narratives doesn't get you anywhere. What does this substitution accomplish? Why, one has to ask, didn't people rush to ask about Guatemalan women, Vietnamese women (or Buddhist women), Palestinian women, or Bosnian women when trying to understand those conflicts? The problem gets framed as one about another culture or religion, and the blame for the problems in the world placed on Muslim men, now neatly branded as patriarchal.

The British in India and the French in Algeria both enlisted the support of women for their colonial projects (i.e., part of the colonial enterprise was ostensibly to "save" native women). Do you think the current rhetoric about women in Afghanistan suffers from the same problem? Is there something about the colonial/neocolonial context that lends itself to this kind of representation (which would explain, as you point out, why such rhetoric cannot be employed in the case of African American women in this country)?

Yes, I ask myself about the very strong appeal of this notion of "saving" Afghan women, a notion that justifies American intervention (according to First Lady Laura Bush's November 2001 radio address) and that dampens criticism of intervention by American and European feminists. It is easy to see through the hypocritical "feminism" of a Republican administration. More troubling for me are the attitudes of those who do genuinely care about women's status. The problem, of course, with ideas of "saving" other women is that they depend on and reinforce a sense of superiority by Westerners.

When you save someone, you are saving them from something. You are also saving them to something. What violences are entailed in this transformation? And what presumptions are being made about the superiority of what you are saving them to? This is the arrogance that feminists need to question. The reason I brought up African American women, or working-class women in the United States, was that the smug and patronizing assumptions of this missionary rhetoric would be obvious if used at home, because we've become more politicized about problems of race and class. What would happen if white middle-class women today said they needed to save those poor African American women from the oppression of their men?

You mentioned that the veil or burqa has been spoken of and defended by Muslim women as "portable seclusion," and that veiling should not be associated with lack of agency. Can you explain why this is the case?

It was the anthropologist Hanna Papanek, working in Pakistan, who twenty years ago coined this term "portable seclusion." I like the phrase because it makes me see burqas as symbolic "mobile homes" that free women to move about in public and among strange men in societies where women's respectability and protection depend on their association with families and the homes that are the center of family lives.

The point about women's veiling is of course too complicated to lay out here. But there were three reasons why I said it could not so simply be associated with lack of agency. First, "veiling" is not one thing across different parts of the Muslim world, or even among different social groups within particular regions. The variety is extraordinary, going from headscarves unself-consciously worn by young women in rural areas to the fuller forms of the very modern "Islamic dress" now being adopted by university women in the most elite of fields, including medicine and engineering. Second, many of the women around the Muslim world who wear these different forms of cover describe this as a choice. We need to take their views seriously, even if not at face value. Beyond that, however, we need to ask some hard questions about what we actually mean when we use words like "agency" and "choice" when talking about human beings, always social beings always living in particular societies with culturally variable meanings of personhood. Do we not all work within social codes? What does the expression we often use here, "the tyranny of fashion," suggest about agency in dress codes?

You argued that the interesting political and ethical question that the burqa raises has to do with how to deal with difference. You ask if it is possible for us to think of Afghan women being free in ways different from our own conception of freedom, that is, can we only free Afghan women to be like us?

Yes, I think we need to recognize that even after "liberation" from the Taliban, Afghan women (and one can't presume any uniformity of views even within this category) might want different things from what we (Westerners, of course also a diverse category) might want for them. What do we do about that? I don't think we need simply to be cultural relativists, advocating respect for whatever goes on elsewhere and explaining it as "just their culture." I've already talked about the problem of "cultural" explanations in my criticism of the focus on the category of "Muslim women." And it should be recalled that Afghan or other Muslims' "cultures" are just as much part of history and an interconnected world as ours are.

What I think we need to do is to work hard to respect and recognize difference—as products of different histories, as expressions of different circumstances, as manifestations of differently structured desires.

We might still argue for justice for women, but consider that there might be different ideas about justice and that different women might want, or choose, different futures from what we envision as best. Among the most difficult things for American feminists to accept is that these futures might involve women in developing within a different religious tradition, or traditions, that don't have as their primary ideal something called "freedom."

Reports that came out of the Bonn peace conference in late November 2001 revealed that there were even differences among the few Afghan women feminists and activists present. Some, like the representative of the Revolutionary Association of the Women of Afghanistan (RAWA), refused to be conciliatory to any notion of Muslim governance. But others looked to Iran as a country in which they could see women making significant gains within an Islamic framework—in part through an Islamically oriented feminist movement that is challenging injustices and reinterpreting the religious tradition. The situation in Iran is itself the subject of great debate within feminist circles, especially among Iranian feminists in the West. It is not clear whether and in what ways women have made gains, and whether the great increases in literacy, decreases in birthrates, presence of women in the professions and government, and a feminist flourishing in cultural fields like writing and filmmaking are because of or despite the establishment of a so-called Islamic Republic.

The concept of an Islamic feminism itself is also the subject of heated debate. Is it an oxymoron, or does it refer to a viable movement forged by women who want another way? Still, the representatives at the Bonn peace conference thought it was more realistic to look to the Iranian model than to a secular Western one if they wanted to have any appeal to local women and to have a chance of transforming women's lives and gender relations from within.

The last point I would want to make about "difference" is that even if we have strong convictions about what might be the best path for Afghan women, wouldn't we do better to keep our sights trained on what we can do, sitting here in this part of the world? We might do better to think how to make the world a more just place rather than trying to "save" women in other cultures. Of course we can ask ourselves how to support those within different communities who want to, and are working to, make women's lives better—here the concept can be that of alliances. But we can also ask ourselves, living in this privileged and powerful part of the world, what our own responsibilities are for the situations in which others have found themselves. We don't stand outside the world, looking over at those poor benighted people elsewhere. How might we make the world a place where certain kinds of forces and values can have an appeal? How might we help create the peace necessary for discussions, debates, and transformations to occur? We need to ask what kinds of world conditions could we contribute to making such that popular desires won't be determined by an overwhelming sense of helplessness in the face of forms of global injustice. Or where those who can point to rich powers swaggering around the world can sway people to their hatreds. Those seem like more productive lines of thought and action. Let's leave the nineteenth-century missionary work of saving Muslim women behind, where it belongs.

TEN | Saba Mahmood

Your work positions itself as a critique of liberal conceptions of political rule and its social and ethical norms, particularly in relation to Islamist movements and politics. Could you please clarify at the outset what you mean by "liberal" in your writing? And why do you think liberalism has such a purchase in the Muslim world?

In my writing when I use the term "liberal" I am referring to liberalism as a tradition of political thought and philosophy with a distinct conception of the subject, ethics, and politics. The liberal tradition as it emerged over the course of the eighteenth and nineteenth century in Europe is coincidental with the development of capitalism and modern governance. Among the principles central to liberal political and moral philosophy that I address in my work on Islamism is the principle of liberty and freedom as an individual and political ethic. While the notion of freedom is valued in a number of premodern traditions, liberalism presupposes a particular anthropology of the subject wherein freedom comes to be primarily understood as an individual capacity to act autonomously in accord with one's own desires and interests (interest here is largely defined in economic terms). Insomuch as autonomy is regarded as a "natural" human attribute, it presupposes a necessary antagonism between the individual and the social, and individual interests are understood to stand in opposition to community values and interests. The liberal maxim that the good life is necessarily a freely chosen one in which a person develops his unique capacities in accord with his "own will and interests" has now become the most dominant ethic of our age.

Beyond this, classical liberal thought also links the principle of liberty intimately with private property, insisting that an economic system based on private property is uniquely capable of delivering and facilitating individual liberty—particularly by enabling a person to employ her labor and her capital in whatever manner she pleases. Classical liberals and libertarians indeed have gone so far as to argue that property itself is a form of freedom (property here is understood in a double sense: the property of labor that one holds within oneself and property as a material possession). These conceptions and ideals not only are presupposed by social theorists and philosophers but are normative to the logic of the modern state—to its juridical, administrative, civic, and executive operations. Liberalism, however, is not simply a state doctrine or a set of juridical conventions: in its vast implications, it defines, in effect, something like a form of life with vast implications for how we imagine ourselves to be human and worthy in this age.

The precepts of liberal political philosophy were introduced into non-Western societies (including Muslim societies) through colonial rule and an expanding system of global capitalist power (through institutions of law, governance, trade, and commerce) over the course of two centuries. Liberal presuppositions about politics and society have over time become an intrinsic part of the sensibilities and institutions of these societies and form an important resource for indigenous critiques of Western power and domination throughout the colonial and postcolonial period. It is precisely because many aspects of liberal discourse have become a part of the language of resistance to Western forms of power that I think it is important to attend to its hegemonic qualities, its normative assumptions, and the ways in which it remains peculiarly blind to other kinds of political and social projects and moral-ethical aspirations. Let me elaborate on this by giving you two examples.

Recall that anticolonial struggle against Western imperialism in the Middle East and South Asia was inspired by the ideal of self-rule, an ideal that liberal political philosophy made available universally while simultaneously denying its extension to the colonial subjects of European empires. The struggle for national self-determination and representative government on the part of colonized peoples against this exclusion is premised precisely on the argument that liberal universal claims of equality and fraternity be extended to the colonial subjects of British and French empires. Anticolonial struggle for self-determination may be seen both as an outcry against the self-limiting character of liberal political rule as much as an extension beyond the limits of what its founders envisioned it to be. You can see in this the productive capacity of the ideology of liberalism, its mutation and extension by those who are simultaneously both ruled *and* excluded by it. (Incidentally, the story of women's suffrage and Black suffrage in European and North Atlantic countries is similar in this regard.) Such a mutation of liberal ideology suggests that liberalism is not simply an imposition of Western values on non-Western peoples since many of its precepts are now constitutive of the modern postcolonial imaginary.

A second example I want to give here of the hegemony liberalism commands in discourses of resistance is the prominence given to the ideal of individual freedom and autonomy within postcolonial feminist projects. One of the most cherished goals of postcolonial feminism—a movement aimed at improving the collective situation of "Third World women"—is to secure conditions under which women can live more autonomously and learn to distinguish between their "own desires" and those of the society, tradition, culture, or community. Despite the critiques leveled against Eurocentric feminism, it is quite common for postcolonial feminists to continue to reproduce many liberal assumptions, key among them the idea that the individual's desires and interests stand in a relationship of opposition to the demands of tradition, society, and community. It is quite common, therefore, to hear that one of the failings of traditional societies is to subsume the individual within the collective (the family, the *biradari*, etc.), thereby extinguishing the opportunities for women to learn how to distinguish between their own desires and those of the society, the elders, the culture, and so on. But one might ask as to whether such an opposition between the individual and the social is universally valid: indeed, such an opposition hardly applies to how life is lived and experienced in Western liberal societies.

In my work I have tried to unpack the limits, prejudices, and blind spots that the adoption of liberal ideals and discourses has produced within the political imagination of postcolonial Muslim societies. Thus, for example, in my book *Politics of Piety* I have tried to problematize the liberal valorization of the value of autonomy and the concomitant ideal of freedom that animates contemporary feminist thought. In doing so, my aim is not to dismiss the utility of these ideals for women's struggles, or to suggest that they are wrong, or to propose a better model of the relationship between the individual and the social. Rather my aim is to question the validity of these distinctions as universally valid and to urge feminists to challenge this rather narrow and parochial way of being human in the world. Some of the questions I am interested in exploring are: What are the different conceptions of the self that are now part of the postcolonial Muslim world that stand in tension with liberal conceptions of the self that are often upheld as more enlightened ways of being human in the world? Because liberalism does not map on to the geographical divide of the West and non-West (in other words, it is not a "cultural" trope) but commands a much broader set of allegiances, what sorts of mutations and genealogies of the self exist in our postcolonial world? What structures of power and authority, with different kinds of political imaginaries, do different conceptions of the subject presuppose? And what desires, other than freedom, do people live by? What do we mean by freedom, from what, and toward what end?

You have said in an article in the Boston Review *that Muslim scholars bear the burden of having to prove their liberal credentials whereas one of the questions that is never posed is what it might mean to "take the resources of the Islamic tradition and question many of the liberal political categories and principles for the contradictions and problems they embody." What do you think such questioning might illuminate? What do you mean when you suggest, later in the same article, that such questioning is rare because of the hegemony that liberalism exercises over Muslim thinkers?*

My complaint in that article was not so much that Muslim scholars have to bear the burden of proving their liberal credentials. The question that I posed to myself and my interlocutors was how is it that liberal ideals have come to command such power in our assessment of what ails Muslim societies today. What consequences does this assessment have on our capacity to imagine a future for ourselves as Muslims in today's world? The article to which I was invited to respond in the *Boston Review* was written by the well-respected legal scholar Khaled Abou El-Fadl and is an exploration of the resources found within the Islamic legal and theological corpus that might make Islam compatible with liberal ideals of democracy, pluralism, and tolerance.[1] What I found problematic about this piece, along with others like it, is the uncritical embrace of the liberal ideal of democracy and concomitant notions of pluralism and tolerance.

First of all, it is important to point out that the values of tolerance and pluralism are not intrinsic to liberalism but have always been an object of struggle by people who were dispossessed and excluded by the very ideology of liberalism (its universalist claims notwithstanding). Liberal forms of governance did not simply hand out a charter of political, civic, and economic rights (as we understand these rights today) to dispossessed peoples; these rights were struggled for (and continue to be struggled for) by people of all sorts, including women, minorities, and colonial subjects. This means that there has never been a single measure of tolerance, pluralism, and democracy within the liberal tradition, but these notions have been a product of intense power struggles and historical contingencies. (Recall here that some of the most heinous crimes committed against humanity—including the Holocaust—were under the rule and rubric of democracy.) So when Muslim scholars unproblematically today uphold "liberal democracy" as the ideal to emulate, I am forced to ask: What form of democracy, where, for whom, and with what conceptions of the collective good?

One of the reasons why Muslim intellectuals tend to champion a rather narrow version of liberal democracy today is because of its purportedly unique ability to manage religious diversity—through, for example, making religion a private matter and granting citizens the right to freedom of conscience (provided their religious practices do not interfere with a citizen's obedience to the laws of the state). I question the certainty of this vision in my article in *Boston Review* at a number of levels. For one, it is wrong to assume that religious coexistence is the achievement only of modern liberal societies: a number of premodern empires, including the Safavid, the Moghul, and the Ottoman, practiced various kinds of social arrangements in which a wide range of religious communities existed peacefully together. These arrangements were not without their faults, but neither is the liberal model. In the Ottoman system, for instance, non-Muslim communities were vertically integrated into a hierarchical ruling structure but had their own independent legal systems. This mutual accommodation enabled different social groups living under a shared political structure to practice distinct ways of life: these life-worlds (that were sometimes incommensurable) were the preconditions for the individual's existence, rather than the objects of individual interests as they are conceived within liberal political thought. The Ottoman system did not make non-Muslims the social or legal equals of Muslims, but it did grant them a certain autonomy to practice and develop their traditions in a manner that is almost inconceivable under the present system of nation-states. I raise this issue not because I think that this system is superior to what we have now or that we should bring it back (one cannot reverse the course of history). But this older model does offer us theoretical resources to ponder a number of questions that are absent from the current debate among Muslim intellectuals about how to think about the problem of religious and ethnic coexistence. These questions include: How does this premodern history make us rethink the politics of tolerance and pluralism beyond the confines of individualism to include the rights of social groups? Is the liberal meaning of tolerance the best or the most desirable one, and if so, in what way? What does such a conception preclude, under what kinds of presuppositions, and for whom? Again, I want to make clear that to think critically about the different ways in which religious or ethnic differences have been negotiated historically is not to argue simply for the superiority of one model over another, but to challenge ourselves beyond the confines of what the present offers precisely so as to think beyond the impasse of our existing ways of imagining and living with difference.

What troubles me about the current state of debate among Muslim intellectuals is the assumption that all roads lead to Rome wherein Rome is imagined on the model of American (and sometimes British or French) liberal democracy. It is seldom if ever asked what the different ways in which Rome might be imagined are, wherein Rome represents not simply another variation of a single model but a different kind of social and political possibility. I think that debate about what might constitute a worthy ethical and moral life (with all its political and economic dimensions) has become increasingly constrained in the last twenty years, often abiding by the confines of a rather narrow definition of free-market liberal democracy in which political participation is reduced to the casting of votes. Recall that it was not too long ago, before the fall of the Soviet Union, when it was customary for Muslim and other postcolonial intellectuals to debate the merits of different models of political life, where each model was equally encumbered by its own particular set of promises, problems and impasses. The utopian self-portrayals of socialism and liberalism notwithstanding, the distinct sociopolitical visions of the good-life each model offered generated a wide-ranging debate in the Muslim world that at least held open the possibility that postcolonial Muslims might have to create and imagine a future that might well be an amalgam of different kinds of ideological, cultural, and political visions. This openness to different kinds of political futures and arrangements is almost completely gone, and what is held out in front of us today is a singular vision of what "democracy" could be, with hardly any discussion or debate about the ideals and horizons such a vision forecloses and the forms of violence it endorses.

Do you think that the rise of Islamist movements complicates this picture somewhat? It is often argued that these movements are the cry of the dispossessed against the failures of postcolonial Muslim states as much as they are an expression of resistance against Western domination, or some combination of the two. Your book Politics of Piety *takes issue with this understanding. Why?*

Well, I think that Islamic movements do complicate this picture in that they have articulated a robust, if disparate and at times inarticulate, critique of secular-liberal models of governance and visions of ethical and political life. Before I go into this though I think it is important to emphasize the plurality of Islamic movements given the homogenous picture that is often painted both in the academic and popular press. The Islamic movement (or what is often called the "Islamic Revival") comprises a number of different strands, including the much publicized militant strand but also grassroots political parties whose aim is to broaden the scope of electoral democracy through civic activism and public participation. Their efforts are often thwarted by authoritarian Middle Eastern governments—as we saw in the 2005 Egyptian elections but also earlier in Tunisia, Turkey, and Morocco.[2] The broadest current within the Islamic movement, however, is what I loosely call the piety movement (in some places it is referred to as the *da'wa* movement), which consists of a network of charitable nonprofit organizations that provide welfare services to the poor (often through mosques) as well as a range of networks and groups whose aim it is to make ordinary Muslims more religiously observant and devout in their daily conduct and practice. Notably, this latter strand of the Islamic movement does not target its efforts at electoral or state reform but seeks to transform the cultural and social ground on which politics is conducted. It is for this reason that I do not regard this strain of the movement to be apolitical (as some other scholars of Islam do) precisely because I think ethical and moral conduct is consequential for how politics is conducted in any modern society. Now it is crucial to note that these various tendencies that comprise the Islamic movement differ not only in the kinds of critiques they offer of Western hegemony and Muslim elites, but also in the social and political imaginaries they endorse and enable. As a result, I do not think it is quite correct to assume that the Islamic movement has a singular critique of either Western hegemony or postcolonial Muslim governments precisely because the various strands are quite distinct from each other.

The assessment that Islamist movements are a form of resistance and outcry against Western hegemony and the injustices committed by post-colonial Muslim governments is not entirely wrong, but in its simplicity it misses some crucial aspects of this plural movement—a pluralism that requires serious reflection on the part of any thinking activist or intellectual today. Consider, for example, the fact that the efforts of Islamic political parties (such as the Muslim Brotherhood or the Nahda party) target the policies and practices of the state (particularly in their demand to end single-party rule, the promulgation of free and fair elections, restitution of political rights, and so on). These parties therefore take the nation, with all of its juridical and distributive functions, as the locus of their activism. As a result, in their ideology and practice, they share many of the presuppositions of their most trenchant critics, namely, secular nationalists with whom they share a nationalist horizon of politics with the citizen-subject as its most natural inhabitant (with her particular form of belonging, rights, and duties). This stands in contrast with the piety activists for whom it is the moral, social, and ethical fabric of society that requires work, and the nationalist horizon of politics, while important to them, is not the prime locus for moral action. It is the pious Muslim who is the normative subject of their activism (rather than the citizen-subject) with her moral and ethical responsibilities and obligations geared toward the moral requisites of the *umma*. Given these differences, it is not surprising that these two distinct strands of the Islamic movement stand in tension with each other. In fact, as I show in my book *Politics of Piety*, secular *and* Islamic nationalists in Egypt often share their critique of the piety movement in that both regard the form of religiosity practiced by the pietists as backward, mired in the inconsequential minutiae of practice as opposed to the abstract spiritual ideals of Islam.

So the simple assertion that Islamic movements are an expression of resistance to Western hegemony misses this complexity completely. Moreover, to read the Islamic movement through the reductive trope of resistance is to fail to interrogate what specific aspects of Western hegemony, postcoloniality, or even liberal-nationalism these different Islamic formations oppose and toward what ends. What distinct and contrasting ethical and political projects do they enable or foreclose? Mind you, these are not simply academic questions. They should be of concern even to those secular Muslims who are critical of the Islamic movement. Indeed, my argument is if the practice of critique entails not simply the annihilation of those one criticizes, but also engagement and debate, then it is crucial that Muslims critical of the "Islamist turn" engage with the specificity of this wide-ranging movement and the diversity of its various projects and aspirations.

I am afraid that the trend among progressive-liberal Muslims (among whom I have often included myself) to characterize the Islamists as one monolithic block—blind in their rage against the West—reproduces the current U.S. and European rhetoric of "Islamic fundamentalism" wherein all distinctions among Islamists are erased so as to secure a homogenous enemy whose annihilation becomes the condition for one's own survival. I find this zero-sum way of thinking not simply misguided and arrogant, but also dangerous, jeopardizing the future of Muslim societies in a way that I fear will be very destructive.

Your suggestion stands at odds with the assertion among many secularists in countries such as Pakistan, Turkey, and Egypt that it is the Islamists who foreclose dialogue and engagement and not the secularists. How would you respond to this?

Yes, you are quite right, this is the claim but I am not sure it holds up to scrutiny. I believe that intransigence exists on both sides: on the one hand you have the intransigence of Muslim clerics in contemporary Iran and Saudi Arabia, and on the other hand, you have the case of Turkey and Algeria where it was secular authoritarian governments that annulled the results of free and fair elections that put Islamists into power in the 1990s. This has historical antecedents with the suppression of the Muslim Brotherhood by the secular regimes of Jamal Abdul Nasser and Hafez al-Assad in Egypt and Syria (in the early 1980s between 10,000 and 25,000 suspected members of the Brotherhood were killed by Assad in Hama). Given the particular geopolitical context in which we are situated right now, it is important to realize how the agenda of the secularists in the Muslim world has converged with the strategic interests of the United States which, under the rubric of the "war on terror," is targeting a wide swath of Islamic activists regardless of their social agenda. It is customary, for example, for Western journalists to refer to the Muslim Brotherhood as a "fundamentalist and terrorist" organization even though the Brothers have not been engaged in any kind of militant activity since the late 1940s and early 1950s. The

U.S. State Department, in addition to its military operations, is currently engaged in a wide-ranging cultural and media campaign to promote the cause of "Islamic liberalism" with the explicit aim of "secularizing Islam from within." I have written about this in another article and I will not repeat my argument here.[3] An important strategy of this project is to paint the diversity of Islamic movements with the single brushstroke of fundamentalism and to render all shades of Islamic activity as suspect, deserving of a clinical excision and punishment.[4] Many secular liberal Muslim intellectuals and activists are guilty of reproducing the reductive assumptions of undergirding this programmatic vision—evident, for example, in the oft-repeated assertion that groups like the Muslim Brotherhood are a different face of Islamic militancy. This reductionism helps legitimize the current U.S. administration's vicious campaign to target and shut down a range of Islamic charities and traditional Islamic reform groups. An unfortunate and dangerous result of such a strategy has been to increase the sympathy (if not the ranks) of Islamic militants, leaving it as the only viable option in a zero-sum war of terror.

The current U.S. policy has in fact given a green light to a number of dictatorial regimes in the Middle East—such as Egypt, Jordan, and Morocco—to increase their persecution of Islamic reformists who constitute an important oppositional voice for democratic change in these societies. The U.S. government continues to abide by its standard hypocritical policy of ignoring such human rights violations while paying lip service to the need for democracy in the Middle East. This was blatantly obvious in the 2005 parliamentary and municipal elections in Egypt: when the Muslim Brothers made a strong showing in the parliamentary elections, the Mubarak government unleashed its goons and police forces on the voters and candidates to limit their electoral gain. The U.S. government barely protested this violation, and even the American press made far more of the Egyptian government's persecution of the secular Kifaya party than of the Muslim Brotherhood—despite the fact that the Kifaya party won far fewer seats in the elections than the Muslim Brothers. All of this has been reported and analyzed by Anthony Shadid in an excellent article recently published in the *Washington Post*.[5]

The fact that religious movements have come to play a significant role in a number of countries (including Islamic countries) seems to be a surprising development for many. These movements, particularly the Islamist movement, are often criticized for politicizing religion. However, the following argument you make in your book seems to unsettle this reading: "[The] conditions of secular-liberal modernity are such that for any world-making project (spiritual or otherwise) to succeed and be effective, it must engage with the all-encompassing institutions and structures of modern governance, whether it aspires to state power or not." Could you elaborate on this?

I think that the ascendance of religious politics in the world today—of which Islamic movements are only one part— has put into question the modernist prediction that religion will eventually decline in importance for people around the world. There are a number of different ways in which this defunct modernist prediction is being rethought today. One strand of thinking involves empirically describing where and when religion has become an important player in social and political fields, and providing a more variegated picture of what it means for religion and politics to coexist in modern societies. A second strand entails rethinking the conceptual ground on the basis of which the truth of the modernist prediction has been taken for granted for so long. It involves a reconsideration of what secularism means, what conceptual and practical transformations it entails, and how secularism is related to its putative nemesis, religion. Perhaps no other scholar has done more to help us rethink these questions than Talal Asad. His work compels us to conceptualize secularism as a historically specific process, one in which religion is not so much banished from the realm of politics (as the doctrine of secularism often claims) but rather rearticulated and reformulated along specific lines. In modernity, religion is conceptualized as a matter of privatized belief, the prime locus of which is the individual (rather than religious authority, scripture, or tradition), squarely rooted in secular conceptions of time, space, and causality. The modern individual owes her primary allegiance to the modern state: when and if her religious beliefs intervene with this obligation, the state steps in to regulate such behavior often through punitive means.

This secular conception of religiosity has come to be instituted in part through the legal and administrative powers of the modern state. It has entailed not simply the curtailment of religious/church power (as is often argued), but also the rearticulation of religion—from its spatial entailments to its worldly aspirations and the epistemological claims it is allowed to make. This massive reorganization of religious life needs to be thought through in terms of the history of secularization (and not simply as the "history of religion") precisely because it shows the constitutive ways in which modern secularism and modern religion are two sides of the same coin. Viewed from this perspective, it is clear that the relationship between modern politics and religion, or church and state, is far more porous and intertwined than the doctrinal understanding of secularism (as a firewall separation between religion and politics) suggests. This, by the way, applies not only to non-Western societies but also to the self-avowedly secular-liberal societies of Europe and America—albeit in different ways. Historians have repeatedly documented the ways in which Puritanism played a constitutive role in American politics and how its peculiar form of evangelical piety continues to characterize American secularism today; similarly scholars have noted the centrality of the Anglican Church in modern Britain and the role the Catholic Church played in delineating the principle and practice of *laïcité* in France.

Some commentators tend to read this intertwining of religion and politics as a sign of an incomplete and inadequate secularization process, and they prescribe a more stringent path toward secularization wherein the political realm is rigorously purified of any religious presence. I find this reading problematic because it remains oblivious to the fact that secularism also entails a robust notion of what proper religiosity should be—secularism, in other words, does not simply cordon off religion but reorganizes it so that it comes to play a particular role in modern society. It is this positive conception of religion—in all its material, institutional, affective and aesthetic dimensions—that any serious study of the rise of religious movements must contend with.

The quote you take from my book above draws attention to the all encompassing context of modern governance within which any religious activity necessarily unfolds today. While it is customary to criticize Islam for overstepping its boundary, what is often ignored are the multiple ways in which the modern state regulates all aspects of our daily life—from its most public to its most private—so as to render our lives congruent with a particular political rationality. I take this point from Charles Hirschkind who wrote a short critique of the term "political Islam" when it first emerged to point out that the term is often used to index the anomalous character of this kind of religiosity, one that illegitimately asserts itself in the political domain thereby subverting the proper meaning of religion.[6] Hirschkind argues that this line of argument fails to pay adequate attention to the expansion of state power into domains of life that were historically outside of its purview in premodern times. If you think about it, all sorts of institutions—from the family, to the school, to social welfare and worship—have been incorporated into the regulatory apparatus of the state to varying degrees such that we can not imagine giving birth, presiding over someone's death, building a house, or making a business contract without encountering the regulatory procedures of the state. It is therefore not surprising that any religious activity that aims to be effective in the social realm must necessarily engage the regulatory apparatus of modern state power—what comprises the political field in the analytical sense of the term.

Consider, for example, the vast array of social welfare organizations, *da'wa* groups, and charitable networks that comprise the Islamic movement. As I mentioned earlier, the aim of these groups is not to wrest control of the state but to provide a range of services (medical care for the poor, building mosques, etc.), and the teaching of pious Islamic practices through community action. As Hirchkind argues in his article, all of these activities engage the domain we call the political, both in the sense that they are subject to restrictions imposed by the state (licensing, etc.), and in the sense that they must compete against state-sponsored models of family, religiosity, worship, leisure, charity, and community. The efforts of even a spiritual movement, therefore, that seeks to institutionalize alternative models of social behavior must necessarily engage the legal, bureaucratic, disciplinary, and technological resources of modern power that shape contemporary societies. This means that for any Islamic activity to be effective it *must* be political, not because Muslims do not understand the distinction between politics and religion, but because modern conditions of governance make it impossible *not* to engage with the realm of the political even if the aim is to change how one lives religiously.

I want to point out that this argument is quite different from one that says Islam does not subscribe to the separation of *din wa dawla*—religion and state. This oft-repeated statement ignores the fact that Islamic history has accommodated different arrangements of administrative and civic power, and the fact that Islam, like any other religion, has gone through crucial theological and doctrinal transformations so as to adjust to the rigors and demands of the modern state. Apart from this historical point, what distinguishes the argument that Hirschkind makes is that it forces us to take seriously what it means to think about religion in the modern world, one in which the omnipotent force of modern political rationality, with all of its disciplinary and regulatory apparatuses, transforms "religion" such that its worldly performance becomes crucially dependent on this political rationality. Viewed from this perspective, religion or Islam does not have an ahistorical essence that asserts itself over and over again in the political domain in its will to power. Rather, one needs to understand how religion itself (from its doctrines to its practices) comes to be transformed through the exercise of modern power, one important vector of which is the ideology and practice of secularism.

Secularization is often viewed as a panacea for the ills of much of the Third World and certainly the Muslim world. In your research in Egypt you found that people you worked with had a different understanding of secularism. How does this understanding complicate the emancipatory reading of secularism?

Yes, indeed, the rise of religio-politics in the last two decades in a number of postcolonial societies has provoked cries within academic and policy circles for the reinstitution of secularism both as a political ethic and a political doctrine. The rise of religious politics is taken as a sign of the failure of these societies to adequately modernize, and the solution is supposed to reside in embarking on a more assiduous and stringent program of secularization. Secularism in this view is understood as a cure—rather than a cause—for the ills these societies are supposed to be suffering from. This understanding is quite distinct from the views of the people of the Islamic Revival that I worked with. These people perceived secularism to be a destructive force that was slowly dissolving a particular life world and its ethical commitments, which they considered to be valuable and worth preserving. They explicitly talked about how the modern secularized conception of religiosity—as a system of privatized belief that has little bearing on how one organizes one's daily practical conduct—was corrosive of their understanding of Islam as a system of ethical and moral virtues. Their commitment to an entire set of rituals and practices—such as strict adherence to Islamic obligations, modes of personal and social conduct, and forging an ethico-political community—was seen from this normative conception of modern religiosity as backward, regressive, and traditional, if not outrightly dangerous. Here I want to be clear that the people I worked with were not interested in wresting control of the state; rather, their interest lay in creating a pious Islamic sociability in which Islam was not promulgated top-down through the state but practiced within the context of a virtuous community where the focus is on how one lives (rather than what one believes). For such people, secularism is perceived as a deleterious force that makes it impossible to practice such a form of life.

In articulating their critique of secularism (as a social, governmental, and cultural logic), they were often confronted by a system of governance that claimed they were violating the principal divide between the moral and the political, a divide that their secular critics assumed was necessary to the sustenance of a modern polity. Yet many of the women and men I worked with from the Islamic Revival understood clearly that this divide between the moral and the political, which liberal political rationality claimed as "natural," is a putative divide that is continuously violated through a set of disciplinary procedures by the state aimed at the regulation of religion. How else, they claimed, was one to understand the history of religious reforms, the cultural practices through which secular norms are propagated and sustained, and the ongoing violation of Islamic cultural and political groups? The violence imminent to secular projects and reforms is often ignored by secularists, the participants of the Islamic Revival claimed, as a sacrifice necessary in the creation of a secular-liberal polity.

I am reminded here of Marx's searing critique of capitalism that not only recognized the powerful and liberating potential of capitalism but also exposed the violence and injustice capitalism unleashed upon the human and natural world. Despite his condemnation of capitalism, Marx was also clear that "traditional and feudal" societies had to undergo this violent process precisely so as to render them more amenable to the possibility of revolution. Marx, as is well known, viewed the British colonization of India positively, as a necessary step toward the eventual realization of a communist polity. I think that a similar attitude characterizes liberal and progressive tolerance toward the violence internal to secularism, which is often justified as the sacrifice necessary for the establishment of a "tolerant liberal polity." This I am afraid is a problematic vision, one that is begetting more (rather than less) violence in the world today.

You say that your writing about the Islamic revival is in part prompted by a desire to question normative liberal assumptions about human nature, such as the belief that all human beings have an innate desire for freedom, that all human beings try to assert their autonomy when permitted to do so, that human agency is primarily exercised in acts that challenge rather than uphold social norms, etc. How is it that these assumptions do not hold in the context of the Islamic revival?

My engagement with the Islamic movement, as I explained in the prologue to my book, is a product of the kind of secular arrogance I have described above, which, by the way, I have been equally guilty of myself in the past. In my book I recount how I came to question this arrogance in myself and others as Islamic politics gained ascendancy in the last three decades in South Asia (where I grew up) and the Middle East (where I conducted my research). I increasingly became dissatisfied not only with the explanations that are given for the rise of the Islamist movement but also with the destructive role that they are supposed to be playing in the Muslim world. This questioning led me to examine the very basis of my own secular suspicion of religion and secularism's claim to reasoned criticism. Mind you, my background in feminist politics was deeply informed by Marxism, and as a result I have always regarded liberalism with a healthy dose of skepticism. Yet a philosophical examination of modern attitudes toward religion reveals how deeply liberal Enlightenment thought informs Marxist and neo-Marxist dismissals of religion. The idea that religion is a less mature, sentimental mode of apprehension of reality, whose force is best understood in psychological or symbolic terms, cuts across liberal and Marxist traditions. If liberalism reduces religion to a kind of sentiment best appreciated within the private space of individualized belief, then historical materialism reduces religion to an affect of a repressed and subjugated consciousness. Religious truth within Marxist accounts is read as force, a play of power whose machinations can always be traced back to the logic of capital and domination. This is a very reductive understanding of power, if not religion, and of the complex relationship between power and ideology.

The more time I spent studying Islamic politics, the more I realized that one cannot have a sane discussion about what this form of politics means without at the same time problematizing secular-liberal assumptions through which the failure (or efficacy) of Islamic movements is measured. This does not mean, as I make clear in my book, that Islamic political and ethical projects (in all their plurality) are necessarily incommensurable with liberal and secular presuppositions. As I said in my answer to your first question, the relationship between Islamism and secular-liberalism is one of proximity and coimbrication rather than negation or opposition. For example, it is impossible to imagine Islamic politics in Egypt without modern forms of political life that were put into place progressively since the 1920s—such as syndicalist and union politics, forms of electoral democracy, the use of public and print media, and mass education. Similarly many secular-liberal ideals, such as those I mentioned earlier (self-determination, universal suffrage, equality) are a crucial part of the ideology and self-understanding of Islamic movements.

This does not mean, however, that all forms of Islamic ethics and politics are a regurgitation of liberal principles and practices. Many aspects of the Islamic movement challenge, reformulate, and stand in tension with liberal valorizations of autonomy, freedom, and equality, just as this movement calls into question the liberal presupposition that politics and morality must be necessarily separated in modern societies. My interest lies in understanding what these tensions are, when and if they occur, and exactly what kind of challenge Islamic politics poses to liberal, progressive, and nationalist forms of politics.

The remarks I made that you quote from were a product of the dissatisfaction I had come to feel with feminist analyses of the Islamic movement in particular and conservative religious movements in general. These analyses often present two supposedly different accounts of women's participation in the Islamist movement. On the one hand, you have accounts in which feminist scholars portray Islamist women as the antithesis of all that feminism stands for, women who instrumentally appropriate feminist symbols, imagery and language, only to make these symbolic resources serve patriarchal ends and goals. On the other hand, there are monographs that desperately search for "Islamic feminism," trying to unearth the feminist potential within Islamist women's discourses even when this language is not a part of Islamist projects. These two accounts, in my opinion, are the mirror opposite of each other: the political and analytical worth of this movement is to be measured in terms of whether it is profeminist or antifeminist. What changes in this equation is the valuation of Islamism vis-à-vis feminism, but we learn little about the goals, projects, and practices of Islamism itself. It is seldom asked whether feminism is the relevant lens through which to analyze women's participation in the Islamist movement: Are there other notions of what it means to be human in this world, competing conceptions of human flourishing and collective and individual good, whose logic does not map onto the ideals that feminism represents and advocates? How might these movements expand feminist politics and analytics beyond what this tradition already knows and values?

Feminism, as I discuss in my book, admittedly is a wide ranging tradition that encompasses socialist, liberal, radical, and other interpretations. But what is common to this tradition and indeed what gives it a certain analytical and political coherence, is the position that women are the subservient members of any society and it is the task of feminist scholars both to render this subservience visible within a given society and to suggest ways in which this subservience might be subverted and changed. While I consider both of these aspects of feminist scholarship to be a worthy enterprise, I also think that in order for feminism to be a vibrant and expansive tradition, it must expand its horizons to a consideration of projects, aspirations, and desires that do not reproduce its liberatory assumptions and telos—but indeed challenge it. In other words, if feminist analysis aspires to be more than a regurgitation of its moral superiority (which these days often translates into a simple denunciation of Islam's abuses), then it must seriously contemplate the idea that it can learn something from nonliberal movements; that these movements might have something to teach feminists about what it means to be human in this world and to live in a variety of ways that do not map onto the logic of anti- or profeminist positions. Such a way of engaging nonliberal movements requires that we question the idea that all women, regardless of their historical and social location, are necessarily interested in expanding their freedoms, that they all seek to become autonomous individuals against the constraints of social and cultural norms.

In your article coauthored with Charles Hirschkind, "Feminism, the Taliban, and Politics of Counter-Insurgency," you discuss the social and political conditions prevailing in Afghanistan in 2001 and their representation in the American context, and ask: "Why were conditions of war, militarization, and starvation considered to be less injurious to women than the lack of education, employment, and most notably, in the media campaign, Western dress styles?" What do you think accounts for the relative weight given to the latter factors? Is it not the case that the former were not targeted at women in the way the latter were?

I think one of the reasons why the *burqa*—or the veil—took such center-stage in the feminist mobilization against the Taliban in the United States is due to the overdetermined status of the veil in Western history, particularly the colonial and Orientalist legacy that made the veil a symbol of Islam's inferior status vis-à-vis "European civilization." What Charles Hirschkind and I tried to point out is that American feminist preoccupations—along with the Western media's—came at the expense of ignoring (or downplaying) the conditions of war and starvation that women were subjected to at that time in Afghanistan. Let me remind you here of the immense feminist mobilization we saw in America against the Taliban: it was led by the Feminist Majority whose broad-based campaign bore fruit as a wide array of popular women's magazines (such as *Jane*, *Glamour*, and *Vogue*) and television and radio shows honed in on the burqa as the primary symbol of Afghan women's oppression. Mind you, this was *before* the events of September 11, 2001, when the Bush administration instrumentally used this vast feminist mobilization to justify its bombing of Afghanistan and the overthrow of the Taliban regime. At the time, there were other Afghan women's organizations that had also been trying to draw international attention to women's plight under Taliban rule, but their efforts never seized the American imagination on the scale or in the manner that the Feminist Majority campaign did—with the burqa as its potent and singular symbol.

We need to recall here that when the Taliban came to power in 1995, the situation of Afghan women was already dire as a result of twenty years of war in which the two superpowers, the United States and the Soviet Union, had turned the region into an orgiastic field of violence. The United States alone poured over three billion dollars into Afghanistan, the largest covert operation in U.S. history since the Second World War, to destabilize the Soviet occupation (with Saudi Arabia and Pakistan, the two most dictatorial regimes in the region, as partners in this project). It has been widely reported that the vast majority of U.S. financial aid was given to the most extreme militant groups in Afghanistan with the understanding that "religious fanatics" would fight the godless communists better. When the Taliban came into power in 1995, they made the situation for urban women worse, but, as was reported even in the popular media at the time, women's situation remained much the same in rural areas.

The Feminist Majority campaign, by virtue of focusing exclusively on the burqa and the Taliban regime, in effect ignored these other issues and the larger context that had enabled the Taliban to come into power in the first place. In doing so, American liberal feminists overlooked the U.S. government's culpability in promoting extremist groups like the Taliban and in creating the conditions of war and starvation to which women were particularly vulnerable. In the Feminist Majority campaign literature, there was hardly a mention of the fact that the United States had practically created the likes of the Afghan *mujahideen* (of which the Taliban were a product) or the brutal history of U.S. involvement in the region. The focus on the burqa made the Taliban issue sexy, it caught the attention of the popular media. Celebrities, who would not have been moved by accounts of poverty and starvation, were galvanized by the image of the burqa. The question we asked in this article was a simple one: Why were images of starving women and children, ravaged by twenty years of war, not as moving for Americans as the image of a burqa-clad woman?

It was clear to us that what mobilized the sympathies of ordinary Americans was the shared judgment that the veil is the ultimate symbol of Muslim women's oppression, which, once removed, would give Afghan women the freedom to do what they wanted. Now this judgment, as we argued, is not simply wrong but a fantasy, produced by a certain kind of an imaginary that has an overdetermined reading of the veil. It does not take much intelligence to understand that Afghan women's freedom depends not on an article of clothing but on the kinds of resources they have access to and the general social conditions in which they live: simply put, an unveiled starving woman is no better than a veiled starving woman. Furthermore, as has been proven over and over again in history, groups that are most devastated by conditions of war, militarization, and starvation are women, children, and the elderly since they are the most vulnerable members of a society and their access to the material resources of a community is limited. It was the silence of the feminist and the media campaign in America against this far more injurious form of victimization of women (enabled by billions of dollars in U.S. financial and military aid to the region) that was absolutely astounding to us.

Given the campaign's success, it was hard for us not to reach the conclusion that the preoccupation of liberal feminists and the Western media with the veil had more to do with the long-standing colonial fantasy to disrobe the Muslim woman than with an interest in securing her "liberation." This is not a difficult deduction to make especially if one follows the events in Afghanistan since the ouster of the Taliban. When the American forces marched in, there were joyous celebratory articles and reports in the U.S. media about how the overthrow of the Taliban would result in Afghan women unveiling themselves, which in turn was represented as an act that would restore their freedoms and rights. Of course, subsequently, we learned that not all women wanted to unveil and that the custom of donning the burqa continued to be practiced in many areas of Afghanistan. More importantly, women's situation became much worse than it was under the Taliban because of increased lawlessness and ethnic-tribal warfare, and the escalation of poverty and militarization in Afghanistan (numerous human rights groups have documented this).[8] Yet none of these disturbing reports have galvanized the Feminist Majority, media celebrities, or popular media (all of whom rallied in support of the U.S. military campaign obscenely named "Operation Enduring Freedom") to take up the cause of Afghan women. One reason for this ongoing silence in the U.S. media—all the more deafening against the pandemonium that accompanied the ouster of the Taliban—might be that women's victimization under conditions of starvation and war does not titillate the Western imagination in the same way that the symbol of the veil does. Perhaps this is why concern for Afghan women has declined—if not altogether disappeared among the veil-hungry consumers of this tragic saga.

*The anxiety that the veil (*hijab*) provokes seems to cut across Western and non-Western societies as is evident from developments in Europe but also Turkey and Egypt. This anxiety seems all the more interesting given that women in many of these regions have adopted the veil out of choice rather than being forced to wear it. In your writings you suggest that the anxiety that attends the veil cannot be understood without adequate attention to norms of secular-liberal sociability. Can you elaborate?*

I often tell my undergraduate students, many of whom express their deep revulsion against the oppressive symbolism of the veil, that they should think about how another article of clothing, the miniskirt, was once viewed by some important sections of the feminist movement in the 1960s and 1970s. As you might recall, a number of Euro-American feminists condemned the miniskirt on the basis that it symbolized a male valuation of women's bodies and women's donning of it, they argued, represented an uncritical embrace of this valuation and therefore its internalization. It is quite rare to find a young woman (or man) these days who would uphold such an opinion, and indeed many prominent feminists in Europe and America don such garments quite regularly. This is in part because we have come to realize that women's attire is a far more complicated matter and cannot simply be treated as a barometer of their feminist consciousness. Nor can one's bodily conduct be mapped onto the logic of coercion and consent so easily. Is women's adoption of regimes of dieting, exercising, and various body enhancement techniques in Euro-American societies simply an expression of their false consciousness or is one's relationship to cultural values, its standards of sexual, physical, and personal worth, more complicated than the false consciousness thesis allows? The notion of false consciousness presumes an omniscient self-transparent consciousness that can step out of the fog of ideology to reveal the "true conditions" of one's oppression and a pathway out of it. Such clairvoyance is crucially dependent upon a calculus of more and less enlightened beings, wherein the destiny of the latter is clearly to be determined by the former. As must be clear, my objection to such a formulation is both analytical and political.

I do not think that the concept of "choice" is very helpful here either, even though it is the term often used in debates around the veil—both by its champions and detractors ("I choose to wear it" versus "The veil is a cultural imposition"). Liberalism often formulates choice as a measure of freedom (societies that have "more choices" are supposed to have "more freedom" and those with fewer choices have less). Yet such a calculus must be clearly rejected precisely because of the ways in which choice has been rendered an instrument of domination in liberal capitalist societies. Not only does this liberal formulation resurrect the fiction of the autonomous sovereign subject, but it also blinds us to the powers and processes that produce such a subject. Clearly, neither the veil nor any other form of attire can be easily mapped onto the calculus of less-and-more choice (or less-and-more freedom) precisely because one's relationship to a religious-cultural practice is far more implicated and complicated.

Contemporary discourse on the veil in the West seems to be relatively untouched by these basic insights. In reading the current literature on the veil, it seems to me that the debate has shifted very little since the eighteenth century when the veil was primarily viewed as a symbol of Muslim misogyny and Islam's oppression of women in colonial meditations. It was particularly startling to watch how this position was wholeheartedly adopted in the Stasi Commission's report that recommended the ban on the veil in French public schools. As you know, the position that the veil is a symbol of Muslim women's oppression was espoused not only by French feminists and public officials but also by a number of Muslim women who testified for the Stasi Commission. It continues to surprise me the ease and regularity with which a number of prominent secular postcolonial feminist writers denounce the veil as a symbol of Islam's oppression of women. Nawal al-Saadawi is a case in point. Upon seeing veiled French women protest the ban, al-Saadawi wrote in *al-Ahram Weekly*: "Strangest of all . . . was the spectacle of young women in the streets of Paris and Cairo and other cities demonstrating against the French government's announcement in defence of their right to wear the veil, and of God's divine commandments in defence of this symbol of their servitude. This is a signal example of how 'false consciousness' makes women enemies of their freedom, enemies of themselves, an example of how they are used in the political game being played by the Islamic fundamentalist movement in its bid for power."[9]

How is it that an anti-imperialist like al-Saadawi can so easily parrot the views of an Islamophobic French government and public? Part of the answer lies in the secular legacy so central to the historical formation of feminism (in Western and postcolonial societies). Given this history, it is common to see an uncritical adoption of the normative liberal position that religion *must* be privatized in modern societies, and when it takes a public form, its outward manifestations *must* be in accord with protocols of secular sociability. Contrary to its own claims, secular ideology is not indifferent to how people conduct themselves socially and in public. Rather, secular norms dictate when and how religious affiliation should be expressed in public life. It is only from this standpoint that one can begin to apprehend the enormous anxiety the veil has provoked in countries as disparate as France, Turkey, Britain, the Netherlands, and Egypt. I think in the context of Europe it is important to understand how the veil sits at the intersection of a longstanding discourse of civilizational superiority vis-à-vis Islam, on the one hand, and, on the other, the norms and protocols of secular liberal culture, now often glossed as "secularity."

You also point out in your book that in several countries, not only is the number of women participating in Islamist movements increasing but it is expanding to include women from the middle and upper-middle classes. How would you respond to the question you then ask in the same context: "Why would such a large number of women across the Muslim world actively support a movement that seems inimical to their 'own interests and agendas,' especially at a historical moment when these women appear to have more emancipatory possibilities available to them?" On a related note, would you agree that women's participation in these movements may be further evidence of their subjugation (within a patriarchal order) or perhaps the result of false consciousness?

As is obvious from my previous answer, the trope of "false consciousness" is of little value here. I think that women's mobilization in support of the Islamist movement should provoke us to rethink the feminist assumption that the values this movement embodies are necessarily injurious to women. It is clear that women who are joining Islamic movements around the world (in countries as diverse as Turkey, Egypt, Indonesia, and Malaysia) find something of value in them; minimally, these movements make possible a form of flourishing that secular life does not. Yet secular feminists (and I include myself in this category) have few resources to think about what these values represent beyond women's oppression; and how these values might challenge many of the core beliefs and assumptions of feminist politics and feminist analysis.

My book questions the assumption that all women (regardless of their historical and cultural location) are motivated by the desire for freedom from relations of domination—particularly male domination. Insomuch as feminism (like other liberation movements) seeks to secure the conditions that maximize women's freedom, there is a tendency among feminists to naturalize the desire for freedom from relations of domination as something that animates all women (by virtue of their subordinate status in a given society). When women (such as Islamist women) are judged not to enact this desire for freedom, they are often understood to be victims of false consciousness, entrapped by the patriarchal ideology they should be wise enough to resist. This line of assessment is seldom, if ever, reversed to ask: Why should we assume in the first place that women (or any subordinate group in a society) are necessarily driven by the desire for freedom? Are there other desires, aspirations, and projects that take precedence over the desire for freedom? If the answer is yes, then how do we understand these projects and the force they command in people's lives? Finally, how does our consideration of these projects help us reassess our own propensity to think that the desire for freedom is definitive of the modern age and its subjects? As must be clear to even the most casual observer, despite the ideology of freedom, most aspects of our lives do not abide by such an ideal; nor do they fit the rationale "coercion." Just as we would not render our lives within the narrow confines of such terms, why continue to explain the aspirations of millions of Muslims in such simplistic terms?

ELEVEN ∎ Gayatri Chakravorty Spivak

In the context of India, and perhaps in much of the postcolonial world, you write about the "class apartheid" produced by the system of education in place since formal decolonization (and prior to it). How does this class apartheid manifest itself and what are its effects?

Above a certain line, education takes place to explain what the material is; below a certain line, the purpose of education is simply to memorize without understanding and to take exams so that the answers replicate *exactly* what has been memorized. This is completely in place and ubiquitous below a certain class line.

The effect of such an education, of learning by rote, is that from a very early age, the ability to use one's intelligence, in other words, to perform intellectual labor, is killed. This means that a certain class is *only* capable of manual labor. The only part of the mind that is able to do any work is that bit which can perform small tasks in order to get security for oneself, fraudulently or otherwise, in a life without social security or upward social mobility. That is kept alive because everything else is counterintuitive. So the larger effects are that there can be no democracy, since people below this class line, learning by rote, are not capable of intuiting the public sphere simply because it would be counterintuitive to think that *anything* exists to serve them. So forgetting everything else—poverty, disease, other external circumstances—the only weapon with which the *extremely* deprived can fight is effectively taken away from them at a very early age. That is the main effect.

You have argued that education in the Humanities attempts to be an "uncoercive rearrangement of desires." What do you see as the emancipatory potential of an education so defined? What are the limits of humanities education as it is currently dispensed in the American academy? By what means could this practice be extended—should it be extended—to other areas of the world?

Education as such, if it educates, is an uncoercive rearrangement of desires. I am obliged to use the word "humanities" because there is a division of academic labor that has been in place now for many centuries and is the model that we follow. I do not know that the potential here is emancipation. Whatever can happen will happen if this kind of education is undertaken through the agency of the educated. This relates to the first question. Education can be used for any purpose: you can also rearrange desires for profound corruption, so I do not, I cannot, assume at all that this kind of education is necessarily emancipatory. In fact the educative efforts that have used this basically cultural instruction have generally been—if they have not been in the service of violence—in the interest of reproductive heteronormativity. And that is not emancipatory. So I am not so idealistic or indeed immature as to think that this kind of education is necessarily emancipatory. No. This is a *form* I am talking about. The filling of it with content is another matter and can take any shape. If I may cite my favorite philosopher, Immanuel Kant, to think that this *form* is emancipatory would be what he calls the "dialectical illusion." He says that the only thing we can really assume is that logic can give us the *form* of knowledge. In an implicit critique of Hegel, Kant says that if we then believe that this can immediately tell us what the substance of things will be, it is a deception of the dialectic. And I don't want to make that mistake. The Left has made that mistake, and therefore it has given resources to the forces of reaction to write off what we do. So, no, I will say again that I do not think this form of education is necessarily emancipatory. I would like to insist, again, that rote-style teaching, which is pervasive among the bottom-feeders (I do not say "grassroots"), is destructive, but that does not make the form of teaching I am supporting necessarily emancipatory. That is what has to be understood. The other kind of nonteaching is destructive of human intelligence and human capabilities, whereas this form of teaching has no guarantee that it is emancipatory but frees the intelligence to do whatever it would want to do, but there is another task beyond just teaching in this way.

As to the second question, the limits of humanities education are many. In fact I am simply obliged to use the word "humanities," as I explained. I am not particularly interested in discussing the limits of humanities education because we are in such a bad situation right now that my role as a humanities professor cannot simply be to launch an autocritique. I think my role is to say that with the corporatizing vision of the university, and perhaps of everything else, the model of education is increasingly becoming management, and since the humanities are neither income-generating nor necessarily funds-generating, they are trivialized. They are not seen as an important item on the capital agenda. Therefore it is difficult really to make many claims for what the humanities can do even if that model of education had emancipation built into it, which it does not, and even if I did make those claims, it would be unrealistic to consolidate such claims through a critique of the humanities. We have our backs to the wall. We are doing whatever we can, making many compromises, restructuring ourselves, so that we can get (and keep) a foot in the door of the corporatist university.

As for such an education being extended: Who will extend it? Americans? That is my first question. I think we should rethink what it means to "extend" our models to the rest of the world. So I need to have that question rethought. I see this humanities education as a collective project where people work in small, decentralized ways rather than something that is extended from this end of the world to the rest of it.

You have discussed in various contexts the work you do with training teachers in parts of rural West Bengal, an attempt driven by your commitment to education for "the largest sector of the future electorate in the global South—the children of the rural poor." What informs your teaching practice in that context, and how would you differentiate it from your pedagogical practice at Columbia University? How, if at all, do the two inform, or relate to, each other?

In the context of rural West Bengal, my main work is to think through what would be a plausible way of persuading the people I work with that this other way of teaching and learning is at all useful. So in a sense I am on the way to cultivating an intuition of the public sphere without using the defunct model of "awareness seminars" or "consciousness-raising." At this end, at Columbia, there is, if anything, too much of a concept of the public sphere as an agency of, as you asked in your previous question, "extending" benevolence all over the world. So here, then, at Columbia, I have to teach how to read, to teach how to read so that it becomes a habit of mind, and one hopes this is, in the long term, productive of that rearrangement of desire which, by itself, is neither emancipatory nor nonemancipatory. As you can see, I am only talking about the *form* of teaching because that is all that one *can* talk about. The substance of teaching informs or is informed by this form. I am not talking about "what" because that is the problem: people think that just giving a lot of "what" actually does work *as* teaching. The trouble to teach is no longer undertaken.

Let me assure you that the "what" is not, in its own context, unimportant. I have worked long and hard and joined with other workers all over the world to expand the canon, and further, to encourage language teaching so that the expanded canon is not always taught in translation in the hegemonic languages. What I am talking about here, however, is that we cannot stop with the "what" especially when we are working with the subaltern. We have to think about *how* the teaching is being done.

I am often there, in rural West Bengal, the day after these consciousness-raising people have left: the legal awareness seminar organizers or the literacy effort-*wallahs* or the urban radicals (actually there are no urban radicals who come to where I have my schools). I am often there the day after such initiatives have taken place. So when I try to find out what has been retained by the recipients of this consciousness-raising, what I learn is not only *nothing*, but worse: what has been retained is against the spirit of what the people thought they had been doing when they held the well-intentioned awareness seminars. The fact that the human mind is an instrument that has to be worked with rather than simply loaded down, this seems to be against the grain of those who want to "extend" things by extending awareness. This extending awareness is based on an unquestioned model of the mental theater as something nourished by good living, and it simply does not work.

So in these areas (I am not sure what to call them: one cannot say "villages" because of course these people are not allowed to live in the villages, and there is no name for where they do live. There is a name for the *sub*-urban or the *ex*-urban, but there is really no name for the sub-rural or the ex-rural, but that is what these areas are), I am trying to learn from the class inferior, the ones made unintelligent by the wrong system of education. I am trying to learn from them how to make a philosophy. And here in New York, I am trying to make people unlearn their confidence without taking away their power, if you like, without—as the horrible word goes—"disempowering" them. And the two sides are very deeply connected.

A phrase that figures prominently in your work is "enabling violation." You use this in particular with respect to colonialism, but the reach seems to be even wider. Could you explain what you mean by this?

I am not against the British. I was against bad colonial policy. I am talking about the enablement: we got railways, a regular currency, schools, hospitals, a system of education, a civil service, an army, and of course a hegemonic language. There are plenty of Indians who would say that as a result of having been imperial subjects, particularly of Great Britain, we have an advantage. I forget the name of the guy who devised call centers, but that is relevant in this context too. I have heard this also in China: I speak English well because I was *owned* by the British (in these exact words). So that is an enablement. It is an enablement that comes through violation.

The relationship of women, for example, or Dalits, to benevolent colonialism is very different: very oblique and very ambivalent. On the other hand, because there is the violation, one can also think about the ways in which one could undo the violation, or rather how to sustain the enablement with a minimum of violation. This should be the real meaning of the word "sustainable"; rather than sustaining economic growth as far as possible we should think instead of how to sustain the enablement of colonialism (and there are others) with a minimum of violation. My very dear friend, Anthony Appiah's recent book, written from a, frankly, aristocratic point of view, for example, seems to suggest that there was no violation—and there Anthony and I will have a long conversation. That is the real question, for all benevolence is "colonial." I cannot discuss this due to time constraints, but it is a very important fact to realize, even for parents.

Relatedly, in your article "Righting Wrongs," you say that the alleged European provenance of human rights is "in the same category as the 'enabling violation' of the production of the colonial subject. One cannot write off the righting of wrongs. The enablement must be used even as the violation is renegotiated." What is the relationship here between human rights as it operates today and the history of colonialism?

In a recent issue of the *New York Times Magazine*, David Rieff, with whom I almost never agree, surprisingly had a piece that I found quite acceptable[1]. I quite like Rieff personally, but I normally find it hard to accept his positions. In this article, he makes it quite clear that, in the current conjuncture, if a small group of nations wants to right the world's wrongs, other places are not to be blamed if they think that this has some connection with nineteenth-century colonialism. In the middle was the Cold War. That is the point of view that most people of goodwill hold today. What I was trying to say in my previous answer was that you cannot escape the colonial impulse, that is why I do not try but rather see how that kind of thing is kept at a minimum. Also you give to the people to whom you are giving things the wherewithal to question this in a persistent kind of way, otherwise it does not work.

Also the point that you bring up later in one of your questions about the changeover from the white man's burden to the burden of the fittest quite clearly shows how the colonial impulse has displaced itself in the current conjuncture. I would also say that, at the first postcolonial moment, when the Bretton Woods organizations were established, they hardly had a kind of alibi or even declared purpose of establishing something like a humane international socialism, not like what they perceived to be the totalitarian problems of actually existing communism. This idea of bringing about social welfare, of establishing a social welfare kind of world, was of course not really there. So that very soon, as many people have argued, after the establishment of the World Bank and the International Monetary Fund, their actual goals changed almost 180 degrees. In fact what happened is what we are seeing again today with this kind of loose, utopian, socialist talk becoming an alibi for the advancement of capitalism. Today's globalization is almost exactly the same story again with a conjectural displacement because capitalism has changed and the mode of production has changed. I am giving you a fairly straightforward Marxist account of this. Especially with the silicon chip, the disappearance of the Cold War, and the two coming together, the mode of production has changed. We have the same kind of thing, however. When free-market globalizers suggest that this will establish a level playing field, that is the promise of a socialism, small "s," equally shared welfare for the whole world; international socialism by peaceful means, as we used to say when we were young. But of course that is an alibi for capitalist globalization with constant subalternization at the bottom, giving a uniform mindset to folks who can seem visibly diverse. This is where Anthony Appiah makes a mistake in thinking that diversity lies simply in national origin. We are talking about, as I say later in my conversation with you, the monocultures of the mind. So this is the same chain of displacement into which colonialism can be integrated. First there was real colonialism, that is to say, the establishment of colons in Greece not so much, but certainly in Rome, and then slowly, slowly, mercantile capitalist colonialism, buying cheap and selling dear, in Latin America. Also at the other end there are the great multiethnic empires, the Ottoman, the Russian, which cannot be called colonialism. That sort of imperialism has to be distinguished. Some people are suggesting that post-Soviet studies should become Eurasian postcolonial studies. They are trying to bring together that imperial formation with our ideas of colonialism, which begin with monopoly capitalist, single-nation, market-expanding colonies. If you look at it that way, then there is a huge chain of displacements within which you can clue in both the transnational agencies at the middle of the twentieth century and what's happening in the twenty-first after the fall of the Berlin Wall.

You argue that "the human rights aspect of postcoloniality has turned out to be the breaking of the new nations, in the name of their breaking-in into the international community of nations." What do you think might be gained by the "breaking" of nations? And what does this say about how we should read the term "international community"?

I am not sure what can be gained by the breaking of nations, but I do know what can be gained by the breaking of *states*. In order to bring in globalization, you have to establish the same system of exchange internationally. You therefore have to remove the barriers and establish a kind of continuity between international capital and fragile national capitals. This concerns abstract economic structures of the state. Our model of free-market globalization is capitalist. What is the accountability and the role of the state in this model? Believe me, I am not so idealistic as to think that the state before restructuring was perfect or was interested in redistribution; I am aware, though, that people who wanted to engage with the state—which supposedly came into being through elections—had ways of constitutional redress that have now become completely useless. The model of the state, like the model on a much smaller scale of the university, becomes management rather than redistribution; both models are driven by the market. The consequences of this are clear enough: to take only one example, the market is never going to produce demands for clean water for the poor. So then it is given over to international civil society to take up these tasks about which we have already had discussions. So this is apparently what the breaking of states brings about.

As for the breaking of the nation, what is to be gained is addressing some of the problems with nationalism (moving toward fascism and so on), but I think that a critical regionalism may be a way of not breaking the nation, but *bending* nationalism. The idea that China and India may support Iran and may not allow Iran to be reprimanded by the United Nations, and that India and Pakistan are coming together in spite of the conversations that Manmohan Singh has had recently with Bush about becoming a nuclear partner, these are signs of a critical regionalism, which one finds useful in a world where there is no longer any bargaining power because there is only one superpower. In the event, it was only Venezuela who supported Iran at the United Nations. Rising Asia could not come through. Think of Bolivian President Morales's visit to Cuba, India, China! Maybe the new Latin America, leaning left, will lead us in the direction of critical regionalism.

In elaborating your reservations with global human rights practice, you use the phrase "subordinate cultures of responsibility," explaining that the term "subordinate" here signals that these cultures are now the recipients of human rights bounty, a bounty that is "the burden of the fittest" and which has the "ambivalent structure of enabling violation that anyone of goodwill associates with the white man's burden." How would you define a culture of responsibility? And why is that characterization important in determining, if at all, that these cultures are now recipients (as opposed to dispensers) of human rights assistance?

When I was talking about cultures of responsibility I was talking about responsibility-based rather than rights-based cultures. We must rethink the word "responsibility" here. I believe in that article I did discuss this.[2] The idea of responsibility here is not "what I ought to do"; there is plenty of that in the richer countries, of course: it is this entire culture of "generosity" (think of the tsunami, Hurricane Katrina, Iraq, Afghanistan, Palestine). This is a sort of litany of "our responsibility" and so on. But that is not what I was talking about. Just as I said earlier that this kind of education—rearranging desire—is not necessarily emancipatory, this responsibility base is not necessarily emancipatory either. I am talking about a *form* here. You can even say that reproductive heteronormativity is at work in this one as well. There is a kind of cultural formation where the individual is defined in terms of a response to something that is radically other. I am born within a Hindu cultural formation, and we call this *adrishta*, the unseen, something that is written; it is only, to quote Barthes, writable rather than readable. Every civilization that suggests that "In His will is our peace"—that is Dante of course—puts human matters as a mere moment in a much larger narrative that, because it is beyond the human players' grasp, is other, in another mode from the world, and written or righting itself. That is putting agency—to use theoretical language—in radical alterity, and the task of the individual is to respond. Quite often, this means that the gendered subaltern is whacked into shouldering the burden, much greater burdens than she should. The female queer is subsumed in this system. The male queer is either tolerated for philosophical entertainment or despised for breaking God's law. You cannot recognize radical alterity because it is radical. You suppose it in order to be responsible to it rather than out of an enhanced self-interest. Mind you, this is all people's imagination. It would be completely wrong to think that this "actually happens," but this distinguishes groups from each other much more than individualism and collectivism: something else wills me (and I am translating a famous eighteenth-century Bengali song). So from that point of view, I am talking about a structure, rather than the substantive notion of "I am responsible, I must do this," etc.

I just gave you a bit of what I think comes from Hindu cultural formations, but I should say at the same time that as we see it in my neck of the woods, there is no such thing as a pure Hindu cultural formation in Eastern India, at least not in the way we were brought up within the *bhadralok* class. I have tried to argue in my little book *Imperatives to Reimagine the Planet*[3] that the idea of what we in Bengali call *al-haq* also has a similar sense that responsibility is kind of a birthright, rather than responsibility in the sense of what one ought to do. This is a very different kind of basis for collectivities. I don't want to use the word community because it is so often put in binary opposition with developed societies. It does not look like responsibility as the narrative goes in the United States at all. It may look like fatalism sometimes, just as the great technological advances and the great advances of science are transformed by most of us into versions of magic.

Do you mean that technology presents itself to us in such a way that we can only respond "fatalistically," the way we respond to our particular cultural formation? Technology as radical alterity?

I am using our idea of "something else wills me" and comparing it to the way in which technology is seen by us as magic. I am not identifying the two. But your idea that technology has given us the view of a much larger world, including the nano-world inside ourselves, which, in the case of genes, literally *writes* us, is also of course a good idea, and one that Derrida thought about already in *Of Grammatology*.

So it seems to me that I was just *describing* something when I said that these people are the recipients of human rights bounty, since the kind of social formations and class levels I am talking about are really subordinate.

You say in a footnote in the same essay that you "have been thinking of the access to the European Enlightenment through colonization as an enablement for twenty-odd years" and that you recommend "using the Enlightenment from below" or "ab-using" the Enlightenment. What does this mean? What elements of the Enlightenment are you invoking in this recommendation? Why do you think that any wholesale rejection of the Enlightenment—if such is possible—is dangerous and in bad faith?

Enlightenment here is a codeword because if I were really to think of the word in its concept-metaphorical meaning and not think of the Treaty of Westphalia, or again, the establishment of a public sphere, or the welfare state, or the public use of reason, whatever that might mean, it has not taken place, because that kind of thing does not take place. How can we possibly invoke a *general* enlightenment, given that every generation has to be educated? So let's just use this as a codeword for the kind of regularizing of the public sphere and of the defeudalizing of the polity that took place with what old-fashioned Marxists would call the bourgeois revolution in Europe, and the attendant colonial formations elsewhere. This is not a correct narrative, but since we are speaking with this *huge* word that is colloquially understood by lots of people who think the narrative that I just outlined is correct, I want to make clear that I don't think this is what really happens. I am not going to be reprimanded by Aijaz Ahmad here. No, this may not be what happens, but a very large section of the world thinks that this is what happens. So that is where I am starting from because that is how I am using the word "enlightenment."

In the article I listed some structures that I said the British had "given" us. Now I am aware that there are historians who would say that India—whatever India was—had come to a place in its own capital formation that would have allowed it to devise these things on its own

182 | FEMINISM AND HUMAN RIGHTS

sooner or later, as in China. That is completely possible. But I am not talking about counterfactual narratives ("How many children had Lady Macbeth?"); I am rather describing something that is taken for granted by a very large section of the world, so in fact, when oppressed minorities ask for civil rights and political rights they are making a demand within what, in this rough-and-ready way, we can call Enlightenment discourse. Therefore it would be bad faith to say that we are rejecting Enlightenment discourse completely. So to use the Enlightenment from below, for me, means to look at how the Enlightenment was fashioned and think of the forms of the fashioning—this is why I quoted Kant a little while ago—as something that we can use to think through substantive problems, rather than think that the Enlightenment itself is emancipatory. This is why I corrected the idea that my notion of humanities education is in itself emancipatory, because to think that anything is *in itself* emancipatory is to make a mistake. So what we do then is loosen the Enlightenment from its supposedly natural, organic, substantive content and begin to look at the forms of questioning that brought about what we call the Enlightenment and see if we can use them in any other way.

Why do you insist to those located, spatially and otherwise, in the metropole the importance of "unlearning one's privilege"? What sort of privilege do you mean, and how does one go about unlearning it? What might such unlearning enable?

I would ask you to look at the first time I used that phrase. It was a long time ago. In many interviews I have tried to clarify what I meant by this. I am not certain if I have done this in actual print because I, unlike many of my good friends, generally do not occupy myself with constantly correcting people's perceptions of my old work. So I may not have done this in actual writing but certainly have in interviews.

Once I started really getting into doing something about this, about unlearning my privilege, I took it away. It is "learning to learn from below," if you want a formula. I have also become extremely suspicious of the fact that people like my little formulas: to take another example, "strategic use of essentialism," I have put that to rest many times, but people have not given it up. As far as "unlearning one's privilege" is concerned, I think one should use one's privilege in order to get some things done. As I said before, all benevolence is colonial; you cannot fully unlearn your privilege. You may say perhaps that one could unlearn it by seeing it as instrumental more than anything else.

I am saying that even with "learning to learn from below" it is a problem to think of it in terms of a formula since I am talking about the *form*. I try to take recruits into these schools because obviously at some level I want people to do this. I think it is a good idea. And when in the city or even in the country I talk about learning from below, people are very much in agreement with me. Then they come and I see, within the week, or within three or four days, that there is so much unacknowledged feudality in the person, because they *really* want to help, they *know* what they are going to do. Even in the assumption that the other person, the person below, as it were, *knows* what they should want, this is in itself an idealistic piece of nonsense. You don't oppress people for centuries and then expect that their intelligence somehow remains unscathed. Remember the class apartheid argument that I made: it is wrong to think that they would have a clear intuition of the public sphere and know exactly what they need and want. This is a very Christian way of thinking about the below.

So as a formula this unlearning in order to learn from below is very easy to agree with and *extremely* difficult to practice, as I am learning. I am making mistakes, I have been doing this for fifteen or sixteen years, and I cannot say that I have really got the hang of it yet. I do think that this kind of effort has to be undertaken in order for any kind of good work to be sustainable in the long run. And although I gave you the formula, I don't suggest picking it up in an "Oh yes, this is exactly what I am doing" kind of move. The unlearning one's privilege was bad enough!

Now that Derrida is safely dead, for example, I get so many articles that I am asked to read for journals that pretty much say this: "My life situation is an exact example of Derrida's theory." This is pure narcissism. So I offer this formula, "learning to learn from below," with the fear that people will immediately think that their life practice is an exact example of learning to learn from below. So that is what has happened to unlearning one's privilege.

You often emphasize the importance of being aware of one's complicity. To whom does this imperative apply, and what kinds of effects might such awareness produce?

The awareness can lead to just unending breast-beating. That is also extremely narcissistic. In the old days, when there was no awareness of one's complicity, we spent our time writing about ourselves. In the new days, when we are totally aware of our complicity, we spend our time writing about ourselves!

So although I believe that one should be aware of one's complicity, again, I am afraid I am very jaded and cynical these days after these long years of being in the academy, I don't know that with the awareness comes a necessary good for the world at large. On the other hand, there is also a way in which we can transform complicity. I offer this here with the proviso that if you feel that you are doing it, you should probably think the game is lost. If you get support from the so-called grassroots that you are doing it, you should put it down as a class narrative at work. But here is what it is. If you can think of com-plicity as being folded together, you begin to work at the other's texture much more carefully. It is a textile metaphor, being folded together. As a literary person, this is a gain for me as a worker.

In Death of a Discipline *you insist that "We must take the languages of the Southern Hemisphere as active cultural media rather than as objects of cultural study by the sanctioned ignorance of the metropolitan migrant." The phrase "sanctioned ignorance" frequently appears in your writing. Could you explain this further? And what do you imagine would be enabled, what might be changed, by an active engagement with the languages of the Third World?*

Well you know I don't use the expression "Third World" anymore. I don't know what is meant by that.

One of the reasons why I talk about languages as cultural media is that sanctioned ignorance is all around us. It is somehow alright not to know certain things. I am unable to think of a big example at the moment, but to take a minor and rather ubiquitous one: we had recently a very fine speaker, Professor Wang Ning, here at Columbia University. He writes "Wang" in huge, block capitals and "Ning" in lowercase cursive. Why is it so difficult for people simply to be aware that in China, last names come first? Why is this mistake being made by people all the time here? This seems to me to be a ridiculous kind of behavior. But this is not a very good example.

Another example: the language center here cites a language called "Filipino." I am sorry to fault the language center because it is not by any means the most privileged bastion at Columbia, god knows, but what kind of sanctioned ignorance lies behind that claim? From Northeastern University Press I have even received a communication about a language called "Indian." It just seems to me that this is not what is called "cultural literacy," as E. D. Hirsch would have it, which involves learning tiny little bits about all kinds of things so that you would solve the problem of sanctioned ignorance in a kind of cocktail-party way. Hirsch is unfortunately still a political reactionary. I could provide you in any given day many, many, many examples of sanctioned ignorance, a problem that is going to become even worse.

There is another fine example, but I am going to talk about it and publish it elsewhere. Let me simply say this: I have published an article in *Radical Philosophy* where I have made this language argument, generally a kind of rhetorical answer to the question, "Is language local?" This is given as it was presented in Korea, where I went right after Derrida's burial.[4]

Let us try a few lines that are going to sound utopian. What unifies people beyond physical generalities is storytelling and making unneeded things. If you want to access this great unifier, paradoxically, you have to confront the immense diversity of languages; the loss of a language is the loss of an entire possibility of meaning. To quote A. L. Becker, each language carries a lingual memory within itself that is highly specific and can be accessed only through immersion-style labor—the way in which people strive to become experts in English. If we want a just world, we have to admit that this project cannot be centralized. Not everyone can learn every language. There is no hierarchy of lingual memories. Mechanical language-learning cannot trap this. The event of language escapes its conventions.

You have often invoked the notion of the "epistemic violence" of imperialism, at times in conjunction with "the international division of labor." What form did the epistemic violence of imperialism take, and how, if at all, has this violence continued by other, or the same, means in the wake of formal decolonization? What is its relation to the international division of labor yesterday and today?

Well, the "international division of labor" now is almost a meaningless term because given that with globalization, especially if one thinks about finance capital—markets and foreign exchange, as it were—then labor is still a category, but it is so much an abstract category, a spectral category, that it retains little of its old meaning. Labor also belongs to the area of data that is itself a spectral category (let us bracket for the moment world trade, where labor has some kind of old substantive meaning).

I take the idea of the spectral from Derrida's very careful distinctions. Spectral is not totally abstract because a ghost has some kind of peculiar body—it is a concept-metaphor—which is not a real body because it is a ghost. Its appearance is periodic but unanticipatable. Inside everything that is data there is the possibility of its transformation. Just like money could be realized out of capital in the old days, now in all data there is the possibility of its *reali*zation into some actual situation. That is the spectrality because there is some kind of possibility of embodiment (in a trade situation, for instance). On the other hand, that periodicity is not a required periodicity (it has to occur every three days or three hours or whatever; it doesn't). That concept-metaphor is exactly what spectrality is: embodiment but something other than that; the data is there for the sake of the data, it is not there for the sake of whatever the embodiment might be, and offhand you don't know what it is. So what I was trying to say is that it is a displacement of what in the nineteenth century for Marx was a huge step ahead to understand that there was something called abstract average labor power. This data stream, the flow of data, is a displacement—there have been other displacements, but after two centuries this is where we are, that is why it is spectral; it is unseriously embodied, but embodied. The body-ness is not its serious thing, the data's. It is unseriously embodied, periodically appearing but unanticipatably so. Therefore the idea of the international division of labor comes into consideration, strangely enough, quite cogently, in the lower reaches, and also in an area in the global South where it is not going to remain like this for very long: this middle part, where software tasks, like outsourcing and call centers, are undertaken by workers who are in fact upwardly mobile as a result of being employed in these outsourced industries. I used to write about the electronification of the stock exchanges in the 1980s because I didn't know anything and therefore didn't know that what I was talking about was globalization, but in the humanities corner, that was a pretty early invocation of this whole phenomenon. So the international division of labor has to be rethought. It is also to be rethought because of the fantastic phenomenon of outsourcing, which of course came about first with post-Fordism when you could in fact diversify the factory floor through fax machines and computers, but that was even welcomed by some British socialists, and now we have to deal with the international division of labor in this other way. We also have to think of the constant subalternization of folks, which does not really have to do much with a capitalogic division of labor. It is not like the international date line, let me put it that way.

As for epistemic violence: in a sense, education is epistemic violence. It is what happens when a way of thinking is changed so that you construct your object of knowledge in a different way; in other words, *how* you know is changed. When Marx asks the worker to think of himself or herself as an agent of production rather than as a victim of capitalism, that is epistemic violence. You have to change completely the way you think, the way you construct your object, your knowledge. I should not have used this phrase because the word "violence" has a kind of paleonymy that suggests bad stuff. How about people who like violence, not in a bad way; I am thinking of S&M for example. Violence is not just killing people. Violence is all kinds of other things. It is not a plus and minus.

I am not sure what it has to do with the international division of labor. I am not sure how I would establish a continuous relationship between the international division of labor and epistemic violence. In fact, most of the time, epistemic violence has allowed people to become upwardly class mobile. Epistemic violence produces the colonial subject who becomes a worker for the master, or a nationalist, or a captain of industry, or a revolutionary, but not directly a victim of the international division of labor.

How is epistemic violence continuing? It is continuing through what Vandana Shiva has called "the monocultures of the mind." Now the moment I invoke Vandana Shiva, people like Meera Nanda will say, "Oh Gayatri Spivak is mystical!" No. I am taking this phrase, "the monocultures of the mind," as a useful way of thinking about what happens when you provide a uniform kind of education in a few uniform languages; this is a kind of epistemic violence. But I cannot say that that is necessarily bad. Or necessarily good. We want it. Let me give you an example of how this works. This is an old story, which is a true story from my family (not my direct family, but through my marriage). A bunch of them live in Scotland and a bunch of them live in Bombay. The Bombay family visited the Scotland family, and the Bombay child was speaking in English and the Scotland child said, "Eeey, baratey angreji bolena, humra Bengali!" ("One doesn't speak in English at home. We are Bengalis!"). So the Bombay girl responded (in Bengali), "If you don't speak in English at home, you will not get entry into an English-medium school."

So this is also a question of bad faith. Here we are, metropolitan diasporics, speaking to each other in English, waxing eloquent on epistemic violence. We have to think of what we are up to. Trying to learn even Chinese for me is *so* difficult and god knows, Chinese is *not* a subaltern language. Who do you think is interested among us in the actual labor of language learning? As I was saying at a session mourning Edward Said at the Lower Manhattan Cultural Council, the one thing that has remained the same with the assimilation or integration model of immigration, even as that is constantly questioned by the new diasporics, who claim we are a salad bowl, and we are this and that, but what has not changed, the one thing that has remained *exactly* the same is that the kids simply do not *like* the language of the parents. So in fact nothing has changed. These diasporics can talk as much as they like about how different they are, but in fact that epistemic violence has continued.

So I do not know how to say we will undo it. Of course it is continuing.

You have translated a number of works by Mahasweta Devi into English. What prompted your interest in her work? Can you say a little about how her work has been received in the English-speaking world? Is there a way in which your translation itself may have enabled a particular reading?

I met Mahasweta Devi in 1979. This is a story I have told often, but I will tell it again. In 1981 I was asked to contribute to the *Yale French Studies* volume on French feminism, and to an issue of *Critical Inquiry*, where I was asked to write on deconstruction. Instead of rejoicing at the fact that I was not European in origin and was politically quite vocal and yet had managed to brave the bastions of this fortress and been asked by these two really rather lily-white—in every sense: there are people whose skin color is not white, but they are as lily-white as can be—journals to opine on these matters, instead of rejoicing, I was young then, thirty-nine years old, and foolish enough to think this, "Oh dear, oh dear, what has happened to my identity," kind of crap! Who would believe that today? For *Yale French Studies* I wrote "French Feminism in an International Frame," and to *Critical Inquiry* I proposed that I do a translation of Mahasweta Devi, because of course I was already so influenced or so ridden by deconstruction that that is how I read. So I felt that I could write on deconstruction in this text quite easily. The funniest thing was that of course I had been asked to write on deconstruction, but when I said that I would do a translation of fiction in Bengali, I was put on spec. They would see: I would submit it to them and they would decide. As it happened, of course, they did take it. So that is what prompted my interest in translating her.

As for my interest in her work, I just liked what she wrote. I read Bengali fiction quite regularly, and I liked her stuff.

Her work has been received very well in the English-speaking world, and one of the reasons is that there are not too many serious translations of Third World texts. As I said, in general I don't use the phrase "Third World," but one has to use it in this context.

Why? What distinguishes its usage here?

Because that is how they put her in course lists, that's why. It is a completely artificial category that has nothing to do with the original economic project. People talk about Mahasweta who don't do any infrastructural work in anything. What I mean by this is: Flaubert's *L'Éducation sentimentale* is about the Revolution of 1848, and it is impossible to teach Flaubert without having any sense of what European revolutions are like. Or to be critical of Flaubert's view of the revolution itself. But it is also possible to teach Flaubert very appreciatively, really liking Flaubert, but nonetheless being able to situate his own situating of the revolution. So that is the difference between some distracted young junior faculty looking for tenure, finding Mahasweta and giving a paper on her at the MLA, knowing absolutely nothing about the complexities of the postcolonial situation in India regarding aboriginals. This is very diversified. I just received a newspaper cutting from Mahasweta herself that complains about the destruction of tribal cave paintings in the state of Jharkand, which is a new tribal state. Mahasweta sent this to me through my Indian publisher because apparently there is a picture of a dinosaur; how on earth did someone put up a picture of a dinosaur ten thousand years ago? So it is rather like the story "Pterodactyl."[5] To know all of this is to be a step ahead. So my relationship with Mahasweta's text is such that the written text itself is a moment in a *much* broader flow of textuality. At the other end stands the poor American junior faculty person, who, wanting to get tenure in a liberal department, is madly teaching Mahasweta, knowing nothing.

At a recent conference on translation at Columbia, one of my points was precisely that translation has to become an activity, a practice rather than a convenience. I don't think that the people who are reading my translations of Mahasweta are necessarily moving toward learning Bengali. In fact people in India who are perhaps my worst enemies have said that I should not write my introductions—someone said this in *India Today*—and have accused me of writing introductions that are "sermonizing." They also said that I should not italicize the words that are already in English, which I do in the interest of future research.[6] I am not sure what to think about this. They don't have anything to compare her to except other works that they read in translation from outside of Europe: Tayeb Salih, and other writers from the Third World; this is ridiculous! I have contributed to this also, and I don't know that this has been a good thing.

Mind you, I am very glad that people are reading her. And yes, my translations have enabled a particular reading. That is exactly what I am saying. Before I translated her, no one had translated her into English. She has received many prizes, and I say to her, "I recognized your excellence before you received any of these damned prizes! And they're not reading your Bengali, they're reading my bloody English!"

In the foreword to Mahasweta Devi's story "Draupadi," you write: "My approach to the story has been influenced by 'deconstructive practice.' I clearly share an unease that would declare avant-garde theories of interpretation too elitist to cope with revolutionary feminist material." How, then, do you respond to the question you ask about what the practice of deconstruction has enabled in this context?

That is a bad-faith remark that was not made in bad faith because I just recounted to you the peculiar state I was in at the time, which I am thoroughly irritated by. It has led to certain kinds of work, but nonetheless, what kind of nonsense was that?

I have no problems with avant-garde theories of interpretation coping with revolutionary feminist material. I have a problem with those who, because of social conditions, latch on to avant-garde theories, and their laziness. This has nothing to do with the theories themselves. In fact, a colleague in women's studies from the University of Chandigarh, the University of Punjab, has not found it difficult to say to me that she uses my translation but that her students really don't like the introduction, and then later, a second time, she told me she is no longer using it. People think that I am not human; they can just say anything to me. The idea that there may be a problem, that perhaps the fact that she herself does not like my introduction has something to do with the way her students respond, that perhaps she ought to show her students what it is that I am trying to say, this is not something she addresses. But what really strikes me is that she has found it necessary to tell me this twice. Then—and this is *ressentiment* of the worst sort—she wrote me a letter asking permission to include a translation of mine, making it quite clear that she was including theoretical essays by my friends Chandra Tal-pade Mohanty and others but not anything by me. So from that point of view, I truly withdraw that earlier remark of mine. I do insist that we see where these theories are accepted, how far people go with them, and so on. This is a sociological fact that one has to see. I have also read in Nivedita Menon's book, *Recovering Subversion: Feminist Politics Beyond the Law*, that she shivered with delight when she met the legendary Étienne Balibar, especially when he said—it so struck me that a white male should produce this semi-orgasmic delight that could actually be spoken of unashamedly right in the beginning pages of a book—"I told Michel Foucault. . . ."[7] Put this over against this kind of *ressentiment*, a refusal to acknowledge that it is possible that there is something useful in stuff that one does not understand.

Mind you, I do not defend the turgidity of the prose in that early essay because I was myself quite self-conscious about not being counted a member of the theoretical club. So over the years I have simplified my language, but that does not mean I have become more understandable, or that the *ressentiment* of others of a certain kind has diminished. I have friends, and I have students, and certainly I am happy to say that I have a real kind of intellectual community all over the world, so that is not a problem, but there is a certain kind of intellectual or activist who feels deep *ressentiment* toward the kind of stuff that I do, especially straddling a gap between the two ends of a spectrum—high theory and extreme subalternity. I can't do anything about it. When my mother was alive, she would put everything in context. But she died two years ago, and it is difficult to remember the things that the old lady used to say. She actually supported me against the arch-conservatives, as well as against these kinds of resentful folks. It was very useful, I now realize, apart from everything else, to have that kind of daily conversation, which oiled the wheels of the machine.

What do you think has been the significance of the kind of history writing inaugurated by the Subaltern Studies collective? What has been your own contribution to this school? What do you think accounts for the singular appeal (and interest) of the U.S. academy for so many members of the collective?

I cannot speak to the last question because they are different people and everybody has their careers, so who knows? And we are not similar people so it is hard to say. Something can be advanced, which has nothing to do with them; it is not their fault. The United States, being what it is, and I generalize, is eager to be active *conveniently*. Therefore the subalternists fill a gap: *authentic* Third World material. It is funny also how many of them have become involved in this kind of implicit or explicit assertion of "This is *not* Europe" or "This is *not* the United States." Shail is not—Shail Mayaram goes her own way. I find that very interesting. Perhaps Shahid Amin does too, I don't know. I shouldn't really name names, these are all my friends.

On the other hand, if we go to the beginning of the question, I think it has been very significant to look at what does not enter the purview of disciplinary historiography and to devise a method for looking at it. This has been a very useful contribution of Subaltern Studies. It is right up there with the changes wrought by the Annales School, and I think this is good.

I will say that I had thought my contribution to the collective had been very small. In the beginning this small contribution was exaggerated by many people who came out in print, beginning with David Hardiman, but then K. N. Panikkar and others, who said that my insertion into the group diluted their interest in history-writing because it turned everything into fiction. It was something like this. I am sorry I cannot summarize exactly what they said, but my work was seen as a deleterious influence. Partha Chatterjee, on the other hand, at the conference commemorating the twentieth anniversary of the delivery of the lecture that became "Can the Subaltern Speak?" was gracious enough to say that my intervention introduced questions of representation into the group. I think that is exaggerated; I myself don't think there was much. I did perhaps make it possible for them to think that there should be a feminist element. And now there are people like Susie Tharu who are part of the collective. This is all to the good.

In your article "A Literary Representation of the Subaltern: A Woman's Text from the Third World," you say: "If 'the need to make the subaltern classes the subject of their own history [has, among other] themes . . . provided a fresh critical thrust to much recent writing on modern Indian history and society,' then a text about the (im)possibility of 'making' the subaltern gender the subject of its own story seems to me to have a certain pertinence." How would you account for the singular difficulty involved in making subaltern woman the subject of her own story, indeed of inserting subaltern woman into history?

I think it is easy to account for this because agency is institutionally validated action. For people who do not have the wherewithal, the social power to claim agency within any real institutions, the only recourse is to fall back on the oldest and broadest institution in the entire world: reproductive heteronormativity. Therefore everything conspires against having women and queer folks be the subject of a story.

Could you explain what you mean by reproductive heteronormativity?

Reproductive heteronormativity simply means that it is normal to be heterosexual and to reproduce, and it is in terms of that norm that society is made: legal structures, religious structures, affective structures, residential structures, everything. It may be displaced into that corner, this corner, and so on, but it is a very tough perennial. It is not something that will go away. It will never go away because that is what writes (and rights) being human, as it were. So it will never go away. Just like death will not go away. The thing to do is not to make of the norm anything more than a convenience. To deny it is stupid. There is a place where Irigaray in her questions to Levinas actually acknowledges that women making love is not the same thing as a man and woman making love. Generations of my students have had great difficulty with this because what they want of course is the reversal, to level the distinction and say it is the same. But Irigaray is smart enough to know that you acknowledge the norm, acknowledge that it is an instrument, it is a means, it has its limits, and it should not think of itself as an end. We should fight against this being the institution of last resort, we should fight against this being confused with the source of ethics and morality, and so on. But that has nothing to do with the acceptance that this is an enduring institution. It is the same kind of absurdity as to deny the fact that we reproduce and we excrete from the same area; to quote Yeats, "Love has pitched its mansion in the place of excrement." We reproduce and we excrete with the same thing, and we have to accommodate that in some way into eros. It is quite interesting to see who accommodates it, who revels in it, and what happens. That is a whole language. Nonetheless what you have to do is not make the mistake of denying it. If you make that mistake you forget that a civil structure, so-called governmentality, is also an instrument; there is no such thing as a bottom-line critique. To be able to make reproductive heteronormativity only an instrument is much harder than simply saying, "Down with it," and then to keep on using it. *That* is the thing: I was born of parents. Can't get around that one! And there's no *need* to get around that one. Melanie Klein is so interesting precisely because she makes the biological itself a kind of semiotic ingredient. I am not going to explain this. I have published on it a great deal.

It should be clear, to get to the end of your question, why it is so hard for subaltern woman to be included in historical narratives. To be subaltern means to be cut off from all lines of social mobility, so how are you going to insert yourself into history? I must say that to be a subalternist historian, which is a wonderful thing, is not to insert the subaltern into history. It is to insert the subaltern into historiography. They are two different kinds of things. One is a task of thinking, another is a task of doing. One has to keep that in mind. Both are fine things, but they are not the *same* thing.

You have said in an interview elsewhere that one has to see "how much development is an alibi for exploitation, how much it's a scam: the responsibility for the entire world's ills is between the legs of the poorest women of the South." Why do you think that development as it is currently constituted is exploitative? And why are women particularly vulnerable given that (or perhaps because?) they are among the primary recipients of such assistance? You have suggested in another context that tribal peoples in India (and elsewhere) too bear the burden of development. Could you elaborate on this?

Where was this taken from?

The quote is taken from the interview you gave to Peter Osborne, which appeared in A Critical Sense. *You were commenting on the Cairo UN Conference on Population and Development. You said, "I have just seen what happens when benevolent First World women are clueless about this (the superexploitation of women) in the farce of the Cairo conference. There was no concept of transnationality there. You have to get into it to see how much development is an alibi for exploitation, how much it's a scam: the responsibility for the entire world's ills is between the legs of the poorest women of the South."*

It was so clear that everybody, some in a benevolent way, some in a hardly disguised malevolent way, were thinking that to stop poor Third World women from having children would solve all the world's problems. It was just amazing! The fact that one Euro-American child consumes 183 times what one Third World child consumes was never thought of, much less articulated. I probably mentioned this in that long-ago interview as well. Secondly, the other thing that was never talked about was the idea of the gross infringement of human rights entailed by this kind of pharmaceutical dumping, forcible sterilization, and so on. Finally, they also never thought about the fact that having children had something to do with social security so that the change does not, cannot in fact, come through aid.

I could say something now that I did not say then. People often think I am just being benevolent and starry-eyed. I just heard Juan Somavia, the director general of the ILO at Davos, and he was interviewed just once whereas everybody else who was saying the opposite thing was on a loop, endlessly repeating the same things. Everybody was talking about Europe's identity problems because of the riots in France and so on. Somavia simply said that politics has to change so that the economy is run differently. There is no problem with keeping uniformity for global capital, but local economies also have to remain viable so people won't want to leave in such large numbers. The woman who was interviewing him, who was obviously totally clueless and was just aware of the received ideas, said, "Yes, but that wouldn't really work in sub-Saharan Africa, where people are dying of hunger." So he said, on the contrary, it is precisely in a place like sub-Saharan Africa that this is what should be tried rather than just giving aid.

I was reading a review of Eric Foner's latest book in the *New York Times Book Review*. Foner points out very ably that the real problem with reconstruction is that everybody thought that those Southern blacks were just not as good as full human beings, so their future had to be in the hands of white people. And that is what we are looking at today. So I have moved a little forward from between the legs of women. But it is all of a piece. I spoke precisely of between the legs of women because I was coming from the ICPD [International Conference on Population and Development].

Development remains an alibi for exploitation as long as we understand sustainability as sustaining the maximum economic growth. And I am by no means in a minority when I say this. A number of mainstream economists have written plenty of quite quantitative articles—I actually try to plow through them—showing that economic growth does not necessarily mean redistributive parity. The classic text remains *Hunger and Public Action* by Amartya Sen and Jean Drèze.

Of course in this country we know this very well: the minimum wage has not been raised for decades, and it was just published in the *New York Times* that the wages of CEOs are four hundred times those of workers. So redistribution is clearly not concomitant with economic growth.

In A Critique of Postcolonial Reason, *you write that "imperialism used Woman, freeing her to legitimize itself." How, as you have also suggested elsewhere, is Western feminism a form of colonial benevolence?*

You can look anywhere and see the same justification for intervention: even Bruce Ackerman writing about liberal capitalism gives the same excuse, namely, liberating women. I am not saying it's bad to liberate women, but the argument that I made in "Can the Subaltern Speak?" was that although it was absolutely fine to criminalize *sati*, the actual effort to engage with the minds of women who were convinced that *sati* was a good thing was never taken up except in a class-fixed way, which had nothing to do with *sati* because middle-class women were not committing *sati* anyway. There are all kinds of dimensions to that claim to liberate women.

God knows where I said that *Western* feminism is a form of colonial benevolence; I generally try to stay clear of saying anything about *Western* anything. Let me recount another anecdote by way of explanation: I met someone, now I forget her name, on the Chakradhapur passenger train in India, which is a *totally* nondeluxe train (most of my nice, radical, academic friends in Calcutta don't get on trains like that). On such a train I have met *Indian* women who have completely internalized the idea of this kind of so-called *Western* feminism. I was transfixed because I have never known the steps that are taken to get to this point, although I knew about gender training and what kind of consciousness raising it was: one, two, three, four, all the steps, and she spoke to me very openly because we got into a conversation and she found out that I taught abroad, so she was very happy to tell me that she had actually followed these steps for gender training. There was not a Western person in sight. So I think one should have some *other* criterion, criteria other than West and non-West. Minimally it has something to do with the educational models in the world. There is a certain kind of international feminism which, again, impatiently follows a structure given from outside and tries to approach women who are so internally—not just externally—separated from these issues. The woman did not speak, for instance, of poverty or disease eradication, getting microcredit or winning in the gender struggle. So what I am saying is that it is not *Western* feminism that is the problem, but something like a change in thought where this kind of stuff is taken to be normal by people.

What is taken to be normal?

The things that are being so-called corrected. In fact, of course, if you really want to take it up, you will see that even in the ones who are correcting in this way, much of this stuff is internalized. You only have to look at advertisements, like the ad about One Pass miles: two white people at a photocopy machine, a man and woman in conversation, the guy wants to be her date, and she says that she has gone with somebody else who has more One Pass miles. This kind of commodified, free-enterprise marketplace of sexual favors is internalized by many of these missionaries, number one. Number two, they also go in thinking that they are not going to be self-interested but are in fact morally outraged for the sake of these poor people. And they go into these places and teach people self-interest. What does that mean? That you teach people what you think is not a good thing? It is too inconvenient, of course, to bring them into that other arena. So I don't think *Western* feminism is a form of colonial benevolence. I think it is really a kind of ignorant goodwill if you like, to quote Yeats once again. It is a way of thinking that these are the nice ways in which all problems can be solved. You go in, and you actually *do* the things that are solving the problems rather than solving the problems. If, like myself, someone the next day actually approaches these women and simply asks, "Well, what happened?" one realizes how little actually goes across. So that is why I think Western feminism, colonial benevolence, is not really the issue. It is rather a certain kind of international feminism that has no concept of mental theater, unless it just talks about cultural difference. I am not talking about cultural difference here, I am completely culturally different from many people here, but I have no problem negotiating because I am on a level where I can negotiate. It is not a problem.

So even the provenance of this feminism, the origins of it, that is not relevant?

Today, what is Western? All education is in a certain way the Western model. All universities everywhere, all schools everywhere, except for a few very unusual models, progressive schools like Shantiniketan.[8] And even that, just look at what it has become: it was so Western in its ideas of being culturally authentic that it was not difficult for it to follow an almost completely Western model after Tagore died.

Historically certain things win. The question then is: What made them win? Is there anything we can learn from the losers? Not to throw away or not acknowledge that *something* won; after all, in the Indian context, the Indo-European languages won. So what are we going to do? Put the clock back? I am talking about North India especially, of course. You cannot deal in fairy stories, or ahistorical utopianism. Right from the start, I talked about colonialism as an enabling violation. That was a risk. What is surprising is that nobody picked me up on that, nobody took issue with that claim, even though *everybody* picked me up on epistemic violence. I would think though that colonialism as an enabling violation was a much harder thing to acknowledge. No one criticized me, they did not notice it or simply chose not to engage with it. People like Meera Nanda, who clearly only looks at the enablement even though in her latest book, *The Wrongs of the Religious Right: Reflections on Science, Secularism and Hindutva*, she has somewhat understood that this was problematic and I congratulate her for it, but nonetheless, when she, and others like her, criticize me, it is because I am totally anticolonial, and therefore I like religion, and so on. They never see that right from the start I had the courage—and I use that word advisedly—to talk about an enabling violation.

But to return to your question, I am not sure that I am interested in criticizing something called Western feminism, especially today, when, under globalization, the demographic frontiers have shifted.

In talking about the present and projected economic dispensation, you frequently invoke the phrase "the financialization of the globe." What are the features of this trend, and what do you see as its implications?

Of course we basically have an idea of what world trade is. With respect to the financialization of the globe, let me first of all recommend a very simple, good book: Amit Bhaduri's *Intelligent Person's Guide to Liberalization*, published by Penguin.

Marx said in the nineteenth century that capital wants to travel at the speed of thought because it is an abstract thing. Now that is neither good nor bad. When you want to establish the same system of exchange all the world over, then you remove the barriers between fragile national capitals and international capital, and the model of state-ship changes from redistribution, ideally, to management, and constitutional redress becomes impossible. So in that situation, what we look at generally is how world trade operates. But of course a much bigger thing is at work because of that abstract desire, in the Deleuzian sense, within capital to move at the speed of thought. That too with the silicon chip at this point—the bio-chip does not work in this way quite, but that is another argument. What happens is that there is a tremendous market in foreign exchange and in negotiable instruments. *That* is finance capital, which goes around fifty times more in a day than world trade. That is what I call globalization as such. That is the issue rather than merely the ancillary, crisis-management-type phenomenon of world trade. That is what I meant.

Can you tell us a little about your forthcoming book, entitled Other Asias?

Today we need to think about how we invoke a sense of place. There is this idea that, with the globalization that I just described, we are operating in a kind of postplace episteme, so to speak, a space-episteme, to quote Castells, and I do not believe this is so. I think the idea that the kind of institutional change that I just described in answer to the previous question signifies a continuous epistemic change is really rather a simplistic notion of what subjects are, of subject-formation as such. But how do we then argue a sense of place? Because on the other side there is a ferocious identitarianism. I never put myself in an opposing position. It is too easy to solve problems that way. So I kept moving down the line—Ballyganj (my neighborhood), Calcutta, West Bengal, India, Asia, and then, immediately, the universe, as we used to write in our junior high school textbooks. And the buck stopped on Asia—because on the other side of it now is thoughts not of the universe but of how the globe is produced to counter such thoughts. I was asked a question at Thammasat University in Thailand, in a very identitarian way, about how I was an Indian and so on, and I realized that I was not an Indian in any way that I could describe. So I began thinking about what sort of work I was doing and I realized that I wanted to look at that abstract and unlocatable word "Asia," which people generally claim as just the name of *their* neck of the woods in Asia: West Asia, Central Asia, South Asia, these three places have rather little to do with each other, in any continuous way, and then of course there is all of East Asia, which relates to Southeast Asia somewhat differently from the way in which South Asia does, and so on. And then there is the important new idea of the Asia-Pacific—the east coast of Asia and the west coast of the United States, jumping over what is called the Pacific, Oceania, Polynesia—everything from Taiwan to New Zealand, with the mysterious Easter Islands as well as Hawaii, the fiftieth state.

So I realized that that is why I was looking at that word, Asia, a kind of phantasmatic sense of place. So I have pieces on Bangladesh, on Afghanistan, on India, on Indian America, on Hong Kong, on Armenia, and that last piece, which is not even specifically Asia, is taking me clear out of the postcolonial model into these various kinds of contemporary models of international civil society. Basically that is the description that I can give.

When is it coming out?
　　Sometime in 2007.

What kind of audience do you write for, and what kind of audience would you like to write for? Is it not the case that a number of the issues you touch belong also in the public sphere, that they might also be the subject of wider engagement outside of an academic setting? What do you see as the role of public intellectuals in the United States, and how would you like to situate yourself within this context?

I write in such a way that all the generalizations would be acceptable to that very poor sector of tribals who are the parents of the children whose teachers I train and have been training for the last sixteen years. It is the other side of Longinus's injunction to his students in search of the sublime style when he said that if you write keeping the illustrious dead in mind, you will write sublimely. Well I do have these absent interlocutors who will not be able to understand either the English or the sophisticated vocabulary, but, on the other hand, I can imagine them as being the judges of some of the generalizations advanced. So that is who I write for.

What kind of audience would I *like* to write for? Well, people who are not veiled racists and sexists. Someone was just cited to me by one of my colleagues, for example, as saying about my essay "Three Women's Texts and a Critique of Imperialism" that its effect on criticism of Victorian literature has been: "She who must be obeyed." And then I read in Nivedita Menon's book, *Recovering Subversion*, that I think I am the "high priestess" of deconstruction. In other words, I would like to write for an audience who would not be alarmed by a powerful, female voice. I would also like, of course, to write for an audience who would be generally left of center. That is already too much to expect, right? And an audience that would not be full of sanctioned ignorance. An audience that would not think, to quote a very well-known writer who said at a recent meeting at Princeton that if she reads something in the middle of the day after a good meal—I am paraphrasing freely here—and she reads it three times and it is still too difficult, then she thinks it is the fault of the text. Anthony Appiah then murmured in my ear, "What about Kant?" and I was thinking about Kant too. Anybody who has that kind of a notion that material is written to match the size of their intellect rather than to cultivate a judgment, the ability to distinguish between vocabulary and jargon and so on, these are not the people I have in mind. I think I would like to have an old-fashioned audience who think that one should try to understand rather than simply reject anything one cannot understand. Finally, I would also like to be read by people who are not monolingual. This is a very general kind of thing.

I never think about what kind of audience I would like to write for because I write without thinking about an audience, except for that judgment thing that I told you about to begin with. But since you ask, I kind of made up something. So don't hold me to it because I am sure I could go on forever adding qualities to the kind of audience I would like to have, but I have given you a general idea.

The answer to the public sphere question is yes.

The phrase "public intellectual" has become too much of a buzzword. Given the way in which power has become centralized in the United States, I think intellectuals can do rather little. Not only has power been centralized, there is a great rift between the electorate and intellectuals. At the most basic level, political campaigns are not affected by real intellectuals in any sense in terms of the entire country. So I think the role of a public intellectual, or organic intellectual, in the sense of Gramsci, who is a permanent persuader, has been taken away from us. And I don't believe I belong within that context at all because if I were a public intellectual in the United States, I think I would have some kind of a New York voice. I don't believe I have a New York voice at all. I have my own sense of why that is so, but I don't think I want to talk about it. So you will just have to take this unsatisfactory response as the final answer to your very astute and interesting questions. Thank you.

PART FOUR I SECULARISM AND ISLAM

TWELVE ▮ Talal Asad

You have suggested in your essay "Religion, Nation-State, Secularism" that the term religion is often used anachronistically. Why is it that the term religion does not exhaust all the components—the practices, the ways of being—that comprise it? How did this understanding of the term come about, and why is it that you place such emphasis on an alternative conception of the term?

I think there is a slight misunderstanding here. I'm not really concerned to give another definition of religion. I am not concerned to say that we can get a more comprehensive, a more dynamic conception, and so on. I wish only to point to the fact that religion as a category is constantly being defined within social and historical contexts, and that people have specific reasons for defining it one way or another. Religion is associated with various kinds of experience, various institutions, various movements, arguments, and so on. That is what I am pointing to. In other words, it is not an abstract definition that interests me. People who use abstract definitions of religion are missing a very important point: that religion is a social and historical *fact*, which has legal dimensions, domestic and political dimensions, economic dimensions, and so on. So what one has to look for, in other words, is the ways in which, as circumstances change, people constantly try, as it were, to gather together elements that they think belong, or *should* belong, to the notion of religion. People *use* particular conceptions of religion in social life. This has really been my concern.

My concern in the *Genealogies of Religion* was to trace some of the ways in which this notion has come to be constructed historically, rather than to provide a cross-cultural definition of religion that can be applied to any society. This is what I have been trying to say.

It has frequently been argued that processes of modernization should culminate in the retreat of religion to the private sphere, so that wherever religion manifests itself in public life, this can be attributed to an incomplete or failed project of modernization, or as the vestiges of tradition forestalling the inevitable triumph of the modern. How would you respond to this?

Well, certainly that is the theory, but, of course, for a long time it has been recognized that this is not the way history has gone. Indeed, it is not even clear that the so-called retreat of religion has been quite a simple thing even since the beginning of the nineteenth century. The way in which people have thought about secularism—that is, the separation between state and religion—has in fact been adapted to very different kinds of states.

Let's think of three examples of states in the West that are supposed to be liberal, democratic, and secular: France, Britain, and the United States. What you have in France—very schematically speaking—is a state that is secular and a society that is secular. In England, you have an established religion and you have a very secular society. In the United States, you have a very religious society and a secular state. There are therefore very different ways in which the negotiation between religion and politics works itself out. There are different kinds of sensibilities, even in these three *modern* states and societies. There are different kinds of reactions that people have toward what is a transgression against "secular" principles.

For example: such sensibilities are found in the debate in France (*l'affaire du foulard*) about whether Muslim girls should be permitted to wear the veil in public schools. It is interesting to note, incidentally, that this has led to a negative reaction by secularists, whereas wearing a yarmulke to school has not. What is it that makes the wearing of the veil a violation of secular rules of politics and not the yarmulke? My point is not that there is unfair discrimination here, but that even in a secular society there are differences in the way secular people evaluate the political significance of "religious symbols" in public space. Or take America. There are clear rules in the United States about the separation of state and religion, but that doesn't prevent "nonsecular" interventions in the politics of the present regime. As we all know, the Christian Right is at the heart of the Bush government. It is an anti-Semitic ally of the

Zionist organizations in America, and its political imagination embraces the war against Iraq as a step toward Armageddon. A "secular" war is supported by them for "religious" reasons. Again, I say this not in order to express my disapproval of the Religious Right (although, of course, I do dislike them), but to point to the fact that a secular state can without difficulty accommodate such politics.

So to come back to the question of what is modern and what is not, and what ultimately is expected of a liberal, modern state: I think one has to recognize, first of all, that the transformation of societies in what is called a modern direction included all sorts of accommodations and all sorts of changes, all sorts of readjustments as well as concessions. The "secular" politics that is emerging is partly the result of these changes. And in that sense modernization/secularization is not really a simple story.

I myself am very skeptical of the notion that modernity is some kind of straightforward destiny for everybody. There is a sense in which modernity can be thought of as a historical periodization, as temporality, but also as particular ways in which people live—must live. I am not at all sure that the "modern" necessarily presupposes everything that people in one or other of the so-called liberal, secular states want or think it should be.

Secularism has always been considered a crucial component of the process of modernization. How would you define the relationship between religion and secularism?

In *Formations of the Secular*, I try to look at questions of sensibility, of experience, of the embodied concepts that orient subjects' sensorium and guide public understandings of truth. I also look at the political doctrine of secularism itself, and at the secularization of law and morality in modernizing states. I think these are complicated questions. I think we don't understand fully what all the implications of the secular modes of everyday existence are for secular politics. I think we need to think about such matters far more deeply in the human sciences than we have done so far.

Secularism as a political doctrine I see as being very closely connected to the formation of religion itself, as the "other" of a religious order. It is precisely in a secular state—which is supposed to be totally separated from religion—that it is essential for *state* law to define, again and again, what *genuine religion* is, and where its boundaries should properly be. In other words, the state is *not* that separate. Paradoxically, modern politics cannot really be separated from religion as the vulgar version of secularism argues it should be—with religion having its own sphere and politics its own. The state (a political entity/realm) has the function of defining the acceptable public face of "religion."

In your book Formations of the Secular, *you write: "The difficulty with secularism as a doctrine of war and peace in the world is not that it is European (and therefore alien to the non-West) but that it is closely connected with the rise of a system of capitalist nation-states—mutually suspicious and grossly unequal in power and prosperity, each possessing a collective personality that is differently mediated and therefore differently guaranteed and threatened." How would you characterize the significance of this dissymmetry in terms of the global politics of secularism?*

A common criticism of secularism in the Third World, especially in Arabic-speaking countries, is that it is not appropriate to Muslim societies because it is foreign. This doesn't seem to me a sound position. From the very beginning these societies have adopted and adapted ideas and practices from "outside." In fact what we know as the Islamic world was a synthesis and development of preexisting institutions, ways of thinking and doing, etc., and borrowing of ideas and practices went on all the time. The question is: What kind of problem is "secularism" supposed to resolve? The difficulty that I see with secularism is that it began by articulating problems of power in the newly emerging nation-states in early modernity. The centralization of the state, its monopolization of violence—its assumption that only the state could legally use force (or authorize it) internally, and that only the state could conduct war externally—its attempt to discipline a subject population by homogenizing it, all this was the project in which secularism developed. We know that at first the centralizing state in Western Europe attempted to impose a single religious identity on its subjects. When this failed the solution tried was the privatization of religious belief. This was a process that took different forms in different states, involved different institutions and discourses. On the other hand, regardless of the intentions of different actors in each state, the "material" in which everyone worked—the main problem they confronted—was the rearrangement of social power and authority within "the state." But all of this didn't take place in self-contained, isolated political units. Political thinkers and actors in one state interacted with those in other states—in fact many of them moved from one West European state to another when things got difficult at home. And the princes themselves made alliances and fought with one another, and protected the foreign activities of their own merchants in order to enrich their own realms. The development of international law begins with the interaction of nation states within Europe, but it is also and especially connected to the wider world of the Americas and Asia in which colonial properties and commercial empires were being created. (European empires in Africa came later.) The great founder of international law Hugo Grotius was famously engaged in debates about the "legal" conditions of exploiting foreign markets. Whether "legal" treaties could be established between European Christians and non-Christians for commercial purposes was a crucial part of these debates. So secularism—in what ways and for what purposes can the power of the state ignore religious differences?—is a part of all this. In the later Western empires in the nineteenth and early twentieth centuries, understanding of the "neutrality" of the state toward "native" religions and also toward Christian missions played a very important part in the evolution of colonial government. In our present, the secular American state seeks actively to impose certain political principles ("freedom of religious belief") on Third World countries on the grounds that secularism ensures both freedom and democracy. I've talked in *Formations* about some of the implications of the American International Religious Freedom Act of 1998 for international politics, and about the close connection between secularism and projects of political redemption.

Although modernity and secularism are often seen as coconstitutive, you point out that the privatization of religion within its own sphere (the process named "secularization") is not essential to modernity. The important point, you suggest, is rather how religion comes into the public domain. You underscore the role of colonialism in this context. Could you elaborate on this?

I think you are referring to my comment on Jose Casanova's argument that modern society did not necessarily need religion to be privatized, as the classical secularization thesis insisted. Casanova suggested that in many cases religion could be seen as furthering modernity and democracy—as in the Catholic Church's role in undermining the communist regime in Poland, and even in the United States where the Church often espoused "progressive" political positions. I was concerned to point out that it was only certain forms of religion—liberalized, secularized, religious movements—that were given as positive examples by him, not "troublesome" ones. In other words, champions of "modernity" were led to maintain that so long as religion didn't challenge the secular state, so long as it espoused all the values encouraged by the secular state, religion would be allowed to make a public appearance. But then, as we've seen recently, this is not how the French see the question of secularism.

Is it not also the case that even in terms of its own self-understanding, "secularization" never occurred in the West? Examples could be the persistence, throughout the period of secularization, of the "Jewish question," and the large conversion of Jews to Christianity in Europe. Also, the fact that the West continued, indeed continues to this day, to send out missionaries throughout the world, which in the period of colonialism—largely coeval with the period of "secularization"—was all but synonymous with civilization and the civilizing mission. In other words, is it not the case that far from disappearing, Christianity and Christian theologies underwent important, indeed dramatic, mutations in the modern period?

No, I would disagree with your initial statement. Remember that "secularization" is a process, not a completed end state, and *that* process has certainly taken place according to "Western self-understanding." But it has taken place in different ways in different Western countries, and therefore generated different contradictions and tensions. I recently wrote an essay on French secularism in which I argued at length that in my view there was no such thing as a single, ideal secularism. So my response to your concluding question is: yes, of course Christianity still exists (and plays complicated roles at home and abroad), and of course Christian theologies have been profoundly reshaped in the modern period. But that doesn't mean that there's no such thing as secularism in the West. An important part of my argument in *Formations* is to reject the idea that many critics espouse, that the Western secular state isn't really secular. I don't think there is any such thing as "real" secularism. There are only different, historically loaded, forms of secularism—meaning by this, that there are different responses to what is seen historically as a major problem of power in modern society: "the threat of public religion to political freedom and to progress."

You argue that "No movement that aspires to more than mere belief or inconsequential talk in public can remain indifferent to state power in a secular world." If this is true, then why is it so often asserted that Islamists are "politicizing" religion?

Precisley because Islamists are not indifferent to state power, they do not want their religious movements to remain matters of mere personal belief.

You also suggest that "A secular state does not guarantee toleration; it puts into play different structures of ambition and fear." How does this insight unsettle the assumption that secular societies are less prone to conflict and violence than "religious" ones? What is the role of the secular state in managing, fostering, or avoiding religious conflict?

Like all states, a secular state tolerates some things and not others. It guarantees the right of its subjects to believe and practice any religion without let or hindrance—*so long as that isn't seen as a threat to the integrity of the state*. But, of course, the latter rests not only on a particular perception of "a threat," but also (and this is a more difficult problem) on what constitutes "the integrity of the state." Are secular societies less prone to conflict and violence? You have only to examine the well-known forms of violence and repression that characterize secular states internally (race, gender, class, etc.) and externally (neo-imperialist domination, the creation and maintenance of spheres of influence, counterinsurgency wars, etc.) to see how problematic this claim about less violence in secular societies is. Politics in liberal democratic societies is centrally concerned with policies that deal with, employ, manage, repress, violence and conflict at home and abroad.

It has been argued elsewhere that religious revivalist movements—such as (but not limited to) ones in the Muslim world—are not in fact atavistic or premodern, but that the very condition of possibility of these movements is the modern. Would you agree with this?

I think to some extent this is certainly true. I would agree if, in "the modern condition of possibility," you include the nation-state and the ambitions of the nation-state. It seems to me that both kinds of movements—both militant movements as well as the liberal forms of Islam that have emerged since the nineteenth century—are adjustments to the fact that the state has ambitions regarding the formation of subjects and the regulation of entire populations, of their life and death. These things were the concern of various other agencies previously—including what one might call the religious—or there was no such function at all. But now a single political structure, the modern nation-state, seeks to deal with them.

I think it is true that, if you like, both the radical forms of religious movements as well as the liberal forms are accommodations to the modern state. The liberal ones obviously because they represent attempts to adjust to that overarching political power and the spaces it authorizes—to the forms of privacy and autonomy that it enables and legitimizes. The radical ones too belong to the same modern world because what is at stake for them primarily is the state since that is the seat of power determining all sorts of things in ways that previously were left unregulated.

So in that sense, yes, these movements are modern. They are also of course modern in the sense that there are all sorts of modern techniques that are now available and employed by them (electronic techniques of communication, scientific forms of knowledge, the various means through which knowledge is produced and circulated, etc.). So it is quite true: various aspects of these movements are constituted in a modern way. At the same time one should not forget that they draw on traditions of reform and reinterpretation that are part of an old history—a history of disagreement, dispute, and physical conflict—that is drawn on and re-presented.

Can or should contemporary Islamist movements make us rethink Western conceptions of secular modernity?

On the whole, neither radical Islamist movements nor liberal Islam appear able to make people rethink Western conceptions of secular modernity. In part this is because many of their projects, insofar as they are modern, have taken over modern assumptions of politics. In part also it is because there is an enduring antipathy in the West toward Islam and ideas coming from the Islamic tradition. And of course the mere fact of the enormous disparity in power between apparently successful Western societies and evidently weak Muslim societies also plays a part.

But I think that the phenomenon as a whole—that is, the phenomenon of Islamism—as well as comparable religious movements elsewhere in the world *ought* to make us rethink the accepted narratives of triumphant secularism and liberal assumptions about what is politically and morally essential to modern life. The very existence of these phenomena should make us rethink our assumptions about what is necessary to modernity.

There has been much discussion recently of the fact that Islam is antithetical to liberal democracy and all it entails (equality, individualism, human rights, pluralism, tolerance, and so on). How would you respond to this claim?

This is connected to the previous question. If you think of Islam and the Islamic tradition as fixed, as having a certain kind of unchangeable essence, then it might well be argued that Islam is antithetical to liberal democracy: what is modern is not really Islamic, and what is Islamic cannot really be modern. So it's a Catch-22 situation that many critics insist on putting Muslims into.

Of course there are people who are trying to rethink the Islamic tradition in ways that would make it compatible with liberal democracy. But I am much more interested in the fact that the Islamic tradition ought to lead us to question many of the liberal categories *themselves*. Rather than saying, "Well yes we can also be like you," why not ask what the liberal categories themselves mean, and what they have represented historically? The question of individualism, for example, is fraught with all sorts of problems, as people who have looked carefully at the tradition of individualism in the West know very well. The same is true of the question of equality. We know that the equality that is offered in liberal democracies is a purely legal equality, not economic equality. And the two forms of equality can't be kept in water-tight compartments. Even political equality doesn't necessarily give equal opportunity to all citizens to engage in or contribute to the formulation of policy. What do Islamic ideas about the individual, equality, etc. tell us about Western liberal ideas?

These are questions worth pursuing, I think. So instead of leaping up and saying, "Ah yes, we can all be liberal," I think it is more important to ask, for example, "What exactly does the liberal mean by tolerance?" It is easy enough to be tolerant about things that don't matter very much. That tends to be the rule in liberal societies. Increasingly what you believe, what you do in your own home, whether you stand on your head or decide not to, is up to you as an individual in liberal democracies. So who cares? The liberal tolerates these things because the liberal doesn't care about them. Yet tolerance is really only meaningful when it is about things that really matter. Even in ordinary language we talk about "tolerating pain." In other words, the kind of tolerance that really matters is something we ought to be exploring, thinking more about—and the ways in which the Islamic tradition conceives of tolerance (however limited that might be) help to open up such questions.

So we ought to be thinking about questions like that instead of simply—and rather defensively—saying, "There *are* Islamic traditions that are very liberal, you know. We can also become liberal." It is in fact much more interesting to ask, "What does liberalism mean by tolerance, or by pluralism? Is the meaning of individualism totally clear, is it totally desirable? Does an exploration of Islamic traditions give us a deeper, more critical understanding of individualism, or tolerance, or pluralism?" I would like to see more of this kind of questioning, rather than people trying to prove their liberal credentials.

What is the relationship between modern forms of power and the way in which questions about religion and human rights and secularism are framed?

This is a large question. And short of repeating myself, I would only say that many of the things claimed about liberal tolerance should be questioned. There are various kinds of intimidation and coercion that go on both covertly and overtly to make things acceptable to liberal sensibilities. Power is exerted not only in the ways people are allowed to speak or not speak, but in what it is that makes *sense* to them. Rather than thinking of power only in terms of the question of freedom of expression and its limitations, we should also pay attention to the kinds of power that go into the formation of listening subjects, of subjects who can open their minds to something that is strange or uncomfortable or distasteful.

I think we need much more investigation of what people regard as poppycock and of what they are willing to open their minds to. Secularism has tended to regard religious traditions as either making nonsensical claims about public knowledge or having dangerous consequences when they are allowed to enter the political realm. William Connolly, for instance, has been trying in many of his writings to retheorize the political arrangement of secularism as it is has been understood historically so that a more compassionate, open-minded attitude can be invited into modern politics.

Some Muslim states, such as Nigeria and Pakistan, have attempted in various ways to implement Shariah law, attempts that have frequently been contested and criticized, since there is a prevailing belief that Shariah law is "backward" and antimodern. Would you agree with this? Is it possible for Shariah law to be accommodated by the centralized and coercive system of law that is so crucial to the modern state?

Can it be accommodated? Aspects of it cannot be accommodated and have not been accommodated of course since the nineteenth century—commercial law particularly, but also procedural law, and so on, have long been abandoned in most Muslim countries. Criminal law as well, but that has less to do with how the modern capitalist state works than with certain kinds of liberal values (for instance, ideas of what is really cruel and insufferable and what is not). There is a rejection of punishments that have to do with the body; they are anathema to the liberal sensibility. I happen to have the same sensibilities, but logically Shariah punishments are not inconsistent with the demands of a "centralized and coercive system of law so crucial to the modern state."

As far as family law is concerned, it is quite clear that this has been adjusted and accommodated in and by modern states in all sorts of ways. And now there is increasing demand for equality on the part of women in relation to particular kinds of laws that discriminate against them. Here the Shariah has come under pressure.

Again I would stress that there are movements of reinterpretation going on among various Muslims who are keen to introduce liberal values into the Shariah, who would like to rewrite the Shariah from its foundations, as it were, so that it has both some kind of attachment to the historical tradition but at the same time is more palatable to a Western liberal sensibility. In principle, I do not see why this is impossible, and indeed, it may very well happen to a greater or lesser extent. There is, for instance, an interesting woman, Azizah Al-Hibri, a lawyer and a law professor at Richmond University, who has been very concerned to develop liberal interpretations of the Shariah in this country. Surely there are movements of this kind, and they will be accommodated by a liberal democratic state.

Following the events of September 2001, the media was saturated with commentaries about the possible scriptural (and most often, Quranic) injunctions to violence. What do you think accounts for the belief that acts of violence perpetrated by Muslims can be best understood by a return to religious texts? Does this belief extend to other monotheistic faiths? If not, why?

I'm persuaded that there is a pervasive and long-standing hostility toward Islam (and therefore Muslims) in the West—notwithstanding the sympathetic work done by many individual Western writers. So this is not simply a consequence of September 2001. An excellent book published recently on this subject, incidentally, is *Crusading Peace: Christendom, the Muslim World, and Western Political Order*, by the Slovenian historian and political theorist Tomaz Mastnak. It's a very learned and closely argued work that deals largely with the Middle Ages. Anyway, you'll agree I think that there's something puzzling about the fact that our respected Orientalists and public intellectuals keep trotting out "inflammatory" verses from the Quran without asking themselves how it is that the text has been around for fifteen hundred years without inciting most Muslims most of the time? They don't ask: Why do *some* Muslim militants invoke them *now*? The answer to this question has already been given by many intelligent people who haven't confused their own egos with the real world. The way religious texts are interpreted, the occasions on which they are cited, and the acts which they legitimate have to do with the world as it exists today. And why haven't other monotheistic faiths been charged with violence as Islam has been? Well, because it is only Muslim militants who have directed themselves against the United States and its European allies. Violent Christian movements in Uganda and Christian militias in Lebanon, violent Jews in Palestine, are of no great interest to Western audiences because they don't target Western power. Nevertheless, it is true that there is a growing critique of monotheism as such—of its alleged propensity to be intolerant, etc. It is the sharply bounded, integrated, and totalistic character of its belief systems—so the thought runs—that makes monotheism hostile to difference and jealous of its followers' loyalty. But apart from the fact that "intolerance" may refer to conduct or to creed, to legal discrimination or to popular hatreds, this thesis errs in equating the concept of a unified doctrine (i.e., to be assented to or rejected as a whole) with the content of that unified doctrine (e.g., strict monotheism as opposed to trinitarianism, belief in a hierarchy of sacred powers and persons or only in a unique divine principle, polytheism, atheism), and in assuming that the two together are necessarily attached to a unified political authority that furthermore requires all its subjects to be loyal to that doctrine in every situation. Consequently, no attention is paid to the *practices* of polytheistic communities that generate intolerance, or of monotheistic believers who are tolerant—let alone to the various behaviors in which "tolerance" is expressed and lived. And *indifference* to the public expression of beliefs that no one really cares about is often taken to be equivalent to *toleration* of beliefs that are regarded as offensive. In brief, those who propound the critique of monotheism generally ignore the fact that many polytheist or atheist societies have been highly intolerant of certain forms of behavioral transgression, while monotheist polities have often tolerated varieties of belief.

You write that "it is not always clear whether it is pain and suffering as such that the secularist cares about or the pain and suffering that can be attributed to religious violence because that is pain the modern imaginary conceives of as gratuitous." Could you explain the significance of this difference for a thinking of international intervention, humanitarian or other? Do you think that religion remains an implicit, even hidden, element in the discourse that legitimates intervention?

In my view secularism has to do with particular structures of freedom and sensibilities that conform to them within the differentiated modern nation state. In that sense secularism tries to curb the inhuman excesses of what it identifies as "religion," but it allows other cruelties that can be justified by a secular calculus of social utility and a secular dream of happiness. It replaces patterns of premodern pain and punishment with those that are peculiarly its own. Here are some familiar examples (I leave aside Stalinist and Nazi atrocities): the deliberate destruction of civilian populations in the Allied bombing of German and Japanese cities during World War II, the ruthless American prison system, the treatment of non-European asylum-seekers by EU countries—all of these actions by liberal democracies are based on calculations of worldly pain and gain, not on religious doctrines and passions. Anything that can be used to counter attempted subversions of the state—any cruelty or deception—acquires justification as a political technique. In "a state of exception," liberal democracies defend "the rule of law" not only by issuing administrative orders to eliminate public disorder, but also by the extrajudicial means of secret violence (the inflicting of pain and death) so long as that contradiction doesn't cause a public scandal. Deliberately inflicted suffering in modern war and government blends into the widespread social misery produced by neoliberal economic policies. Thus apart from the enhanced scale of suffering due to modern techniques, the quality of human suffering is often shaped by changed relations and ideas. People are taught that they are free and equal and find to their anguish that they are not: encouraged to believe that they can fulfill all their "normal" desires—even be desired by others—they find they cannot and are not. The modern sufferer's sense that pain is always worldly, or that it no longer has any moral significance, perhaps makes it less easy to bear. Be that as it may, modern poverty is certainly experienced as more unjust—and so as more intolerable. I don't want to suggest that the distribution of pain engendered by modern power is worse than the distribution in premodern societies, but only that it is different. Nor do I make the foolish claim that there has been no progress in any kind of suffering. The cure of various illnesses and improvements in public health and welfare are undeniable social facts that have led to the amelioration of distress and affliction. I don't think that justifies every kind of humanitarian intervention by Western powers in other societies. Whether it justifies *any* is a difficult question, but I'm skeptical. My main point is only that more is at stake in secularism than compassion for other human beings, and the securing of a modern, democratic life. And nothing is less plausible than the claim that secularism is an essential means of avoiding destructive conflict and establishing peace in the modern world.

How would you explain why there are infinitely more reports of human rights violations in the "Third World" than there are in the Euro-American world?

One reason for this is of course the fact that there are quite a lot of dictators in power in the Third World. This applies to Latin America, to Africa, and to China—not only to the Muslim world as the media would have us believe. But I think that there is something more that interests me in this whole question of human rights. Very often, many of the assumptions underlying human rights have to do with ways of life that are recognized as Western. Many things are found insufferable in the Third World merely because they are in the Third World. Things in the West are not found quite so insufferable simply because they are part of a different (more prestigious) way of life.

I was reminded of this again when I was reading the *Christian Science Monitor* recently. There was a long article on Qatar, which is said to be relatively liberal and tolerant, and so on. Qatar is portrayed as a progressive society, therefore as one of the more interesting societies in the region. The examples given to support this claim, quite unself-consciously, are that Doha has Starbucks cafes, that people eat Subway sandwiches, that there are malls. And of course they are also America's crucial military allies in the region at a time when Saudi Arabia is shuffling its feet in the war against Iraq. I am not trying to trash Qatar, of course. What I am saying is that the conception here, automatically and quite unself-consciously put forward, is that "they are becoming more like us." "Us" here refers explicitly to Americans, not even to Europeans (which the Europeans are discovering now, much to their frustration).

There is another important aspect to this human rights issue, one that has international dimensions. Many of the conditions of disenfranchisement in the Third World are due not only to brutal dictators but also to the way in which these societies are connected to the global system.

The point is that conditions inside a country are thought of not as being anybody's responsibility but that of the national government.

The trouble with the way human rights violations are conceived is that they invest the sovereign state with legal responsibility for *all* the sufferings of its people. There is some reason for this, historical as well as political, but increasingly around the world this notion makes nonsense of the way in which the violation of people's rights should be understood. The notion that lack of education, poverty, and misery of various kinds have only to do with those countries themselves is absurd. Of course (it is grandly conceded) we in the West have an obligation to give aid, and they in the Third World have an obligation to follow the sound policies urged on by the International Monetary Fund and the World Bank, which lend them money. But beyond that each Third World country is responsible for its own miseries—and its own human rights abuses.

In other words, the responsibility cannot lie here with Western countries as far as *any* human rights violations in the Third World are concerned. So it is that as well. There are really a number of different things that contribute to people thinking in particular ways about human rights violations, and therefore to more violations "there" than "here."

The Universal Declaration of Human Rights reads that "no one shall be subjected to torture or to cruel, inhuman or degrading treatment or punishment," but this does not seem to apply to the conduct of war, although, as you say, "modern, technological warfare involves forms of suffering, in number and in kind, that are without precedent." What accounts for this paradox? What are its historical sources? And aside from technology, what are the other traits of its modern specificity? What are the specific ways in which "secular" violence is rendered invisible?

War (i.e., violence between sovereign states) is legitimate, whereas rebellion against constituted authority, insurgency, is not. Since the International Committee of the Red Cross was founded in the middle of the nineteenth century, various conventions have been signed in the West to modify the cruelty of war—mainly wars between European powers. Colonial wars were different partly because they were nearly always counterinsurgency wars, so many things were condoned there. But I'm afraid it should be evident to anyone who has read about the conduct of war over the past century that international conventions haven't been very effective—except for punishing military officers of the losing side. The fact that "necessary" and "proportional" use of military force is legal means that all sorts of cruelties can be perpetrated. After all, if the destruction of Hiroshima and Nagasaki can be justified (as it still is) on the grounds that it was necessary to "the saving of many more lives" in an extended war, what more can one say? This kind of violence is secular only in the sense that it is conducted by secular states and justified by secular arguments.

In addition, you suggest that "The use of excessive force against civilians through aerial bombardment is regarded differently from the use of violence perpetrated by particular officials against individual victims. It is not a matter of human rights abuse but of collateral damage." How did this come to be the case, and what is its significance?

This is again a matter of the "law of force." Modern domestic law and international private law emerged at about the same time as did secular conceptions of war. War was no longer subject to Christian doctrines as "just war" had been. War came to be thought of as an active condition in which belligerent states had rights and duties, but these were not to be confused with human rights, which had a separate trajectory and field of application. Violence directed at a particular individual, as in torture, was separate from the anonymous violence of war and couldn't be justified as the latter could. Although some of the arguments about the use of force when questioning militant suspects raise familiar problems: the condemnation of "unnecessary suffering" in those situations implies that some suffering is *necessary* to securing vital information. Anyway, I think the point I wanted to underscore when I made that statement was that liberals tend to regard face-to-face violence with greater distaste than violence at a distance.

Similarly, as you point out, military action is not the only, or for most states most of the time, the most important, form of intervention by powerful states in the affairs of others. The global economic agenda, implemented and policed by various multilateral financial institutions (the World Bank, the IMF, etc.), and championed by the United States, frequently has devastating consequences for individuals in recipient countries. When such interventions result in widespread immiseration and destitution, involving millions of individual lives, why are these actions still not viewed as violations of human rights?

Because one would have to hold foreign states and transnational corporations and corrupt rulers of Third World states responsible for the misery their economic actions cause to human beings. The idea that that could happen in a capitalist world is a total fantasy, of course. It's diffi-cult enough to hold individuals accountable in an international criminal court for the direct physical violence they inflict on individuals belong-ing to a different country. It is common knowledge that not only has the United States refused to sign up to the International Criminal Court statute (as have about half of the states in the world), it has also actively tried to undermine the court by signing about ninety bilateral treaties with individual countries to bypass the authority of the ICC. Certainly people have a sense of the damage done by neoliberal policies through-out the world, and they do regard this as a great injustice. But having this recognized internationally as a violation of human rights, and acting on it legally against agents at home and abroad, is quite another matter.

You have been accused of sympathizing with nativism, "Islamic fundamental-ism," and the like. Recently one critic charged you (along with others) of culti-vating an "aura of authenticity." How would you respond to such a charge?

My first reaction would be to say that I only answer charges in a court of law!

I find this rather disappointing, frankly. It is a reflection of much of the careless thinking that is going around in the human sciences these days. It is the kind of carelessness that has some rather unfortunate and worrying moral implications. The people who say this are not unlike Bush, who says, "You are either with us, or against us," and not unlike people who condemn attempts at understanding disturbing events as nothing more than attempts at excusing. I do not think quite honestly that anybody who has read my work carefully could think that I am for irrationality and for the kind of fanaticism that is associated with fun-damentalism (a term I prefer not to use for theoretical reasons as well as political ones).

I know also that at least one critic has said that I have endorsed an "aura of authenticity"—and that, in his eyes, is clearly a great political failing on my part. What I have to say in response to this is not only that the person concerned has not read my work carefully, but also that he has not read Walter Benjamin carefully, from whom the expression "aura of authenticity" is derived, particularly from his essay "The Work of Art in the Age of Mechanical Reproduction."

Many people in cultural studies and anthropology who invoke that text do not seem to have noticed that Benjamin had a very ambivalent attitude toward "authenticity." If you reread that essay, you will see that, on the one hand, he looks forward with approval to a time when certain kinds of authority are undermined—he particularly expects the end of religious authority with the collapse of cultic aura and envisages a consequent enhancement of freedom that the technique of mechanical reproduction will make possible. We know, of course, that this optimism has not been justified.

At the same time, Benjamin's idea of authenticity and aura is a very complex one. It is also a notion that relates to historicity, to the historicity of the authentic thing. It is precisely because a thing is authentic, because the same thing moves from one time to another, that it acquires, as it were, certain qualities of ancientness and genuineness, an aura. Its authenticity as an ancient thing guarantees its historicity. Benjamin recognized ambivalently that the undermining of aura, in the complex sense in which he was talking about it, might also mean the undermining of historicity. Thus it is precisely the fact that certain ancient documents are authentic documents, that they show, as it were, the "real" wear and tear of their historical experience, which makes it possible to use those documents to construct a reliable historical account of something. In other words, Benjamin had a notion of aura not only as essential to modern concepts of historicity, but also as intrinsic to "tradition." This lends his work a productive tension because it is not straightforwardly progressivist.

I find that what Benjamin has to say there is much more complicated and dialectical, much more suggestive, than is often vulgarly assumed by progressivists. So I would say that whoever accused me of sympathizing with fundamentalism because I'm supposed to have endorsed the idea of "aura of authenticity" that Benjamin dismantled has done a rather superficial reading not only of my own work but of Benjamin's as well.

The historian of imperialism, Frank Furedi, has suggested that the emergence of anticolonial nationalism and eventually the emergence of postcolonial states demanded that assumptions such as the superiority of the West could no longer be stated explicitly, so new "more polite," nonoffensive, more diplomatic ways of articulation were invented that in fact retained the old prejudices just under the surface. Indeed, the characterization of the world into "developed, underdeveloped" could be seen as such a new articulation following World War II. Could one say that a similar process is at work in "secularization"?

Yes, I think Furedi is right (although I haven't read where he says this). I would add that some of that politeness is beginning to rub off in some quarters. And yes, a similar process is at work in the international language of "secularization" that has become integral to the human rights regime.

You have spoken of self-criticism within the Middle East. For strategic reasons, the United States has now also discursively complicated its reading of Islamic tradition; it speaks of a plurality (or rather, a duality—the regressive and the modern) of traditions within Islam and declares its aim to be to encourage the more modern, democratic element. What is the difference between your appreciation of the complexity of Muslim tradition and the U.S. schema? Is there any commonality between the forces that the United States seeks to encourage, and the sources of criticism that you gesture toward? Where would you locate, and how would you read, a possible emancipatory politics today?

Well, first of all, let me distance myself from U.S. policy, and say that clearly, as I read it, U.S. policy is only concerned to find tendencies in the Middle East and the Muslim world, whether they are religious or secular, with which it can ally politically. That does not interest me, of course. Second, these U.S. policymakers have a teleological conception of regional developments, and I touched on that when we talked about Benjamin. In other words, people like the patriotic journalist Thomas Friedman evaluate these movements by reference to what "we" in the United States are. Because that, of course, is what all civilized human beings should become—and if this is not obvious to everyone in the world, then clearly there's something terribly wrong with them.

I do not see it that way at all. I hope that things will not develop that way. In my more pessimistic moments, which are now increasingly frequent, I think that regardless of what one would like, one may end up with a world that the Friedmans of this country want. In other words, we may see a world that is more dominated and hegemonized by a singular power pushing us in a singular direction, with less and less possibility for a multiplicity of experiences, and so on. I see power as being more and more polarized, I see cultural options becoming narrower—even though individuals might have more things to consume, more ways to amuse themselves, more ways to aestheticize their personal lives. I would like to see something else, but what I like is neither here nor there, so I distinguish between how I see things as desirable and how I see things as probable. This is what I fear: a homogenization that may well lead to a victory for the kind of world U.S. policymakers have in mind. So in that sense Friedman and I might agree, but I with sadness and he with great delight.

But then history is full of surprises; that is the one thing I console myself with. The best-laid plans of mice and men go wrong. People who confidently predict particular outcomes of historical developments are often mistaken. I hope that I will be wrong too. What might emerge as this century proceeds is in the end very difficult to say. I think that what kind of emancipatory politics makes sense will depend very much on what emerges. I am not in favor of talking confidently about what kind of politics is emancipatory. We have had too many programs of this kind in the past that have been dismal failures. Clearly, one can try to resist oppressive power in various ways, some big, and some small; one can resist morally, one can resist politically. But I don't think academics have quite as much impact on politics as they sometimes think—except if you happen to be a Kissinger, of course. Then you are a public intellectual integrated into the ruling apparatus. So I don't know, quite honestly, if I have anything useful to say on this subject. All I can say is that certainly politics has always had an oppositional dimension. So we ought to try to make our arrogant rulers uncomfortable at the very least, and insecure, at best. Whether we can do more than that I doubt. In the end it is up to the younger generation that has both a greater imagination and a stronger sense of commitment to fellow human beings to decide what to do and how to do it. At present I see large uncertainties around. We are all in a sense much more in the dark than we think we are.

SECULARISM AND THE THEOLOGICO-POLITICAL

The term "theologico-political" features prominently in The Jew, the Arab: A History of the Enemy, *indeed, is central to the arguments you make. What does "theologico-political" mean, and what is its relation to secularism? How might it help us understand the question of the Jew, the Arab?*

The phrase is meant to signal a singular, if complex and varied, Western configuration regarding the way divisions are massively made that separate the human from the divine, the sacred from the profane, the holy and the eschatological from the secular, and so forth, all terms that are produced at the same time that they are distinguished. At the most basic level, the phrase is also a lever, a way of interrogating, at least, the claim that secularization has occurred (or even that it *should* occur), to question the possibility of separating anything, and, most urgently, religion from politics. This goes beyond the current obsessions as to whether George Bush or Ariel Sharon are governed or oriented by "religious" group interests (of course, they are). It is rather about the dominant, Western understanding of the world as "disenchanted" or simply as "secular." Look at France and the embarrassing ways in which it clings to its "secularism," or look at the all-too-visible and invisible investments in "the Holy Land" on the part of the Western media (and populations). My own interest in writing the book was precisely to come to some understanding regarding the relation of religion to politics, on the actual possibility or impossibility of distinguishing between them. I am informed in this matter by what I am afraid is a very pedestrian understanding of Derrida's work, namely, that, at some level, there is *only* difference. Otherwise put, Leibniz's principle—if two things are absolutely identical, they are not *two* things, they are *one*—works in such a way that, because there is more than one thing, sign, object, and so forth, there are only differences between them. Not identity, which is itself differential.

And yet, the question is: How do you define this or that difference? Where do you say that a difference occurs or cuts? Clearly, there are differences between religion and politics, as there are, perhaps, between men and women. Who will argue with that? Yet does that mean that there should be? Or that one could claim to know, in any exhaustive and fully determined way, what the difference is? The problem occurs at the moment one tries to identify where the difference or even differences lie and what their significance is. We know, in biology as in cultural studies and history, that when there is a claim made identifying where the difference between men and women, male and female, is, something is at stake that has little to do with that difference as such (as if there could be difference as such). Of course, and forgive the banality of what I am saying, much of this has to do with power, but it is not exhausted by the question of power. Even "before" political issues, if you will, the question is: What is at stake? What kind of investment is there in saying *here* is the difference, because there is difference, but who is to say that there is *more* difference between this man and this woman than there is between this man and that man? On what basis will one claim that the differences between men are more significant—or less significant—than the differences between men and women? The same is true of religion and politics; there is difference between and within them, so who is to say that the difference between them is more significant than the difference *within* them? And who is to say, finally, that what occurs in insisting on this or that difference is not sheer obfuscation?

Again, what I am saying is perfectly banal. But the question of the theologico-political may reside in this banality: Why is there a difference *precisely here*? Why is this difference deemed determining or, simply, relevant? How did its terms acquire such weight, and increasingly so today? And to such an extent that some people can assert, "I am on the side of politics" and someone else can respond by saying, "I am on the side of religion." How did that difference even establish itself? How did people come to identify with it in the peculiar way they do today? And why do we believe in this difference? I have been trying to understand why the theologico-political is the site of difference. Everything can be a site of difference; why is this particular site currently invested?

"In light of current events," as they say, this may be a most urgent question, that is, the question of the distinction between religion and politics may urgently need to be resolved (and perhaps even put aside, as the *least* relevant regarding "current events"). Forgive me for repeating myself, but this all truly goes beyond the fact that George Bush is as much a fundamentalist as Osama bin Laden; the urgency, indeed, the emergency (if such is its location) extends beyond, and is far graver than, the immediate context we find ourselves in knowingly. What is at stake is the claim to secularism in the West (which goes hand in hand, by the way, with an extraordinary obsession with religion and religiosity—of others); even, I would say, the claim that secularization has occurred in the West. How do we determine such a thing, that there was religion once and then there was something else? It is clear that there are continuities. That there has been a change is not in question (though perhaps it should be), but the terms in which we consider that change is what make all the difference. Things are intertwined in such a way that in order to understand historical change one actually needs to assert that there is a radical beginning, that the cards are so entirely reshuffled that they no longer resemble at all what they appeared like before. This is a possibility, but then one cannot say that religion has changed or that it has been secularized. Either one makes an argument and explains the continuity and where religion has all gone, or one makes an argument in terms of rupture. This is probably too simplistic on my part, but I will say this nonetheless. It is possible that everything is so different that whatever we call religion today has *nothing* to do with what "religion" used to be (which, incidentally, was not even called "religion," as Talal Asad has taught us). None of this has anything to do with the past, this goes without saying.

I am not certain, then, but I think that right now we are in a place where we might be able to begin asking the question: What is the theologico-political? And what is theologico-political difference? How did it, how *does* it come to be and persist? And how does it come to be so determining? Is it truly so? And although I am referring to difference in the singular, it is obviously much larger.

The next question, then, is how and why is this difference between religion and politics still determining us? We have not thought enough about this, I think, at least not if one judges from the perspective of the enemy. For the question of the enemy is a critical moment here. Whatever history of theology, religion, and politics we would want to write, as long as we have not confronted the enemy, which remains as unconceptualized before as after "secularization," from the beginning until today, to the extent that the enemy is thoroughly theologico-political (and such is my argument), and we have not thought about it, then we are still with the enemy. And to that extent, nothing has happened to distance us from the theologico-political in its most structural dimensions. If history—allow me to be ludicrously grandiose—is also the history of the enemy, then nothing has happened.

Could you explain how this conception of the enemy, and its relation to the theologico-political, is connected to the Jew, the Arab?
Yes, this is what I was just beginning to say. The Jew, the Arab, that is to say, the enemy, constitutes the theologico-political. It is through "them" that it becomes what it is. As a philosophical problem, the massive absence of the metaphysical question par excellence regarding the enemy is, I think, absolutely fascinating. What is a friend? What is a true friend? These are the questions that philosophy (and political thinking) asks, as Derrida has demonstrated. These are the questions that philosophy *begins* with: *philosophia* thinks of itself as love and friendship. It does not concern itself with what the enemy is. So it is a philosophical problem, to the extent as well that what has occurred in the vicinity of this absence, in the unreflected spheres of enmity, has in fact involved theologico-political difference. If I have ventured an answer, then, it will have been to say (without reducing the whole concept) that the enemy *is* the theologico-political, meaning that it *constitutes* the theologico-political. Therefore, I am suggesting that we will not be able to address the question of what the theologico-political is without asking the question of the enemy. This is where one needs to look, it seems to me. The enemy is constituted by religion and politics, and the historical weight of the question is entirely burdened with and constituted by the Jew and the Arab in Europe. Therefore, to the extent that an absence can be shown to be operative, it is a *structuring* absence. The absence of that question of the enemy can, in fact, be shown to structure the rapport to the enemy in the West, the rapport of the West to itself, as well, finally, as the relation between religion and politics.
I will try to explain this by way of contemporary politics. I hope this is not too much of a digression. Political Zionism has been described as

the reentry of the Jews into history, understood in this case as a certain (and quite narrow, in fact) political history; another way to put this is that with political Zionism, the Jews have entered secularized, Christian history (my friend and mentor, Amnon Raz-Krakotzkin, a historian, has written compelling analyses of this, and I am learning from him on these and numerous matters). On what is apparently another front, Islam, which for centuries was denied its theological dimension, has now become the epitome of "religion" and religious fanaticism. And from these two factors, there is much that follows. One consequence, for example, is that the Palestinians are still considered to have no legitimate, *political* claims. They would be Muslim fanatics, so we are told, bent on the pursuit of war and conflict. Another is that Islam is synonymous with intolerance, which is typical, of course, of how "religion" has been described since the Enlightenment. This, by the way, is another curious fact about the secularization thesis: that the West claimed to have lost religion, that secularization became triumphant, at the very same moment that religion was "discovered" in the East. There is a profound link between Orientalism and the "fact" of religion. Islam is not the only example, of course (Richard King has written eloquently on the "Mystic East" focusing on "Hinduism"; think also of the relation between contemporary Jewish studies and the development of "Semitics" in the nineteenth century), but I would argue that it is a crucial one. With "secularization," more or less, Islam became a "world religion."

Clearly, the role of Europe is crucial in this respect. Europe is after all the very site of the theologico-political. In other words, Europe itself has absolutely *not* worked out or worked through the difference it has inherited from its past, the difference, assuming that there should be one, between theology and politics, because secularized Christianity is *still* Christianity, however translated (Schmitt), metaphorized (Blumenberg), or perverted (Löwith). The only tradition that has found itself secularized, that has reinvented or simply transformed itself as secular, is Western Christianity, so whatever changes Christianity has undergone in the last three hundred years are still changes that *Christianity* has undergone as a cultural unit (however porous and problematic and invested in claiming its own "purity" that unit might be).

I will say this quickly and probably all too schematically because it is something I have recently been trying to learn about, and which has become increasingly astonishing to me. When people talk about the Inquisition and about the emergence of the antecedents of modern, biological racism, they often refer to the "limpieza de sangre" (the Purity of Blood statutes), those statutes and regulations identifying *conversos* or "New Christians" (converts or descendants of converts) as having Jewish blood and barring them from certain official positions and functions. Such statutes were first written in Spain in the fifteenth century and became increasingly widespread about a century later throughout Spain and Portugal. Implicit to these statutes is the claim (well recognized by those who opposed them, and they were many) that the holy sacraments do not work, that baptism is no longer sufficient or even efficient to make one a Christian. The implication of these statutes for the "New Christians" was, of course, enormous. More important, it seems to me, is the question of what it means for the Church ultimately to uphold a distinction between old and new Christians. This is a huge problem for Jewish historians, as it is for historians of Spain. As for me, I cannot think of any more antitheological, secular a statement on the part of Christianity than this. The "limpieza de sangre" is, as it were, the beginning of secularization: the de facto abolition of the Sacraments in their efficacy. This is where one truly finds the "New Christians," then. Not or not only among the *conversos*, but among those—the Church—who reinvent themselves as "Old Christians." All of this is still very Christian, of course, very Catholic, done in the name of the Church even as it goes against the most basic principles of Christian theology. What remains, at any rate, is that Catholicism, Christianity in fact, has changed radically at that moment, yet it is *Christianity* that has changed, and afterwards it is still going to call itself or function as Christianity. So one could say that everything is exactly the same, and yet just a little different, to quote Walter Benjamin. Something radical has happened to Christianity, quite apart from what has happened to the Jews and to the Moors. Of course, it is a catastrophe, and Europe has changed at that moment. Western Christendom has totally reinvented itself by claiming to be conservative (and what could be more conservative than the Inquisition?), and that is the beginning of secularization. Secularization is just Christianity by another name. But a different Christianity, of course.

RELIGION, RACE, AND ETHNICITY

In the title of your book, The Jew, the Arab, *the former, "Jew," denotes a religious category, whereas the latter, "Arab," an ethnic one. Throughout the book you refer primarily to the Jew, the Arab (rather than, for instance, and more intuitively perhaps, the Jew, the Muslim). Does it make a difference that one is ethnic and the other religious, and what is the significance of this collapse of ethnic and/or political markers with religious ones?*

This is a very important issue, as you know. There is a level at which I wanted to *submit* to the force of the names I was invoking, and perhaps more truthfully, interpellated and even seized by. In the media, in Israeli political discourse, in discussions about institutions, on Israeli ID cards, everywhere practically, "Jew" and "Arab" are the terms that persist. When people theorize that the "conflict" is theological—it is a clash of religions—they will still use the terms "Jew" and "Arab" (rather than Jew and Muslim).

If they see it as a political problem—as a matter of competing nationalisms—they will still employ the same terminology (even if some try to be more "accurate" and speak then of Israelis and Palestinians). Some people then are trying to be rigorous. But the issue exceeds rigor, of course, as well as the speaker's intentions, and for the most part, the terms that persist are "Jew" and "Arab."

Now, it might all be the effect of a certain confusion. There has been a lot of slippage between the different terms used in Western languages to refer to Muslims (Saracens, Agarenes, Turks, Mohammedans, Arabs). There is thus a broad range of terms that appear in the discourse of Europe, which does not necessarily have a changing referent, or referential range. At some level, though, I would want to say that the terms really do not have a referent; they are, first of all, self-referential. These are ways for Europe to speak to itself, trying to think *itself* and to think itself *without* that which it names as the Arabs, the Turks, the Saracens, and so forth.

Obviously when I indicate that one term is a religious marker ("Jew"), while the other is an ethnic marker ("Arab"), I do not wish to endorse this usage, or even this understanding, which is, after all, narrow. Yet, there is a way in which the historical connotations I spoke of have weighed on the terms of the discourse. One example that comes to mind, from among the many things I have learned from my dear friend and colleague Joseph Massad, is that American Jews are, on the one hand, embracing the discourse of ethnicity (which, in its complicated relation to race, has become more and more popular in the last thirty to forty years in this country). On the other hand, they have really, at the organizational level, entirely *resisted* the discourse of ethnicity, which is why they are called American Jews, and *not* Jewish Americans. In other words, they would just be a religious minority. Jews in America are riding the wave of ethnicity, and yet they are not hyphenated. So at that level, certainly within American discourse, "Jew" is primarily, even if not exclusively, a religious term. It is referring to a religious community, a community that may be ethnic but fundamentally has a religious commitment. By becoming white, Jews can be said to have sought and gained a status that is more social than anything else. Yet, they have done so as part of a historical attempt to distance themselves from the racialization of Jews such as has occurred throughout the nineteenth and twentieth centuries with the consequences we know (in this context, let me recommend the work of Mitchell Hart on the crucial role played in this matter by Jewish social scientists in Europe and the United States).

Of course this suggestion is shot through with contradictions, and with contaminations from other realms. It would be silly to say that Jews in America do not think of themselves as an ethnic group. And yet something inscribes itself in the language that I think demands attention. At the same level, Israel claims to be a secular state and yet in the way in which it inscribes "nationality"—distinguishing it from "citizenship"—Israel both ethnicizes—indeed, racializes—the Jew and erases the religious difference that is nonetheless critical to its myths and policies. It is, after all, the Rabbinate that is in charge of deciding who is a Jew, which creates all kinds of political problems. For the most part it is the Rabbinate that has authority over family law, which is where important *political* decisions are made.

So religious authorities actually decide (which is to say that they are granted the authority of the state) who is a Jew, which means that "Jew" is still a religious term, but when it comes to nationality—meaning ethnicity—religious difference is actually not marked (as with "Arab"). There are many categories on Israeli identity cards, and one of them is Jew, for example, and others include Circassian and Druze. So some of the categories are ethnic, while some are religious. It gets really complicated. There are Arabs who are not Muslim, and there are Muslims who are not Arab, so the terms are not symmetric. So the fact that "Arab" would claim itself in such a dominant nonreligious way makes me consider it mostly, dominantly, at this point, as an *ethnic* marker, whereas "Jew" remains determined by a certain theology.

What is important is that even if Israel would admit that "Jew" is a racial marker—which it would not, of course—such acknowledgment would perhaps put an end to its persistent denegations of its racism, but it would maintain those denegations pertaining to the theological dimensions, the messianic, eschatological, apocalyptic dimensions of Zionism. And not just of the settlers, but of Zionism itself, at its core. Again Amnon Raz-Krakotzkin has demonstrated well the denegation that is at work in Zionism's claims that it is a *political* and *not* a religious movement (whence the vilification of so-called religious extremists, as if one settlement could be built and maintained without the "secular" support of the Israeli government or the approval of the American one).

This is how it seems to me the issue of the theologico-political illuminates the current problems of "Jews and Arabs." I should say that the issue of race and ethnicity has become somehow clearer to me since I completed the book. There was one chapter I was considering writing for the book, but did not include in the end and am finishing now. As a way of marking my debt to Mahmood Mamdani (following his discussion of the "Hamitic Hypothesis"), I called my paper "The Semitic Hypothesis." The paper examines the invention of the Semites and, more importantly, their disappearance. There are no more Semites in the sense that Semite is a term that, when it was invented, functioned so as to indicate an almost *absolute* identity between Jew and Arab, so that whatever is said about one could equally be said about the other.

This, again, has everything to do with Europe. The nineteenth century is the only period where Europe thinks of itself as secular, *really* secular, as having won over religion (of course not in all quarters of Europe, but certainly in intellectual, political, and cultural discourse). It is also the only moment where the theologico-political appears no longer to constitute a problem. And it is the only moment where whatever one says about the Jew can be said about the Arab, and vice-versa. There was apparently nothing at stake in abolishing the difference between them. It is an absolutely fabulous (if also horrendous) and, I think, essential moment to understand. But interestingly enough, it is less about religion and politics—although that is also very much there—than about religion and *race*. What I was saying before about the Inquisition is really the beginning of that process. One could, I believe, tell the history of the relation between race and religion from that very moment. I think the nineteenth century and the invention of the Semites is particularly important, however, because what happens with the Semites is the strange invention of the race said to have invented religion.

At that moment, then, race and religion become two distinct categories that are at the same time collapsed in the figure of the Semites.

What is absolutely fascinating, and Edward Said describes this quite evocatively, is the way in which the Jew "bifurcated," the way in which the animus was transferred from the Jew *and* the Arab to the Arab alone. Thus the Jews stopped being Semites. After World War II, all kinds of complicated things happened between race and religion around the Jews. Most of all, race becomes a word that cannot speak its name when one speaks about the Jews (and some account has to be given of that), whereas the last Semites and the only Semites become the Arabs. So they are a race, and the Jews are a religion. Or if you want, even vice versa. Better yet, the Arabs have become the race that is still attached to its religion, whereas the Jews have in fact become Western Christians and therefore are no longer marked, either by race or by religion.

In the academic realm, at any rate, the distinction between race and religion is complete. Religion has a completely marginal place in race studies. You have race, class, gender, but it still very rarely happens that people will say: race, class, gender, *religion*. Religious studies is a disciplinary field, which, like many other fields, has explored questions of race, but it seems to me that there has yet to be a critique of the distinction between religion and race comparable to the distinction between, say, literature and philosophy, that is to say, as disciplinary mechanisms in the management of knowledge.

The interesting question is not what religion precisely *is*, then, whether it is right or wrong, but rather how it functions (in the same way that "Arab" as an ethnic marker functions), how it is located and contained. There are people who claim to be religious, others who explain things by way of religion, and entire cultures that now assert how fundamental religion is to their self-understanding. The term clearly has wide currency, and so it needs to be looked at in more complex ways. When religion is affirmed as a category, it is reinscribed as distinct. But distinct from what? Maybe there is a difference and maybe there is not, or maybe the difference is not where we think it is, and that is the argument I make in this article I just mentioned ("The Semitic Hypothesis"). There are disciplinary mechanisms (in the Foucauldian sense) whereby something is marked as race, and something is marked as religion. The difference is really not where we might think it is. And it continues to serve purposes we ignore.

One of my favorite examples, by the way, comes from a book called *Exhibiting Religion* by John Burris, which documents the way the World Parliament of Religion was created and looks at the huge exhibits in Chicago and London at the turn of the nineteenth century. Anthropologists had already claimed Native Americans as "cultural" objects, so when religious studies people came along, they expressed no interest in studying Native Americans (already marked as a "culture") and focused instead on those groups said to have a "religion." At some point, then, an entire discourse of resistance is elaborated whereby some communities wished to be recognized as religious communities as well, that is taking the term, appropriating it, and at the same time changing it. But it is a magnificent claim that emerges as a result of new disciplinary encounters: please recognize us as a religion.

So this is what interests me, at least, the way in which the difference between race and religion is articulated, the way it is deployed. And the way in which the history of its becoming has become invisible actually *is* the history of the Semites. It is probably not its only history, but it is one that is crucial in terms of the West. Why did this notion of "Semites" all but disappear? Why is it that what one can say about the Jew can no longer be said about the Arab? What is the dissymmetry, when there used to be so much symmetry, if only for a short century? There are lingering effects, of course: the fact that Jews and Arabs are seen as brothers or cousins, as equally fanatic or bent on destruction. But dissymmetry is now the governing rule of understanding Jews and Arabs. And I want to underscore, once again, the place of Europe in these shifts.

THE JEW, THE ARAB IN EUROPE

How is it that the Arab came to be constructed as an external (and political) enemy of Europe and the Jew, an internal (and theological) enemy? What is the import of this construction, and why, as you suggest, following Schmitt, was it necessary for the being-political, as opposed to, or together with, the being-Christian of Europe, to have an enemy?

I want to reiterate that I am not, by any means, writing the history of the enemy. I know I subtitled the book *A History of the Enemy*, but this was precisely to underscore that there is no such. So I really do not have all the historical answers (or any answer, for that matter); rather, I am looking at the ways of deploying history to begin to account for its nonexistence, its absence.

One of the things that particularly struck me was the early reaction to Islam on the part of Christian theologians, who saw its new adherents as the "new Jews." Some of these theologians simply said, in amazement:

"The Jews are back." Theologically, this was a stunning, almost *unbearable* recognition. To this day, there is no Christian discourse that makes sense of the theological existence of *both* Jew *and* Muslim. In other words—to just isolate the theological, however provisionally and however artificially—I would still say that Christianity does not know how to think both Judaism and Islam in its conception of world history. Is there anything more evident today?

I am not aware of the existence in current Christian theological discourse of any communication between those who advocate a Christian dialogue with Islam and those who speak about Jewish-Christian dialogue. I do not think there is any institutional connection between those two groups within the Christian church. There are Christians—Catholics and Protestants—who advocate a Judeo-Christian dialogue; there are many more Christians who say there should be a Muslim-Christian dialogue. The important thing for now is that those dialogues would need to be conducted at the religious and theological level.

There are those, of course, who argue for the three monotheistic faiths to come together. The possibility of speaking of the three monotheistic religions is first of all a Muslim gesture. "Monotheistic religions" is a Muslim construct that has been adopted—not very successfully—by some Christians and some Jews. That is fine; I am all for dialogue (whatever that means). But such reflections imply a kind of equality or symmetry that seems to me untenable. Moreover, they do not acknowledge the singular anxiety that Christianity bears. As historical revelations, the order of appearance is, I think, particularly unsettling for Christians. Hence, it would be very different to elaborate a Christian position that would make theological sense of both Jews and Muslims (and again suspending the problem of how Muslims are conceived of, racially versus theologically and/or religiously; in other words, it is overdetermined), rather than seek some peaceful, three-way dialogue that does not acknowledge internal tensions and resistances. I wish there were a Christian theologian—and maybe there is one whom I am not aware of—who would attempt to ascertain the responsibility that Christianity bears, or simply the impact (upon "itself") of its relations to the other monotheistic religions (not to speak of the other religions!). Again the absence of a history of Christian Europe in its relation to *both* Jew *and* Arab, Jew *and* Muslim, certainly does not lead me to think that there is some kind of major theological presence that I missed.

Now, to return to the topological aspect of your question. Let me say that I am utterly unconvinced by empirical arguments regarding the "presence" of minorities in the midst of the dominant Christian population. Would anyone want to suggest that the concern about demons, as opposed to the concern about witches, has anything to do with the empirical presence of either? Clearly, there are overdetermined factors that need to be studied before relying on alleged facts of whatever kind. For my part, aside from asserting that the division between theological enemy (the Jew) and political enemy (the Arab) also happens to replicate the exhausted, misleading, and mistaken commonplace that locates Islam outside of Europe and the Jews within it (while recounting a history that often sought to exteriorize, or simply expel, Jews out of Europe, while trying—still trying, as if it meant anything, aside from replicating old patterns of violence—to prevent Islam's "entry" into it), I would only venture to suggest that we look at it as a matter of intimacy. It took some time, there were ups and down, but Christian Europe appeared to have made sense of the Jews (for the better and for the worse), enabling a certain phantasmatic intimacy. Such is much harder to assert regarding Islam, let alone the Arabs (recall that these names are themselves shifty signifiers, only links in a longer chain of names, multiple and changing sites of anxiety). It was thus easier, it remains easier, to see Islam as distant, as if engaging it, acknowledging it, were a matter of contingency (whereas some would still argue that the relation to the Jews and to Judaism was a necessity, a theological one). But this is just a suggestion. Obviously, historical studies would have to attend to different periods, different contexts in order to account for such strange continuities and ruptures. As I said, the history of Europe's relation to both Jew and Arab, attending to the interconnectedness of both, remains to be written. But I repeat myself. Forgive me.

You say in your book as well that whereas there has been lots of material published on Jews and Muslims in Christian lands (although significantly less so on the latter), we still await "a study that would engage together, and in a comparative perspective, the image of Jews and Muslims in Europe, as the history, therefore, of Europe." What might such a study illuminate?

At the very least that Christian Europe is not Christian. That it wants very much to be Christian, that it has even managed to convince a whole lot of people that it is (for example, it has convinced Zionists that Jews have no place in Europe, or in the world for that matter—a position that continues to be maintained by some who do live in Europe and elsewhere, anywhere almost except in Israel). But political Zionism emerges precisely at the moment where Theodor Herzl becomes convinced that Jews should not be in Europe. That is what anti-Semites have been saying all along, and Herzl simply affirms their position. But that is not to say that it succeeds, only that it is rhetorically effective and has far-reaching consequences.

Even taking into consideration the persecution of Jews in Europe and the Holocaust, I *still* think it is good—because it is difficult, and politically enriching—that there are Jews, and numerous other minorities, in Europe. Why should there not be? There is absolutely no reason to agree with the claim that Europe makes for itself, more or less vocally, that it should purify itself of any so-called foreign element.

I should also make this clear: right now, it seems to me ludicrous and irresponsible to suggest that Jews are the endangered minority of Europe. If anything, Muslims are, and—why privilege ethnicity and religion?—so are the poor and the unemployed (who may no longer be a minority very soon, at the rate things are going). Staying with our issue, it is truly frightening to consider the number of Muslims there are in Europe and the kind of discourse that passes as permissible in the public sphere against them. I should also point out that there is a dreadful similarity between the way in which Israel *and* Europe speak publicly about their Muslim populations as a "demographic threat." It is incredible, although it remains an absolutely legitimate discourse to maintain. To invoke an illustration I am loath to invoke, think of when Jews were declared a demographic threat, and think of what happens when a state and public personalities (rather than oppressed minorities living in poverty and without prospects for a future) deploy such rhetoric as if this were no problem at all. Or for a major politician, who is not Le Pen, supposedly not a fascist, to say that the inclusion of Turkey into Europe would threaten the integrity of Europe, a statement that was promptly endorsed by the pope, who of course agrees with it! It boggles my naïve mind. Imagine if a major French politician were to say today that the Jews were a demographic threat to Europe. No one says that. Until then, I will not believe in the so-called new anti-Semitism. Such an irresponsible concept!

THE MUSELMANN IN AUSCHWITZ

Primo Levi, among other survivors of the death camps, has talked about the figure of the Muselmann, the Muslim, in Nazi concentration camps. In Levi's words, "This word, Muselmann, I do not know why, was used by the old ones of the camp to describe the weak, the inept, those doomed to selection." The Italian philosopher Giorgio Agamben has commented that, "With a kind of ferocious irony, the Jews knew that they would not die at Auschwitz as Jews." How does your reading of the understanding of Islam in certain canonical/philosophical texts of the Western tradition—Kant, Montesquieu, and Hegel—help us to understand the use of this appellation in the context of the concentration camp?

I started working on the *Muselmann* (a term I translate as "Muslim" since that is what the German was taken to mean, according to countless testimonies) when I wrote the introduction to Derrida's *Acts of Religion*, although at the time I was not quite sure where it was taking me. By the time I read Agamben's *Remnants of Auschwitz*, which had just come out in French (the English translation had not yet appeared), I was really taken with the book and thought that I would have nothing to add. Agamben is after all the first to take Levi seriously on the crucial importance of the Muslim, and to dedicate an entire book to a figure that, though well known in circles familiar with Holocaust literature, has hardly attracted attention or, indeed, any serious reflection.

I subsequently came to suspect that there might be something to add after all, and this for two reasons. The first is that Agamben reinscribes the historical obscurity of the term "Muslim," its opacity and its strangeness. I do not by any means wish to diminish the strangeness, quite the contrary. I just want to say that this strangeness is even *more* extensive because of a combination of visibility and invisibility. What I am arguing is that the use of the term in the context of the camp has a history that can be read on the very surface of major philosophical texts. This all-too-visible history is, however, also marked by its *invisibility*.

The second reason I thought I may have something to add by way of a footnote to Agamben is that, as complex as Agamben's argument is—touching as it does on numerous issues and dimensions of language, of ethics, of politics, and of law—it has in this particular context very little to say about religion or theology. This is particularly surprising to me since it is Agamben who, after Derrida, alerted me to the importance of the theologico-political (think only of *Homo Sacer*, of his analyses of Schmitt and Benjamin, and so forth).

So there were these two factors: the invisible visibility of the term "Muslim," and of its history, the alleged obscurity of its origins, and the absence of religion and theology in the discussion of the term and the phenomenon in Agamben. Agamben suggests, quite tentatively, that *maybe* the use of "Muslim" relied on a medieval stereotype. Primo Levi, on the other hand, said the term might have come into common usage because of the way in which people imagined Muslims praying, or because of bandages around the head. Like Levi, I have found none of the explanations I encountered convincing.

So I wanted to explore this double absence, and from then on it seemed as though I only encountered symptoms as well as potential, if partial, explanations for this absence everywhere. The first was Kant, who says in his most famous statement on the sublime, in the *Critique of Judgment*: "Perhaps the most sublime passage in the Jewish Law is the commandment: Thou shalt not make unto thee any graven image, or any likeness of any thing that is in heaven or on earth, or under the earth, etc. This commandment alone can explain the enthusiasm that the Jewish people in its civilized era felt for its religion when it compared itself with other peoples, or can explain the pride that Mohammedanism inspires."

Some commentators do quote this passage in its entirety, going all the way to the comment about Islam ("Mohammedanism"), but most of them actually interrupt the quote *before* Islam appears. They just stop, so that the whole passage becomes exclusively about Jewish law and about how Kant paradigmatically implicated the Jews in the sublime, which is one of the reasons why Kant can become "Kant the Jew." Peter Gordon pointed out to me that what I am showing is not that there is *just* "Kant the Jew," but also "Kant the Muslim," which I thought was a lovely remark. When you actually look at the context of the *Critique of Judgment*, you realize that Kant is deploying the language that will later enable Hegel, with the help of Montesquieu, to describe the "religions of the sublime," religions which, according to an overwhelming experience (if one can use the term at all), enslave their constituencies and subject individuals to their power.

In this early example of absolute subjection (as theologico-political!), such as Kant articulates it, it is impossible to ignore that Kant offers two moments, two paradigms, that are at once distinct and indissociable. The basic terms, which will then coagulate with Montesquieu—and his elaborations of the Muslim as the ultimate example of the despotic subject—and finally with Hegel, are formulated in Kant. In the book I hope I have succeeded to show this genealogy of sorts, but what I would want to do were I to write it now would be to claim that Hegel (by which I mean Hegel's time, of course) invented the Semites. He invented the Muslim, no doubt, as he provides the clearest and most thorough formulation of what will then be repeated almost verbatim in Auschwitz and in Holocaust literature. But he also invents the Semites. He is the one who basically begins the tradition whereby whatever you say about the Jews you can say about the Muslims (note that Kant does not collapse the two into a barely differentiated unity), and Hegel does this long before Ernest Renan. He also does it before the category of the Semites really gets disseminated. He is writing at the beginning of the nineteenth century, which is just a few decades after the very notion of a distinction between Aryans and Semites is formulated by Herder and by very few others. Hegel has perhaps not been given enough credit (or blame) for this but to my mind it is really an extraordinary moment in the history of Western thought. And again it is no accident that it is found in Hegel. You could attribute a whole lot of things to Hegel, and of course he is not alone, but I think the formulations are truly momentous and revealing.

The argument, then, is that the "religions of the sublime" are a direct consequence of Hegel's learning from Kant, since we know that Kant and Montesquieu were the two intellectual heroes of Hegel. It is on the basis of their work that he wrote much of what he did. The moment in the *Critique of Judgment* quoted above complemented by the new articulation of despotism in Montesquieu and more importantly of the despotic subject—meaning the one who is subjected to the despot—and of Islam being *the* example, or the Muslim being *the* example par excellence of subjugation, all come together in Hegel. He points out that both Jews and Muslims are thoroughly submitted, they are *slaves*. They are slaves to their god. Aside from that, there are differences, yes. One can compare Islam, Christianity, and Judaism, and there are slight differences, political here, more or less political there. But for the most part, this is what it is, and there is much more similarity between Judaism and Islam than between either and Christianity (this is something that the German-Jewish philosopher Franz Rosenzweig understood well and opposed explicitly). It is critical that the terms of that submission are precisely those that describe the Muslim in Auschwitz.

I presented this material at a conference in France, after which a kind woman, whose name I unfortunately forget, approached me. She told me that she was French but her mother was German and had grown up and gone to school in Germany in the 1930s. This woman had called her mother after having heard my talk, and in response her mother had read out to her the words of a song:

K-a-f-f-e-e
K-a-f-f-e-e,
trink nicht so viel kaffee!
Nicht für Kinder ist der türkentrank
schwächt die Nerven, macht dich blaß lassen und krank.
Sei doch kein Muselmann,
der ihn nicht lassen kann!
C-o-f-f-e-e
C-o-f-f-e-e,
Don't drink so much coffee!
The Turk's drink is not for children,
It weakens the nerves and makes you pale and sick.
Don't be a Muslim
Who can't help it!

This is like a *contines pour enfants*; a children's song that people still learn, as it turns out. I have since met young German people who know that song and I am told it also appears in an opera.

The figure of the powerless, of extreme weakness and subjection, is not shrouded in mystery: coffee will make you *weak*, it will make you into a Muslim, a *Muselmann*. Here the image of Islam in the West is both that it is a political threat and that it is a feminizing threat, a weakness. *They* are weak, and they make *us* weak. Coffee was one of the sites of that Christian anxiety, dating at least from the attempts by the Ottoman Empire ("the Turk") to invade Venice, Vienna, Europe, in short. At some point, though, Christian Europe realizes that the threat may not be as large as initially anticipated. Historians will know this better than I, but if I recall, the battle of Lepanto, and the failure of the Ottoman fleet to invade Venice signals this turn downward in the fear of "the Turk." Here, by the way, is another instance of a strange phrase concerning which I looked but could not find a history. The Ottoman Empire will, in the nineteenth century, be referred to as "the sick man of Europe." This profoundly disturbing and evocative figure, said to emerge after the War of Crimea, seems to me to resonate profoundly with the Muslim, for what is he if not the sick man of Europe? You can do a Google search on the sick man of Europe and find enormous amounts of material. It is simply everywhere. Every Ottoman specialist knows it.

There are thus numerous traces, all of which can be found and followed, read and interpreted, that suggest possible venues for a genealogy of the Muslims of Auschwitz. These traces are both visible and invisible on the surface of the modern philosophical tradition, in children's songs, and in nineteenth- and twentieth-century popular culture. Nothing here diminishes the mystery that the Muslim is, its dreadful paradigmatic dimension. Yet, its genealogy, essentially related to Jews and Arabs as they appear at crucial moments of its articulation in and by Europe, is, it seems to me, less obscure.

The sick man of Europe is like the Muslim: there is no one who knows anything about Holocaust literature or about Holocaust history who does not know about the Muslim. That is the horrifying beauty of it all. It is the most manifest, and yet also the most invisible. Almost *everybody* I talked to tells me, "I have always wondered why the term *Muselmann* was used." It is just everywhere, and yet there has been no explanation for it. It is, as I said, quite horrifying.

In the book I also write about how in Hebrew the term "Muslim" is not translated but rather transliterated (something that could be rendered as *muzelmann*, quite distinct therefore from *muslemi*, i.e., "Muslim," in modern Hebrew). I do not mention the following anecdote in the book, but I had an Israeli student with whom I went over this material in a class on Holocaust literature. After I spoke to her about the Muslims of Auschwitz, she recognized the term and said to her grandfather, himself a survivor of Auschwitz, "Grandfather, you have always spoken with me about the *Muselmann*, but you never told me that the word *Muselmann* means *Muslim*." She later told me that her grandfather flew into a rage such that she had never seen him in before. He adamantly insisted that this was not the case, that it is not what the word meant, that it *never* meant that. It is both tragic and even comic that one could claim that a word *is not* a word, not *that* word. Even in English one finds antiquated spellings of "Mussulman" or "Musselman" for the word "Muslim." But I am not making an etymological argument. I am merely saying that the way the term functioned followed from previous usage, in very different yet related contexts. In Auschwitz it functioned repeatedly by way of pointing to a similarity between certain peoples in the camp and Arabs praying. But how was this "recognition" possible? And why the popularity, the massive dissemination, of the term after the end of the war? When Primo Levi says that "Muslim" is another term like "Canada" or "Mexico" (names given to certain buildings in the camp) that has absolutely no recognizable referential value, or that its connotations have nothing to do with its usage in other contexts, it is simply striking and, to my mind, mistaken.

Of course words function outside of their context, but the fact is that something of the common usage remains or is reinscribed. So that when people say "Canada," it may be a singular name, but it is also overdetermined, culturally and discursively, if you will. The building where all the belongings of the dead were gathered and where it was actually (if only relatively) better to work has nothing to do with Canada, per se, and yet it was Canada that was thereby imagined as a place of plenty, toward which one could dream and, if one survived, escape after the war. And people did. And comparable things can be said of "Mexico," which is where they stored blankets that had stripes that reminded people of the traditional cloth of Mexico.

This is the culture of stereotypes. If one says to a little boy, "You throw like a girl," the question is: What enables the "recognition" of a "girl" in this boy? What are the conditions that make possible such a slur? It is not because a girl "really" throws like a girl; it is because people think that they can recognize in a bad throw a *girlish* throw. This is all I am asking: How did that term—even if that is not what it meant to people—come to function? How did that recognition become possible? How could people say, "This looks to me like a Muslim"? When you have a song that says that a Muslim is weak and pale and submissive and can't help it, and this understanding is ubiquitous in the whole discourse of modern Western philosophy, it becomes no less surprising, but perhaps less opaque.

It is not important that individual people know or endorse what its origins might be (think of the verb "to Jew" in English—would anyone claim that it is not a racial slur if used in a context where Jews are not present, not intended, not known? Or if people do not know, not consciously, that it has anything to do with Jews?). It may well be the case that my student's grandfather did not know, and still does not know, but then why fly into a rage? It is not simply because of a mistake; it is far more loaded than that. So the stakes are enormous, absolutely *enormous*, in denying that there could be any parallel, that the Muslim is alive, against all odds, and *still* dying, in Israel and Palestine. That thought, I would argue, is simply unthinkable, and more: *unbearable*.

THE PROJECT OF ZIONISM

What seems to be interesting to you about Franz Rosenzweig's Star of Redemption *is the way in which he articulates a conception of the enemy through his discussion of war. How does this relate to the way he understands the place of holy war (as opposed to, and together with, political war) in the Abrahamic religions?*

I have to make one point about Rosenzweig before I say anything further. In an oral presentation of the material I have on him, I argued that his relation to Islam must be treated in the same way, and as exclusively, as Heidegger's relation to the Jews (in other words, Heidegger's relation to Nazism). Someone asked how I could draw such an analogy since Rosenzweig never said that Islam should be eradicated, or that Muslims should be exterminated. I reminded them that Heidegger had also never said that Judaism should disappear from the face of the earth or that Jews should face extermination. I do believe that the philosophical problem, the problem of reading, the hermeneutical and rhetorical problems of Rosenzweig and Heidegger are absolutely comparable. In a more informed discussion, Peter Gordon has shown the convergence between the two thinkers. I merely propose a parallel, if marginal, venue on the matter.

I should say that, aside from one and a half articles, almost nothing has been said about Rosenzweig and Islam, which is quite extraordinary (this will change, I hope, thanks to the work of Gesine Palmer and Yossef Schwartz). He is probably one of the most difficult philosophers, but he is certainly not the least written on. A whole lot of people have written about him, even though he is very difficult, and yet virtually no one has commented, in a serious or extended way, on his relation to Islam.

The Star, as Rosenzweig articulates the figure, provides a great image and summary of what is a very architectural argument. To put it simply, he proposes three kinds of subjects: the theological subject or the theological community, that is, Judaism; the theological-political community, that is, Christianity; and the political community, that is, Islam. Each one of these subjects has a particular relationship to war. So the theological subject, Judaism, he says, knows only political war. In other words, when Judaism looks at any war it only sees a *political* war. One reason for this is that, for Rosenzweig, Judaism is outside of history so when it looks at anything that is happening in history, it can only see history, which is irrelevant to it. So the theological subject looks at war as political. The theological-political subject, Christianity, does not know the difference between political and holy war, so it actually does not know how to differentiate between the two. Finally, the political subject, the one that Rosenzweig denies religiosity to, is Islam, and it knows only holy war. The figure of the Star, as he articulates it, is magnificent in the mechanistic way in which it all works.

Rosenzweig is interested in the becoming-theological of the political community or, more accurately, the becoming fully theological of the theological-political community. But he ends up having no interest in what happens to the political community, which is why Islam does not appear in the last book of *The Star*. Rosenzweig was also very Hegelian in a sense, if also anti-Hegelian, and the figures that he deploys from the beginning of the book get *aufgehoben*, sublated, in one way or another in the continuation of the book. But like Antigone in Hegel, which undergoes no *Aufhebung*, no sublation, and who just disappears, Islam also simply disappears from Rosenzweig's argument, and that is what I take to be a philosophical problem. At this level, as my revered teacher Amos Funkenstein has shown, Rosenzweig brilliantly embodies a certain culmination of Christian theology.

What is fascinating in all of this is that Rosenzweig was known to be anti-Zionist. One could say that unfortunately there came a point where no Jewish position—even anti-Zionist—could actually be anything if not determined by Zionism. That is a very long statement to unpack (not to mention, a somehow depressing one), but I will just leave it at that for now. I think it is crucial that even though he was known as an anti-Zionist, there is still a fundamental congruence between what Rosenzweig said and what ends up happening in Israel and Palestine. Again, I am merely arguing that lines of continuity (and rupture) need to be explored, in terms that have yet to sufficiently coagulate.

The alliance between the Christian fundamentalists in the United States and Israeli Zionists would suggest a mutation in the present geopolitical configuration from the discursive terrain that you explore in your book.

My comment on this issue would be the following: there has been absolutely no change on that front. I mean by this that there is nothing new at all. The simplest, and probably the more provocative, way of putting it is that Israel, as a theologico-political project, is the clear continuation of Western Christendom's relation to Islam.

I believe I am, as one says in French, weighing my words, *je pèse mes mots*. The argument I want to make is that it is absolutely essential to continue to insist on the colonial dimension of Zionism, and colonial in the strict sense, absolutely. The claim that there was no colonial basis for Israel is ludicrous. People were citizens of countries and were acting on behalf of Western powers, and Western powers understood this very well. As did Herzl, of course, and others.

So Israel is absolutely a colonial enterprise, a colonial settler state, to be precise. But Israel is also something other than that. This is not to say that it is therefore better or that the state of Israel should be exonerated for what it has done and is doing more than ever to the Palestinians. Rather, I wish to underscore that there are sources and reasons for the phenomenon that is modern Zionism, sources and reasons that *precede* colonialism and that continue to affect and possibly govern, if subterraneously, events and processes in Israel/Palestine as well as in Europe and the United States. The claim that Western Christendom or that the West, Europe, even the United States were solving their Jewish question by exporting it to the Middle East is, of course, quite accurate, but not to consider that they were also exporting their *Arab* problem is, it seems to me, misleading and quite dangerous. It is not just because a group of Jewish or Zionist organizations insisted on going to Palestine (after some struggle as to which "empty land" could be considered as well) that the state of Israel was founded. This was not a peaceful project, as we know, since some people wanted to go elsewhere, and the colonial project was such that they were, in fact, considering Uganda, *or* Argentina, *or* Palestine. So it was not just that the Zionist movement simply made the decision. It certainly did not have that kind of power at the time.

What is more or at least equally important is that Europe has also been dealing with a Muslim question (which is to say, as well, an Arab question, with the slides between names, and because the slide is also between religion and ethnicity, between religion and race), and to ignore this is in fact to reinscribe the enforced vanishing of the Arab and of the Muslim in and from Europe. It is to repeat what Giscard d'Estaing [who said that Turkey's entry into the European Union would be "the end of Europe"] and the pope appear to want to do historically. It is false, and it is wrong. Forget medieval influences and the role of Arabic culture in "transmitting" Greek culture. What I am talking about is a constant, if changing, mode of presence and a lengthy series of imaginary effects, and much more than imaginary, in and on Europe, on a continuous basis, from the seventh century all the way to the twenty-first. There is no moment when Europe is not concerned, occupied, at war, propagandizing, writing, thinking, worrying, admiring, loving, hating the Arab, the Muslim, the Turk, the Saracen, the Agarene, the Moor. There is no single moment in history since the seventh century when someone can tell me that in Western Europe there is not a concern that is, in one way or another, determining of Western culture, music, art, politics, religion, everything. Would someone want to tell me that it is just a Jewish matter that is being exported to the Middle East? Absolutely not. Why, then, specifically, to Palestine? Why did the Western powers want and agree with the destruction of Palestine for the benefit of Israel? Why to the "Holy Land"?

The question must be asked, and the answer must engage "the Muslim question." For to ignore this question is to renew and increase the invisibility of the Christian role in the prehistory and the history of colonialism and postcolonialism. The pope, to take a random example, has not exactly been a peaceful mediator of anything here. No pope has been and no Western power has been. There is no mediation. There is rather an extreme investment in the continuation of the war of Israel against Palestine, that is to say, in maintaining the conditions that make this war possible. I say this, and I include Europe, even though Europe is to some extent more progressive in this respect, certainly more than the United States (mind you, that is not hard), but I do think there is an investment, economic and psychic, in maintaining the enmity. It is after all perfect from a Christian perspective: the Jews and the Muslims are fighting each other, and God knows what it is about. Who can understand these people anyway? That would be the more "tolerant" and relentlessly symmetric statement: well, they are *all* crazy. I am absolutely against any such symmetry, but I am also more and more against any assertion that Christian, Western powers are just like big brothers trying to manage irreconcilable enemies.

On a related matter, somewhat anecdotally, I did consider another cover for the book, which I had shown in some lectures. I was not sure I would like the cover as it now appears, but Janet Wood did a wonderful job, with which I was extremely happy. I was surprised I liked it because I did not want to provide a face, to unsettle and confirm all kinds of expectations. In the end, it is precisely the vanishing of the face and its indeterminability as it appears on the cover that appeals to me so much.

But the image that I had, which would have run the risk of turning the book into some kind of comic book, was a photograph of the pope visiting the Holy Land a few years ago. It was in *Time* magazine (so it probably would have been too much trouble to get anyway in terms of copyright and so forth). On the photograph, the pope appears wearing his full regalia, all white, shiny-white, and on either side he has one of the chief rabbis and a Muslim cleric who was nominated by Arafat (the actual Mufti of Jerusalem declined to attend). And the rabbi and the cleric look *exactly the same*: they are both wearing European dark suits, ties, white shirts, and they both have a salt-and-pepper beard. The only thing that is slightly different is the headdress: the rabbi has a more European hat, whereas the Muslim has a kind of turban, but you can scarcely see that in the picture.

What is fantastic about this is that you could more or less substitute one for the other without too much trouble. I am not sure how observant, in both senses of the term, people have been of the distinction. What is particularly striking, however, is the pope, who sits all in white in the middle, holding his head as if in great suffering (the elderly John Paul II has been quite sick for a number of years). In the photograph, at any rate, he is surrounded by the Jew and the Arab, and he simply cannot take it. And such is the theological predicament of Christianity: the Jew, and the Muslim, and what of the Christian then? A hyphen in between? How is that possible? And there are one billion Muslims? They *succeeded* the Christians? That is why Christianity had to maintain for so long that Islam was not a religion, not even a theological aberration. How could a religion come about and succeed after Jesus? That makes no sense, even if you think of a Second Coming. But another *religion*?

Of course the pope is not really holding his head because of any theological predicament. The structure of the image does perfectly replicate the well-known pictures of a big, *white* brother in between the two dark people who cannot get along. As if the big, white brother was not also *separating*, and *keeping apart*: it is Carter between Begin and Sadat, and it is Clinton between Rabin and Arafat. I cannot endorse those moments. Nor am I saying that if you let everybody just *talk*, everything will be all right.

So to return to the question, there is nothing new about the alliance between Zionism and Christian fundamentalism. It is somewhat new only in terms of the way in which Israel has been more blatant about it. I was reading an article recently that described the last visit of the Israeli minister of tourism to the United States. During this visit, the minister of tourism—one of many outspoken fascists in the Israeli government, but one who is particularly blatant from one of the extreme right-wing parties—for the first time never even contacted any Jewish organization but went straight and only for Christian evangelists.

So in terms of policy subtleties (or lack thereof), this may be new, but at a fundamental, structural level, there is nothing new. Of course there is an alliance. And I am not just talking about eschatological issues, I am talking about a fundamental congruence of understanding concerning

Islam in the world, on the need to fight it, and to establish dissymmetries, and with Jews and Jewish Israelis willingly taking up that fight. It is beautifully choreographed, though I do not think there is one choreographer, not even one team. Things are much more disseminated.

THE PROBLEM OF UNIVERSALISM

How is the question of the theologico-political related to the question of universalism, and all the values that it concretely names: democracy, human rights, equality, and so on?

I will just give you a preview, if I may, of the article I have just completed and which I mentioned to you earlier, entitled "The Semitic Hypothesis." For this article, I decided to have a summary in which one of the phrases I included, somewhat provocatively, was "Secularism is Orientalism." I know I have more work to do on this issue, to continue reading Talal Asad's wonderful *Formations of the Secular*, for example. I therefore do not want to reduce the secular to Orientalism, but I think at this point it is *extremely* important to understand that the discourse on secularism is fundamentally related to *anti-Islam*. Nor is this, by the way, a new development. It is rather, as we saw with Hegel, constitutive of the newly found religiosity of the East that occurred at the same time as the West was "losing its religion." I have yet to hear a convincing argument, at any rate, that would enable me to think that some kind of politically forward move would not be predicated on dictating to one billion people (and that is a conservative estimate) that they have to let go. Which, aside from the ludicrous dimension of it all, is just truly preposterous as a judgment on . . . but on what exactly? Islam as a whole? History? The world?

This is related to what I was saying earlier about secularization being a fundamental change *within* Christianity and therefore, still about Christianity. It is not just that secularization is not something that simply exports itself (nor for that matter was Christianity—read Ines Zupanov on Jesuits in India) as if it were a product or a recipe (although the attempt does have extensive and often devastating consequences—I wish we could discuss the history, but also current size and impact, of the numerous Christian missionary movements when speaking of "globalization"), nor do I mean to deny that there has been a generalization of the use of religion. It would be silly not to recognize that Islamists are now (and they are very much of the *now*) claiming a religious perspective, and that they are calling it religion—which in itself is incredible, given the Latin (which is to say, Christian) as well as modern histories of the term that Derrida talks about in *Faith and Knowledge*. I simply want to underscore the cultural and political effects of a massive translation. The translation, for example, of *din* into "religion," comparable at least to the translation of *adab* into "letters," is simply momentous and reorganizes knowledges, communities, and more. To think that what is happening (or worse, that what should happen) is "secularization" is simply obfuscating. And it is much more complicated than the decision to use a certain word (there are, of course, other processes at work, the usual suspects: colonialism, capitalism, and so forth), yet I would not minimize at all the impact of linguistic changes.

We are desperately in need of another kind of political imagination if all we can come up with at the moment is that no civil society can be constituted with the presence of religion in the public sphere (keeping in mind the continuous identification of Islam as that religion). We also have to go beyond the narrative that now construes Islam (and other "religions") as a "way of life," which then became a religion. There are perhaps terms that may enable descriptions of the changes that have occurred and that occur still, but issues of translation loom large, so much so that the very possibility of speaking of change is dependent on them. The other thing to recognize is that, for the most part, the discourse on secularization, the discourse on modernization and on democracy in the Middle East—itself predicated on some kind of secularization—is conducted for the most part by people who have never learned a word of Arabic or of any language of the area. Knowledge (if we can call it that), and perhaps more precisely "expertise," knows no bounds to its lack of humility.

I have to say that if some expert wants to tell me what *exactly* is wrong with the world, what needs to be changed in order to solve all or most current problems, I have no objection to the "wrong" being identified as "religion," if that is what pleases such expert. I am, however, fascinated by this move: how anybody could claim such a thing regarding what is wrong with the world *in general* and where the solution lies *precisely*. Marx at least was modest enough, for the most part, to limit himself to Western culture. I know he made statements that could disrupt that assertion, but for the most part he was talking about the way in which Western society functioned. So was Foucault. I am sure there is much I still do not understand here, but I do see that as a sign of modesty rather than as sheer ethnocentrism. There has to be some recognition of the fact that one cannot speak about everything especially when one does not know even the rudiments of the *languages* of the area of which one speaks. I am thus not particularly keen on trashing anything religious or on blaming religion more than politics or human psychology or anything else in areas where I can only hope to educate myself a little.

There is, in fact, a level at which I simply lack all understanding. Can anyone seriously claim that the problem with Islamic countries is *Islam*? Well, maybe the problem with countries is that they are countries. Or maybe the problem is that there are people (all such suggestions have been made by respectable people). I do not know what the problem is, so I am not going to advocate a solution that is so *massive* in its claims as to propose the wholesale transformation of entire cultures, societies, and polities. Arguably, an extensive part of said transformation has *already* occurred, but the argument goes both ways. It is already a given that a number of women are wearing a veil in western Europe. Let us concede that this may be described as a change. Would one then go on to claim that French culture will stand or fall on either its acceptance of or resistance to such change? The transformation of societies was not done by fiat in the West. It is not as if someone stood up at some point and simply said, "Let's have a civil society," and then it was created ex nihilo. As if it came with a recipe.

Rather than making calls for abandoning religion, or relegating it to the private sphere, or displacing it, or whatever it is that people are advocating, we might think instead of the ways in which religion has already changed, and the ways in which it is helping people *live* (and, like much else, generously helping them die, although I am doubtful it is the main or only culprit on that front). I am not trying to cleanse religion from responsibility. I am just asking whether it is right to consider it as *more* responsible than other elements of human history. As Levinas taught us, it is a difficult thing to attribute responsibility. It is, in fact, highly irresponsible, unless one utters the only responsible assertion, in the first person: I am responsible.

To advocate an abandonment of religion, at any rate, is to my naïve mind the same thing as to suggest that the aesthetic (that other modern invention) should be abandoned, that it is such a problematic thing that we should altogether drop the distinction between the ugly and the beautiful. Never go to a museum again or admire the face of a child. Like art and beauty, and probably more so, religion is still understood in highly contained ways, so construed in simple, oppositional terms such as human and divine, and so on. And perhaps we should in fact abandon that distinction, and forget these terms, human and divine. But who am I to say?

I do not mean to diminish the importance of very serious thinkers who have worked on such questions and issues. I am not arguing that what they say is irrelevant. It is just that my own general ignorance would make such a gesture preposterous, even if it were a gesture of agreement with these illustrious thinkers, all of whom I respect greatly. It just seems to involve a simplification of what religion is in *every* case, and, at the very least, of the history of religion and secularism.

With regard to questions about human rights and democracy, there are people who insist on the endogenous or local reasons for whatever happens in much of the Third World. But really, so many of the dictatorial regimes in the world, and by implication most of the dictatorial regimes in the Middle East, have been put in place by American policy, or are an effect of American policy. The United States has an active military presence in more than a hundred countries.

I do not mean to be deterministic by suggesting that everything comes down to military and economic power. Whatever other reasons there might be for the situation, the fact is that the obstacles thus constituted to the development of indigenous causes and processes are so small that I fail to see the point in apportioning blame that way. That is why I am Eurocentric, if you will; that is why I am only talking about Europe and the West because economic and military power is so dominantly with the West, with the Christian West. That said, I do not talk about economic and military power because I do not know them, and because I have been trained to think that a lot of important things occur at a different level, mostly rhetorical, and indeed "textual." The embodiments of policies today have antecedents that are hundreds and hundreds of years old. I do not know why, but they are still working their effects, whether it is because people are still reading the Bible, because Aquinas is not dead, because Luther is not dead, because St. Paul is not dead (or perhaps they are indeed, which only makes them more powerful, as Freud taught us), and because the Crusades are quite certainly not over. Has the West recovered from them? Has it really? After all, if the first Gulf War was meant to recover from the Vietnam War, who knows what will be needed for the loss of Jerusalem?

INTRODUCTION I

1. See also Nermeen Shaikh, "Interrogating Charity and the Benevolence of Empire," *Development* 50 (2) (June 2007).

FOUR I JOSEPH STIGLITZ

1. This eighth agreement was the result of negotiations called the Uruguay Round because the negotiations began in 1986 in Punta del Este, Uruguay. The round was concluded in Marrakech on December 15, 1993, when 117 countries joined in this trade liberalization agreement. The World Trade Organization (WTO) came into formal effect on January 1, 1995, and over 100 countries had signed on by July. One provision of the agreement entailed converting the GATT into the WTO. Joseph Stiglitz, *Globalization and Its Discontents* (New York: W. W. Norton, 2002), p. 7.

2. Stiglitz, *Globalization and Its Discontents*, p. 7.

3. Ibid., p. 8.

4. In the same editorial in the *Financial Times*, Wolfowitz argued that "It is trade, not aid, that holds the key to creating jobs and raising incomes. It is trade that will allow poor countries to generate growth; forgiving debt alone will not do that." He went on to say that there is a "moral argument" to support better terms of trade for the developing world: "How can we justify spending $280 billion on support to agricultural producers in developed countries—nearly the total gross domestic product of Africa and four times the total amount of overseas aid? How can we justify imposing barriers on the poorest 2 billion people that are twice as

high as on everyone else? How can we accept a system in which Africa's share of world exports has fallen from 3.5 percent to less than 2 percent in the past 30 years?" He concluded by insisting that the United States needs to do more to cut its subsidies "substantially" and that industrialized nations must give up their subsidies and other barriers to free trade. Paul Wolfowitz, "Everyone Must Do More for Doha to Succeed," *Financial Times* (October 24, 2005), A13.

TEN I SABA MAHMOOD

1. Saba Mahmood, "Questioning Liberalism, Too: A Response to 'Islam and the Challenge of Democracy,'" *Boston Review: A Political and Literary Forum* (April/May 2003). Reprinted as "Is Liberalism Islam's Only Answer?" in *Islam and the Challenge to Democracy*, edited by Joshua Cohen and Deborah Chasman (Princeton: Princeton University Press, 2004).

2. Here I am going to limit my remarks to oppositional Islamist movements rather than Islamic groups that have come to power in places like Iran or the Sudan.

3. Saba Mahmood, "Secularism, Hermeneutics, Empire: The Politics of Islamic Reformation," *Public Culture* 18.2 (2006): 326–327.

4. See, for example, two reports recently issued by the Rand Corporation. The first, commissioned by the U.S. government and written by Cheryl Benard, is *Civil Democratic Islam: Partners, Resources, Strategies* (Pittsburgh: Rand Corporation, 2003). The second, commissioned by the U.S. Air Force, was written by Angel Rabasa et al., *Muslim World After 9/11* (Pittsburgh: Rand Corporation, 2004).

5. Anthony Shadid, "Egypt Shuts Door on Dissent as U.S. Officials Back Away," *Washington Post*, March 19, 2007, A01.

6. Charles Hirschkind, "What Is Political Islam?" *Middle East Research Project* 27(1997):12–14. http://www.merip.org/mer/mer205/hirschk.htm.

7. Charles Hirschkind and Saba Mahmood, "Feminism, the Taliban, and Politics of Counter-Insurgency," *Anthropological Quarterly* 75.2 (2002):339–354.

8. Human Rights Watch, "'We Want to Live as Humans': Repression of Women and Girls in Western Afghanistan," *Human Rights Watch Reports* 14:11 (C) (2002). http://www.hrw.org/reports/2002/afghnwmn1202. Also see Amnesty International, "Afghanistan: 'No One Listens to Us and No One Treats Us as Human Beings': Justice Denied to Women," *Amnesty International Reports*, AI Index: ASA (11/023/2003) (2003). http://www.web.amnesty.org/library/index/engasa110232003.

9. Nawal al-Saadawi, "An Unholy Alliance," *Al-Ahram Weekly*, January 22, 2004. http://weekly.ahram.org.eg/2004/674/op2.htm.

ELEVEN I GAYATRI CHAKRAVORTY SPIVAK

1. David Rieff, "The Way We Live Now; A Nation of Pre-emptors?" *New York Times Magazine* (January 15, 2006).

2. Gayatri Chakravorty Spivak, "Righting Wrongs," *South Atlantic Quarterly* 103 (2/3) (Spring/Summer 2004).

3. Gayatri Chakravorty Spivak, *Imperatives to Re-Imagine the Planet / Imperative zur Neuerfindung des Planeten*, herausgegeben von Willi Goetschel (Vienna: Passagen Verlag, 1999).

4. Gayatri Chakravorty Spivak, "Remembering Derrida," *Radical Philosophy* (January–February 2005).

5. The story appears in Mahasweta Devi, *Imaginary Maps*, trans. Gayatri Chakravorty Spivak (New York: Routledge, 1995).

6. For an elaboration of the argument to italicize the English words in the original, see the "Translator's Note" in *Imaginary Maps* (p. xxxi): "The language of the practical everyday life of all classes (including the subaltern), profoundly marked by English, mimes the historical sedimentation of colonialism by the degree to which the words and phrases have been lexicalized, and the degree to which, therefore, they exist 'independently' in Bengali. By contrast, the culturalist intellectual—a group addressed in the 'Translator's Preface'—and the State can affect a 'pure' idiom, which disguises *neo*colonialist collaboration."

7. Nivedita Menon, *Recovering Subversion: Feminist Politics Beyond the Law* (Chicago: University of Illinois Press, 2004), p. x.

8. Established in 1901 by Nobel Laureate Rabindranath Tagore in West Bengal.

LILA ABU-LUGHOD is professor of anthropology and women's and gender studies at Columbia University. She has authored and edited several books, including *Dramas of Nationhood* (University of Chicago Press, 2005), *Writing Women's Worlds: Bedouin Stories* (University of California Press, 1993), *Remaking Women: Feminism and Modernity in the Middle East* (Princeton University Press, 1998), and *Veiled Sentiments: Honor and Poetry in a Bedouin Society* (University of California Press, 1986).

GIL ANIDJAR is associate professor in the Department of Middle East and Asian Languages and Cultures at Columbia University. His next book, entitled *Semites: Race, Religion, Literature*, is forthcoming from Stanford University Press.

TALAL ASAD is distinguished professor of anthropology at the City University of New York Graduate Center. He is the author of *Genealogies of Religion: Discipline and Reasons of Power in Christianity and Islam* (Johns Hopkins University Press, 1993) and *Formations of the Secular: Christianity, Islam, Modernity* (Stanford University Press, 2003). His book *On Suicide Bombing* is forthcoming from Columbia University Press.

PARTHA CHATTERJEE is director of the Centre for Studies in Social Sciences, Calcutta, and professor of anthropology at Columbia University. His books include *The Politics of the Governed* (Columbia University Press, 2004), *A Princely Impostor?* (Princeton University Press, 2002), *Partha Chatterjee Omnibus* (Oxford University Press, 1999), *A Possible India* (Oxford University Press, 1997), *The Nation and Its Fragments* (Princeton University Press, 1993), and *Nationalist Thought and the Colonial World* (Zed Books, 1986).

SHIRIN EBADI, an Iranian lawyer and human rights activist, was awarded the Nobel Peace Prize in 2003. She has published extensively in Persian and has led efforts to change Iran's discriminatory laws against women, to provide more protection for street children, and to free those detained for expressing their opposition to the government.

ANATOL LIEVEN is senior research fellow at the New America Foundation in Washington, DC. In the 1980s and 1990s he worked as a British journalist in South Asia and the former Soviet Union. He writes on a range of security and international affairs issues and has published in a number of journals and newspapers, among them the *Financial Times*, the *London Review of Books*, the *Nation*, and the *International Herald Tribune*. His latest book is *Ethical Realism: A Vision for America's Role in the World*. Coauthored with John Hulsman, it was published by Pantheon in 2006.

SABA MAHMOOD is associate professor of anthropology at the University of California, Berkeley. She is the author of *Politics of Piety: The Islamic Revival and the Feminist Subject* (Princeton University Press, 2005). She is currently working on a comparative history of secularism in Egypt and Lebanon.

MAHMOOD MAMDANI is from Kampala, Uganda. He received his Ph.D. in government from Harvard University. He is currently Herbert Lehman Professor of Government in the Departments of Anthropology, Political Science, and International and Public Affairs at Columbia University, where he was also director of the Institute of African Studies from 1999 to 2004. He has taught at the University of Dar-es-Salaam (1973–79), Makerere University (1980–93), and University of Cape Town (1996–99) and was the founding director of the Centre for Basic Research in Kampala, Uganda (1987–96). Mamdani is the author of *Good Muslim, Bad Muslim: America, the Cold War and the Origins of Terror* (Pantheon, 2004), *When Victims Become Killers: Colonialism, Nativism and Genocide in Rwanda* (Princeton University Press, 2001), *Citizen and Subject: Contemporary Africa and the Legacy of Late Colonialism* (Princeton University Press, 1996), and ten other books. *Citizen and Subject* was recognized as "one of Africa's 100 best books of the 20th century" in Cape Town in 2003 and was also awarded the Herskovitz Prize of the African Studies Association of the USA for "the best book on Africa published in the English language in 1996." His latest book, *Scholars in the Marketplace: The Dilemmas of Neo-Liberal reform at Makerere University, 1989–2005*, will be published by the Council for the Development of Social Research in Africa (CODESRIA) in 2007. Mahmood Mamdani was president of CODESRIA from 1999 to 2002. In 2001 he was invited to present one of nine papers at the Nobel Peace Prize Centennial Symposium in Oslo. In 2004 he presented one of nine plenary papers at the African Union-organized Global Meeting of Intellectuals from Africa and the African Diaspora in Dakar.

HELENA NORBERG-HODGE is a leading analyst of the impact of the global economy on culture and agriculture worldwide. She is a recipient of the Right Livelihood Award, or the "Alternative Nobel Prize," and the founder/director of the International Society for Ecology and Culture (ISEC). She is author of numerous works, including *Bringing the Food Economy Home* and the inspirational classic *Ancient Futures*, which together with a film by the same title has been translated into forty-seven languages.

SANJAY REDDY is an assistant professor of Economics at Barnard College, Columbia University. His areas of work include development economics, international economics, economics and philosophy, and economics and social theory.

AMARTYA SEN is Lamont University Professor at Harvard University. In 1998 he was awarded the Nobel Prize in Economics. He has taught at Harvard University, Oxford University, Cambridge University, London School of Economics, Delhi University, and other academic institutions. His books have been translated into over thirty languages and include *Identity and Violence* (W. W. Norton, 2006), *The Argumentative Indian* (Farrar, Straus and Giroux, 2005), *Development as Freedom* (Oxford University Press, 1999), *On Ethics and Economics* (Basil Blackwell, 1987), *Poverty and Famines* (Clarendon Press, 1982) and *Collective Choice and Social Welfare* (Elsevier, 1970, 1979).

GAYATRI CHAKRAVORTY SPIVAK is Avalon Foundation Professor in the Humanities at Columbia University. Among her publications are *A Critique of Postcolonial Reason* (Harvard University Press, 1999), *Outside in the Teaching Machine* (Routledge, 1993), *The Post-Colonial Critic* (Routledge, 1990), *In Other Worlds* (Routledge, 1987), *Imaginary Maps* (translation with critical material on the fiction of Bengali writer Mahasweta Devi; Routledge, 1994), and *Of Grammatology* (translation with critical introduction of Jacques Derrida's *De la grammmatologie*; Johns Hopkins University Press, 1977).

JOSEPH STIGLITZ is University Professor at Columbia University. In 2001, he was awarded the Nobel Prize in Economics. He was a member of the Council of Economic Advisers from 1993 to 1995, during the Clinton administration, and served as CEA chairman from 1995 to 1997. He then became chief economist and senior vice-president of the World Bank from 1997 to 2000. He is the author of numerous books, including *Fair Trade for All* (Oxford University Press, 2006), *The Roaring Nineties* (W. W. Norton, 2003), *Globalization and its Discontents* (W. W. Norton, 2002), and *Making Globalization Work* (W. W. Norton, 2006).

Abu-Lughod, Lila, 143–47, 259

Academia. *See* Intellectual class

Ackerman Bruce, 196

Afghanistan, 103, 123–24, 165–66

Africa: Algeria, 156; Angola, 102; Congo (former Zaire), 43, 115; debates over colonial influence, 94–95; Hutu-Tutsi violence, 13, 95; independence of former colonies, 102; Libya, 120; Morocco, 157; Mozambique, 102, 103; Nigeria, 135, 214; Renamo movement, 102, 108; Sub-Saharan, 46, 47

Agamben, Giorgio, 239–40

Agriculture: closed Western markets, 54; commodity price swings, 46–47, 49; destruction of rural marketing opportunities, 21; Western countries' subsidies of, 54

Aid, geopolitical, 47–48; relationship to development, 66

AIDS, 64

Ajayi, Jacob Ade, 94

Algeria, 156

Al-Hibri, Azizah, 215

Al-Qaeda, 122–24

Al-Saadawi, Nawal, 169–70

"American Creed," 109, 111–12, 132–33

American imperialism: advantages of moderate, civilized, rational version, 133–34; as bellicosity after attack or insult, 113–14, 134; benevolent aim of spreading democracy and freedom, 115; dislike of expensive undertakings, 114; with goal of world domination, 121; hypocrisy of imposition of democracy, 116; possibility of seizure of oil producing countries, 135–36; presence welcome in East Asia and Eastern Europe, 134; ruling Third World through indirect rule ("comprador model"), 116–17

American nationalism: advantages of spreading democracy by example, 119; "American Creed," 109, 111–12; chauvinism, fear, contempt, hatred of outsiders, 110; Christian fundamentalists entwined with Israeli Right, Zionists, 128–29, 246, 249; as contradictory and disastrous, 110–11; difficulty of challenging myths, 112

Anglican Church, 159

Angola, 102

Anidjar, Gil, 225–53, 259

Annan, Kofi, 10

Apocalypse, 128–29

Appiah, Anthony, 176, 177

Arab, as term for Muslim, 230–31, 232

Argentina, 58, 61–62

Asad, Talal, 158, 205–24, 250, 259

Asia: and sense of place, 199–200; *See also* East Asia

Asian Financial Crisis of 1997, 60–61
Assad, Hafez al-, 156
Authenticity, aura of, 221–22

Baker, Russell, 131
Baptism, 230
Baritz, Loren, 132
Barry, Christian, 53
Becker, A.L., 185
Benevolence, as colonial, 176, 182–83, 196
Benjamin, Walter, 221–22
Bhaduri, Amit, 198
Bible, 128
Bin Laden, Osama, 99
Birth control, 194–95
Blair, Tony, 126
"Blood-drenched century," 12–13
Bolivia, 58
Boykin, William, 128
BPL ("below the poverty line") demarcation, 92–93
"Breaking of nations" in name of human rights, 178–79
Bretton Woods institutions, 6, 35, 38, 51, 177; *See also* International Monetary Fund; World Bank
Britain: considerations of church/state separation, 159, 206; enablement in India by colonization, 176
Burnside, Craig, 48
Burris, John, 234
Bush (G.W.) administration: advocating preemptive removal of threats, 106, 108; Christian Right in heart of, 206–07, 227; desire to democratize Muslim world, 110; failure to decrease U.S. reliance on oil, 135; fluctuating China policy, 112–13, 115, 122; as fundamentalist, 227; on "good" and "bad" Muslims, 98; Iraq as disaster for, 121–22; media's failure to criticize propaganda by, 129; possibility of attack on Iran's nuclear program, 125–26; possibility of ill-considered ventures, 134; pragmatic Russia policy, 112; promoting cause of "Islamic liberalism," 157; radicals wishing to destroy Chinese Communist state, 124–25; relative pragmatism of, 115; suicidal options for, 134; support for

dictatorial regimes, ignoring human rights violations, 157; targeting Islamic charities and reform groups, 157; turning from actual 9/11 perpetrators to "axis of evil," 123; uninterested in Europe and NATO, 113
Bush, Laura, 144

Call centers, 186
Camdessus, Michel, 6
"Canada" as building in Auschwitz, 243–44
Capital, movement of, 198
Capital market liberalization, 61
CARE, 7
Caribbean, 133, 134
Carter administration, 121
Casanova, Jose, 209
Caste movement, 77–78
Catholic Church, 100, 159, 229–30
Central America, 133, 134
Chalabi, Ahmed, 110, 116
Chatterjee, Partha, 71–93, 192, 259
Chechnya, 125
China: after World War II, 6; Bush's fluctuating policy toward, 112–13, 115, 122; health services compared to India's, 15–16; need for oil, 135; possible responses to Taiwanese independence, 125; praise of, in WDR, 35–36; progress and problems, 15–16; role in IMF governing structure, 56; U.S. radicals wishing to destroy Communist state, 124–25; as victim of modernity, 86, 87
Christianity: absence of dialogue with Islam or Judaism, 236; secularism as change within, 250; *See also* religion
Christian Right (in U.S.): affinity for Jewish religious tradition, 128; entwined with Israeli Right, Zionists, 128–29, 246, 249; furthering Armageddon in support of Israel, 206–07; in heart of Bush administration, 206–07, 227; as political movements, 99, 206–07
CIA, 103
"Civilizing mission," 115
Civil rights movement, 97
Civil society, compared to political society, 88–90

"Class apartheid," 172, 183

Clinton administration, 55, 57–58, 60, 112–13

CO_2 emissions, 20

Cold War: Afghanistan as battlefield between U.S. and Soviets, 166; costs of U.S. victory in, 105–06; giving rise to nonstate terrorism, 96; missed opportunities at conclusion of, 55; terrorism as strategy of U.S., 101–03; Vietnam War, 102, 111, 123, 132

Collateral damage, 101, 220

Collier, Paul, 48

Colonialism: anticolonial struggles for self-rule, and nationalism, 78–85, 149–50; authoritarians replaced by bringers of democracy, 115–16; as chain of displacements through history, 178; Christian missionaries as synonymous with civilizing mission, 210; development of international law, 209; and distribution of present-day advantages/disadvantages, 45; echoes of, in West's impulse to right wrongs, 177; as "enabling violation," 176, 198; encouraging production for trade, 17; epistemic violence of imperialism, 185, 187–88; ideological and institutional texture, 94–95; influence of giant corporations and traders, 19; introducing precepts of liberal political philosophy, 149; neutrality toward native religions and Christian missionaries, 209; religious movements as anticolonial nationalist struggles, 13–14; "saving" native women, 144, 147, 196; Zionism as, 246–47

Columbia University, 174

Commodity price swings, 46–47, 49

Complicity, one's own, being aware of, 183–84

Comprador model, 116–17

Congo (former Zaire), 43, 115

Connolly, William, 214

Consciousness-raising, 174, 175, 184–85, 196

Conscription, 114, 115, 121, 134

Conspiracy theory of Asian Financial Crisis of 1997, 60–61

Consumer lifestyle, 20, 21–22

Contact lenses, 22

Contras, 103, 108

Conversos, 230

Corporations as traders, 19

Cost-of-living estimates, 31

Cromwell, Oliver, 128

Crusades, 253

Cultural literacy, 185

Culture: as basis for identity, 97–98, 99; breakdown with trade, 21–22; compared to religion, 141; ethnic and religions divisions and disempowerment, 23; future seen as narrower, homogenized, U.S.-influenced, 223; identity-based conflict, 22–24; misleading as explanation for terrorism, 107; Western influences privileging European, 21–22

"Culture Talk," 97–98, 107, 108

Currency equivalence, 28–29, 32

Dayaks of Indonesia, 22

Debt repayment: crises of 1980s, 43; debt relief, 53, 65, 66; intergenerational burden of, 43; loans to dictators supported by U.S., 142; of "odious" debts, 44

Deconstruction, 190–91

Democracy: democratization as substitute for strategy in Iraq, 112; democratization myth, 110, 133; disproportionate power of rich, 66; erosion in U.S., 107; Islam viewed as incompatible with, 140–41, 164–65, 212–14; need for debate on models of liberalism, 153–54; problem of U.S.-supported dictatorships, 157, 218, 253; as public reasoning, 9–10; purported ability to manage religious diversity, 152; question of sufficiency to guarantee change, 14–16; rote learning as destructive of, 172, 183; threat of strong, detached executive power, 105; tolerance and pluralism not intrinsic to, 152; U.S. messianistic desire to spread, 109–10, 111

Derrida, Jacques, 226

D'Estaing, Giscard, 247

Development: advantages of countries' experimentation, 41–42; advantages of pluralization, 52; as alibi for exploitation, 194–95; ambiguity of goals, 39–40, 52; centralization of jobs, 24; damaging effects, 18, 19, 24; early concern with human life, 3; as economic growth, 3;

Development (*continued*)
encouraging production for trade, 17; eroding trust and cooperation, 51; income inequalities resulting from, 19, 26; influence of giant corporations and traders, 19; need for analysis of development paradigm, 52; need for independent research on, 36–38; need for institutionalized process of review and support, 42; need for public debates, 25; possibilities for positive change, 25–26, 52–53; problem of technocratic perspective, 40–41; progress and problems, 51–52; relationship with geopolitical aid, 47–48, 66; rural versus urban life, 19–21; small-scale production as unfeasible, 23; sustainability as maximum growth, 195; as systems of destruction, 24; uneven progress across countries and populations, 50–51; urbanization pressures and "slumification," 20–22, 23, 25–26; valuing technology instead of human labor, 23; *See also* Globalization; Human development; Trade
Devi, Mahasweta, 188–90
Diasporics, languages spoken by, 187–88
Dictatorships, 142, 157, 218, 253
Difference, difficulties of analyzing, 226–27
Distributive justice, international issues and debates, 42–44
Dollar, David, 48
"Dominance without hegemony," 75–78
Drèze, Jean, 195

East Asia: economic success without Washington Consensus, 60; IMF and World Bank policies contradictory in, 58; Japan, 135; North Korea, 113, 115; Taiwan, 125; *See also* China; South Asia
Easterly, William, 48
Ebadi, Shirin, 139–42, 260
Economic growth: as measure of progress, 3; theory of, 3; "trickle-down" economics, 59; *See also* Development
Education: advantages for development, 47; corporatizing model of university, 174; as epistemic violence, 187; following Western model, 197; ignorance leading to prejudice, 142; mid-day meals and

school enrollment, 41; producing "class apartheid," 172, 183; questioning Bank's expenditures on universities, 37–38; rote learning as destructive of democracy, 172, 183; user fees recommended by World Bank, 34–35; *See also* Humanities education
Egypt, 117, 156, 157
Eisenhower, Dwight D., 119, 122
El-Fadl, Khaled Abou, 151
Elon, Amos, 127
Employment guarantees, 49–50
"Enabling violation," 176, 198
Enemy, the: as Jew and Arab, 228–30, 235–38; as theological-political, 228–30
Energy resources: decentralizing infrastructures, 26; and geopolitics of oil, 134–36
Enlightenment, the, 163, 181–82
Epistemic violence of imperialism, 185, 187–88
Equality, 11–12, 15, 51–52, 164, 165, 213, 215
Ethnicity and race, 230–35; *See also* Identity politics
Europe: absence of historiography of Jews and Muslims in, 237–38; Britain, 159, 176, 206; Bush's lack of interest in, 112; continuous worry about the Turk, 242, 247–48; enemies as Jews and Arabs, 235–38; France, 169–70, 206, 225, 252; French Islamophobic ban on veil, 169–70; justifications of colonialism, 115; minorities in, 238; Muslim populations seen as demographic threat, 238; pressure on Iran to suspend nuclear program, 126; rethinking identities and values, 111–12; as secular in nineteenth century, 233; as site of theological-political, 229; Spain, 230; treatment of asylum-seekers, 217; *See also* Colonialism
Evil Empire (Reagan's term), 102
Eye color, 21, 22

"False consciousness," 168, 170, 171
Falwell, Jerry, 128
Fanon, Frantz, 96–97
Fashion, tyranny of, 145
Feminism: attire as barometer of feminine consciousness, 168–69; challenges to

assumption of desire for freedom from male domination, 171; difficulty of inserting subaltern woman into history, 192–94; as form of colonial benevolence, 196–98; gender equality as universal human right, 11–12; as ignorant goodwill, 197; Islamic, 146, 147; mobilization in U.S. against Taliban, 165–66; need for challenges to liberal assumptions, 164–65; overlooking U.S. culpability for war and starvation, 166; postcolonial, 150–51; women's equality as concern in India, 15; *See also* Veil/burqa

Feminist Majority, 165–66, 168

Finance capital, 198

Finance ministers and governance of IMF, 56–57

Fisher, Stanley, 6

Foner, Eric, 195

Food supply, 20

France: clinging to secularism, 225; considerations of church/state separation, 206; Islamophobic ban on veil, 169–70, 252

Freedom: choice inadequate as measure of, 169; as individual autonomy, with possible opposition to community, 148, 150; Islamic movement challenging aspects of, 140–41, 164–65, 212–14; need for postcolonial Muslim conceptions of, 151; private property as form of, 149; for women in patriarchal societies, need to question assumptions, 171

Friedman, Thomas, 223

Fulbright, William, 110

Fundamentalism: as Christian phenomenon, 99; as kind of fanaticism, 221; Muslim, erroneously viewed as monolithic block, 156; as Muslim and Hindu nationalism, 95

Funkenstein, Amos, 246

Furedi, Frank, 222

Gandhi, Indira, 74

Gandhi, Mahatma, 11, 78, 79

GATT (General Agreement on Tariffs and Trade), 25

GDP (gross domestic product), 31

Gender equality, 11–12, 15, 215; *See also* Feminism

Genocide, 104–05, 106–07

Glass, Charles, 118

Global Development Network, 37

Globalization: for advancement of living conditions, 9; advancing capitalism, 177; ancient history of global contact, 8–9; continuing pattern of 100–150 years, 88; driven by West with disproportionate share of benefits, 54–55; economic agenda as intervention, 220–21; encouraging production for trade, 18; favoring traders at expense of local producers, 19; as "financialization of the globe," 198–99; influence of global democracy as public reasoning, 9–10; leading to breaking of states, 178–79; minimizing role of governments, maximizing that of free markets, 59–60; need for better division of benefits, 9; need for improved policies, 9; need for viable local economies, 195; problem of inequality of power, 8; as tenet of "Washington Consensus," 59; *See also* Development; Trade

Global poverty estimates: alternative methods for determining, 30–33; Bank's defense of its methodology, 29–30; inadequacy of, 27–30; institutional responsibility for, 29–30; need for inclusion of human requirements in, 30; need for international effort with comparability, 32, 33; problem of money-metric approach, 28–29; problems of World Bank overseeing, 32–33

Global warming, 20, 26

Good life, the, 148, 153

Gordon, Peter, 240, 245

Gore, Al, 112

Governmentalities. *See* State, the

Greenhouses, 26

Grotius, Hugo, 209

Guha, Ranajit, 75

Haiti, 133

Hardiman, David, 192

Hart, Mitchell, 232

Hartz, Louis, 110

Health services: advantages for development, 47; AIDS prevention, 64; infant

Health services (*continued*)
and child mortality, 40–41; malaria
prevention, 41; pharmaceutical industry
interests, 57, 63–64; user fees recommended by World Bank, 34–35

Hegel, Georg W.F., 240–41

Heidegger, Martin, 245

Herzl, Theodor, 238

Heuty, Antoine, 40

Hezbollah, 126

Hirsch, E.D., 185

Hirschkind, Charles, 159, 160, 165

Historicity of the authentic, 222

Historiography: absence of story of Jews and
Muslims in Europe, 237–38; difficulty of
inserting subaltern woman into history,
192–94; subaltern studies, 191–92; use of
unconventional sources, 75

Hofstadter, Richard, 110, 111

Holocaust, 127, 128, 152, 238–44

Holy war, 245–46

Human capabilities, 10

Human development: as approach to
economic growth theory, 4; capabilities
as contextual and dependent, 10–12; early
inclusion in economic growth theory,
3; influence of ul-Haq on, 4–5; need
to identify human requirements, 30;
problems of institutions, 5–7; subjective
versus objective measures of, 10–12; *See
also* Development

Human Development Index, 12

Humanities education: American, question
of exporting, 174; for cultural literacy, 185;
debatable emancipatory effects, 173; limits of, 174; as trivialized, 174; as uncoercive
rearrangement of desires, 173; unlearning
privilege, learning to learn from below,
182–83; use of Enlightenment as forms of
questioning, 181–82

Human requirements, 30

Human rights: as bounty bestowed as "white
man's burden," 179; "breaking of nations"
in name of, 178–79; within history of
colonialism, 176–78; as indivisibly civil,
social, and economic, 141; Islam viewed
as incompatible with, 140–41, 164–65,
212–14; little understanding of, at time

of Bretton Woods Agreement, 6; means
of guaranteeing, 141–42; more reports
of violations in Third World, 218–19;
politeness rubbing off, 222–23; problem
of U.S.-supported dictatorships, 253;
in subordinate cultures of responsibility, 179–80; violations as result of global
economic framework, 220–21; West's
perception of "here" versus "there," 218–19

Hussein, Saddam, 142

Hutu-Tutsi violence, 13, 95

Identity politics: arising from expectations of
government services, 92; conflict arising
from, 22–24; cultural/religious versus
political, 97–98, 99; questions of religious
and ethnic coexistence, 153; and sense of
place, 199–200; *See also* Cultures

Imperialism, 114; *See also* American imperialism; Colonialism

Income poverty: global dimension, individual versus systematic responsibility,
44–46; inequalities resulting from development, 19, 26; limitation of, as measure
of development, 3; need for egalitarian
distributive policies, 35; need for international collective action, 66; pessimistic
scenarios for reduction, 40; redistribution
of wealth, 178, 195; regional variations in
reduction, 39–40; *See also* Global poverty
estimates

India: as authoritarian state, 72, 74; BPL
demarcation of sectors of populace,
92–93; Calcutta theater, film, sports, 73;
enablement by British colonization, 176;
health services compared to China's,
15–16; high agricultural yields, 19; interest
in European culture, 73; Maharastra
Employment Guarantee Scheme,
49; Maoist movement, 71, 72, 74–75;
nationalism and anticolonial struggle, 72;
National Rural Employment Guarantee
Programme, 49; postcolonial, 75–78;
progress and problems, 14–16; as secular
state with unresolved tension, 84; social
and demographic changes, 77–78; social
equality issues, 16, 51–52; subaltern studies, 74–78, 87; teacher training in rural

West Bengal, 174–76; women's equality as recent concern, 15

Individualism, 148, 150, 213, 214

Indonesia, 22

Inequalities of income. *See* Income poverty

Infant and child mortality, 40–41

Information technology, 10, 12

Inquisition, 229–30

Insurance, global reinsurance fund, 49–50

Intellectual class, academics, and think tanks, American: anti-Chinese hardliners, 125; conformism, lack of debate, 132; failure to analyze Muslim world, 123; incapable of serious analysis, 132; interest in subaltern studies, 191–92; need for oppositional dimension, 224; as public intellectuals, 200–201; with stake in foreign policy agendas, 122

Intellectual class and academics, nonWestern: Muslim, inflected by liberalism, 151–54; need for independent domestic intellectuals, 37

Intellectual decolonization, 95–96

Intellectual property rights, 57, 63–64

International Civil Service Commission, 31

International Comparison Program, 32

International Criminal Court statute, 221

International Development Association (IDA), 56

International law, 209

International Monetary Fund: advancing capitalism, 177; advocating privatization of social security, 60; advocating value added tax, 58; calls for abolition or reform, 61–62; changes in leadership and approach, 6; as creditor-friendly, not international, 62; criticized for political agenda, 58–59; governance structure issues, 6, 7, 51, 56–57, 62, 67; legitimacy undermined, 66; policies exacerbating problems, 24–25; proclamatory mindset, 63; purpose and funding, 55–57; responses to criticisms, 10; subject to vagaries of U.S. politics, 60; "Washington Consensus," 59–60

Intervention, 217–18, 220

Intifadah, 97

Iran, 120, 121, 125–26, 156

Iraq: Chalabi as pro-American strongman, 110; pre-2003 sanctions, 104–05; as threat to be removed, 106; war as disaster for Bush neocons, 121–22; worries over World Bank role, 65

Islam: disappearance from Rosenzweig's argument, 246; discourses on secularism related to anti-Islam, 250; as epitome of religious fanaticism, 229; as ideological enemy of U.S., 122, 156; viewed as antithetical to liberal democracy, 212–14; viewed as discriminating against women, 141; viewed as incompatible with human rights and democracy, 140–41; Western antipathy toward, 212, 215; *See also* Muslim world

Islamic revival, 161, 162

Islamists: challenging liberalism's autonomy, freedom, and equality, 164–65; concept of jihad justifying violence, 108; engagement with Marxism-Leninism, 107–08; impossibility of not being political, 160; incorporating some secular-liberal ideals, 163; increasing participation of women, 170–71; need to differentiate among objectives of, 155–56; network of charitable and social welfare organizations, 154–55, 160; at odds with Muslim secularists, 156–57; plural strands and criticism of West, 154–55; as political Islam, 99–100, 159, 210–11; as postcolonial phenomenon, 100–101, 154; Reagan's rescue from historical cul-de-sac, 104; settling scores with West, 13–14

Israel: America's special relationship with, 112, 126–28; as catalyst and focus for Muslim feeling of humiliation, 118; coverage in American media, 130; as secular state with religious authorities, 232; Zionism, 228–29, 233, 238, 244–50, 246–47

Japan, 135

Java, 22

Jews: in America, 231–32; as *conversos*, 230; rabbinical decision necessary for Jewishness, 232

Jihad, 108

Jordan, 117, 118, 157

"Justified anger," as universal human right, 10–11

Kant, Immanuel, 173, 240, 241
Kennan, George, 110
Kifaya party, 157
Kissinger, Henry, 102, 132
Klein, Melanie, 193–94

Labor: international division of, 185, 186; as spectral, abstract category, 185–86
Ladakh, Tibet, 18, 19, 24, 26
Language issues: epistemic violence of imperialism, 185, 187–88; language as active cultural media, 184–85; languages spoken among diasporics, 187–88; loss of language with entire possibilities of meaning, 185; neglecting women's identity, 12; problem of ignorance, 252; teaching in other than hegemonic languages, 175; translation having cultural and political effects, 251; translation of works by Devi, 188–90, 257n6; Western influences privileging European, 21
Latin America: Argentina, 58; Bolivia, 58; Contras, 103, 108; Nicaragua, 103; U.S. sphere of influence in, 133; Venezuela, 135; "Washington Consensus," 59, 60
Law: of force, 220; international, 209; International Criminal Court statute, 221; rule of, 217; Sharia, 214–15
Leibniz, Gottfried, 226
Levi, Primo, 238–39, 240, 243
Liberalism: in assessment of ills of Muslim women, 151; assumption of model as American, 153; as basis for postcolonial critiques of Western power and domination, 149; colonial peoples denied basic freedoms of, 149–50; distaste for face-to-face violence, 220; freedom as individual and political ethic, 148; hegemony over Muslim thinkers decried, 151–54; incorporating Enlightenment dismissal of religion, 163; interpretations of postcolonial feminist projects, 150–51; irrelevance through governmental technologies, 90–91; Islam viewed as incompatible with, 140–41, 164–65, 212–14;

tolerance and pluralism not intrinsic to, 151–52
Libya, 120
Lieven, Anatol, 109–36, 260
Limpieza de sangre, 230
Lind, Michael, 130
Luxury goods, 18

Macro-stability, 59
Maharastra Employment Guarantee Scheme, 49
Mahmood, Saba, 148–71, 260
Malaria prevention, 41
Mamdani, Mahmood, 94–108, 233, 260
Maoist movement, India, 71, 72, 74–75
Market economy, 9
Marxism-Leninism: critique of capitalism, 162; critique of Western culture, 251; dismissal of religion, 163; political Islam's engagement with, 107–08
Massad, Joseph, 231
Mastnak, Tomaz, 215
Mawdudi, Abu A'laa, 100, 101, 108
Media, American: exaggerated sense of importance, behaving like senior officials, 131; failure to criticize Bush's propaganda program, 129; receiving constructed information and spin, 131; supporting campaign to "free" Afghan women, 168; use of term "Holy Land," 225
Media, Western, 104–05
Menon, Nivedita, 191
Messianism in U.S. desire to spread democracy, 109–10, 111
"Mexico" as building in Auschwitz, 243–44
Middle East: Egypt, 117, 156, 157; Iran, 120, 121, 125–26, 156; Jordan, 117, 118, 157; Palestine, 97, 126, 229; possibilities for emancipatory politics, 224; Qatar, 218; Saudi Arabia, 117, 118, 120, 156; Syria, 118, 121, 156; Turkey, 156, 238; U.S. inability to question relationship with Israel, 112; U.S. lacking serious strategy for, 134; *See also* Iraq; Israel
"Military-industrial-academic complex," 122
Millenarianism, 129
Millenium Development Goals, 39–42
Miniskirt, compared to veil/burqa, 168

Minoiu, Camelia, 46, 47

Missionaries, 209, 210

Modernity: civil society, compared to political society, 88–90; discursive power of Western, 88; erroneous prediction of decline of religion, 158–61, 206; Islamism challenging narratives of secularism, 212; lack of, in Muslim world, 117–18; local elaborations and domestications, 86, 87, 88; moderns willing to die and kill for causes, 96–97; no longer a gift from the West, 82; in postcolonial Third World, 85–88; radical Islam using modern methods, 118; some religious forms furthering, 209–10; Western, as incomplete and imperfect, 87–88

Monbiot, George, 65, 66–67

Monetary policy reforms, 42–44

Monocultures, 17, 18, 26

Monotheism, 216, 236

Montesquieu, 240, 241

Mozambique, 102, 103

Mubarak, Hosni, 157

Mudimbe, Valentine Y., 94–95

Muselmann in Auschwitz, 238–44

Musharraf, Pervez, 119, 120

Muslim Brotherhood, 156, 157

Muslim women: Afghan, as victims of conditions of war and starvation, 165, 166, 167–68; being "saved" by America, 144–45; importance of recognizing difference, 146; increasing participation in Islamic movements, 170–71; liberalism infusing assessment of, 151; post-9/11 Western interest, 144, 166–68; postcolonial feminism, 150–51; *See also* Veil/burqa

Muslim world: American failure to understand, 123; American hopes of political allies in, 223; American neocons' chauvinism, fear, and contempt of, 110; American patronage of client regimes, 119; Americans' more complicated reading of, 223; ancient kingdoms as positive identity, 14; ancient kingdoms of religious tolerance, 152; Arab states as "tribes with flags," 118; attempts to understand, after September 11, 143; Bush's desire to democratize, 110; demonized by pro-Israeli American

influences, 110; distrust of U.S. desire to bring democracy, 119; economic failure, 118; erroneously characterized as monolithic block, 156; Europe's fear of Ottoman Turks, 242; as extremely diverse, 122; feminism in Iran, 146, 147; "good" and "bad" Muslims, 98–99; immigrants seen as demographic threat in Europe, 238; liberalism inflecting assessment of ills, 151–54; need for debate on models of liberalism and democracy, 153–54; political weakness and lack of modernization in, 117–19; populations in Soviet Union, 103; religious revivalist movements as modern, 211–12; secularists versus Islamists, 156–57; secularization as panacea or destructive force, 161–62; some support in, for invasion of Afghanistan, 124; Sunni revolutionary element as threat to states, 124; unlikelihood of secularism taking hold in, 250–51; West's descriptive terms for, 230–31; *See also* Islam; Islamists

NAFTA (North American Free Trade Agreement), 57–58

Nanda, Meera, 187, 198

Nandy, Ashis, 52

Nasser, Gamal Abdul, 156

Nationalism: and anticolonial struggle, 78–85; bending through critical regionalism, 179; U.S. policy of subverting in Third World, 106; *See also* American nationalism

Native Americans, 127, 235

Nativism, 95

NATO, 112

Neoconservatives in U.S.: contempt for Muslims and Arabs, 110; Muslim world as new U.S. enemy, 122

New Christians, 230

NGOs (nongovernmental organizations), 6–7

Nicaragua, 103

Niebuhr, Reinhold, 110

Nigeria, 135, 214

Nonviolent resistance, 79

Norberg-Hodge, Helena, 17–26, 261

North Korea, 113, 115

Novak, Robert, 129
Nussbaum, Martha, 10

Objectivity, in ethics and political philosophy, 10
Oil, geopolitics of, 134–36
Ottoman Empire, 152, 242, 243
Outsourcing, 186
OXFAM, 6–7

Pain and punishment as secular calculus, 217–18
Pakistan, 56, 118, 214
Palestine, 97, 126, 229
Palmer, Gesine, 245
Panikkar, K.N., 192
Papanek, Hanna, 145
Pharmaceutical industry, 57, 63–64, 195
Place, invoking sense of, 199–200
Pluralism, 151–53, 214
Podhoretz, Norman, 122
Political Islam, 99–100, 159, 210–11; *See also* Islamists
Political society, compared to civil society, 88–90
Politics. *See* Theological-political, the
Poor, the: criterion for identifying, 27–30; debt owed to, 25; *See also* Income poverty
Pope, the, 248, 249
Population pressure, 20–21, 194–95
"Portable seclusion," veil/burqa as, 145
Postcolonial state: as benefitting and victimized by modernity, 85–88; civil society, compared to political society, 88–90; debates over legitimate forms of governance, 78–81; and "dominance without hegemony," 75–78; nationalism, secularism, and religious reform movements, 83–85; need for intellectual decolonization, 95–96; similarity to colonial techniques of rule, 75–78
Poverty. *See* Global poverty estimates; Income poverty
Preemptive war, 106, 108, 125–26
Private property rights, 35, 149
Privatization, 59
Privilege, unlearning, 182–83
Propaganda by Bush administration, 129

Protestant Church, 100
Proxy war, 102, 103
Public debate / public reasoning: for agreement on universal human capabilities/rights, 10; democracy promoting, 9–10; leading to health service improvements, 15, 16; over method of counting the poor, 29–30; over objectives and consequences of development, 25; *See also* Intellectual class
Public intellectuals, 200–201; *See also* Intellectual class
Puritanism, 159
Purity of Blood statutes, 230
Putin, Vladimir, 117

Qatar, 218
Quran, 215–16
Qutb, Syed, 100, 108

Race and ethnicity, 230–35, 233–34
Racism, 230
Radical alterity, 180
Rajan, Raghuram, 48
Rationality, 12, 13
Ravallion, Martin, 29
Raz-Krakotzkin, Amnon, 229, 233
Reagan administration, 43, 101–03, 104
Reddy, Sanjay, 27–53, 261
Redistribution of wealth, 178, 195
Regionalism, 179
"Regulatory Takings" provision in NAFTA, 57–58
Religion: adapting to modern state, 211–12; advantages of considering positive changes, 252; analyzing historical changes in, 227; critique of monotheism, 216; cultural/religious versus political, 97–98, 99, 141; decline in modern times as debatable and naive, 158–61, 252–53; historic roles in America, Britain, and France, 159; ideologization and privatization of war by, 103; inadequate as sole determinant of national character, 143; legitimating violence, 217; local adaptations and innovations, 84–85; "of the sublime," 240, 241; as politicized, 158–61; as politicized Islam, 210–11; postcolonial nationalism,

secularism, and religious reform movements, 83–85; problematic relationship with secularism, 207–08; public, as threat to political freedom, 210; questions of multi-religious and ethnic coexistence, 153; race and ethnicity, 230–35, 234, 234–35; Reagan's political uses of "evil," 102; redefinition within social and historical contexts, 205; religious movements as anticolonial nationalist struggles, 13–14; religious revivalist movements as modern, 211–12; state dictating means of expression of religious affiliation, 170; as term used anachronistically, 205; *See also* Christian Right; Theological-political, the

Religious Right. *See* Christian Right
Renamo movement, 102, 108
Responsibility, cultures of, 179–80
Ressentiment, 190–91
Rieff, David, 176–77
Rosenzweig, Franz, 241, 244–46
Rote learning, 172, 183
Rural versus urban life, 19–21
Russia, 112, 115, 117, 125
Rwanda, 13, 95

Sachs, Jeffrey, 40, 41, 46, 48
Sacraments, baptism, 230
Safety nets, 49–50
Said, Edward, 234
Sanctioned ignorance, 184–85
Sandanistas, 103
Saudi Arabia, 117, 118, 120, 156
Schwartz, Yossef, 245
Science/technology: ancient history of global exchange, 8–9; expansion of information technology, 10, 12; need for research, 26; no longer a gift from the West, 82; response to, 180–81
Second World War. *See* World War II
Secularism: assumption of superiority of developed countries, 222; claiming to be less prone to conflict and violence, 211, 218; as culmination of modernization, 206; curbing excesses of religion while allowing other cruelties, 217; discourses related to anti-Islam, 250;

Islamism challenging narrative of, 212; in nineteenth century Europe, 233; origins in Purity of Blood statutes, 230; pain and punishment as secular calculus, 217–18; postcolonial nationalism and religious reform movements, 83–85; problem of "Jewish question," conversion of Jews, and present-day missionaries, 210; question of, and need for, civil society, 251; reconsidering relationship to religion, 158–61; secularization of Muslim world as panacea, 161–62; and the theological-political, 225–30; varied adaptations of separation of religion and state, 206–08, 209–10; West's claim to, 227

Self, the, 151
Semites, 233–35, 240–41
Sen, Amartya, 3–16, 50, 195, 261
September 11th's aftermath: American analyses of Muslim societies, 143; America's actions, 109–10; atmosphere of debate, 109–10; Bush's policy shift on China, 112–13; Bush turning from actual perpetrators to "axis of evil," 123; feminist mobilization as excuse for war, 166; hunger for information on Muslim women, 144; media commentaries on Quranic injunctions to violence, 215–16; militant nationalist wave and silencing of criticism, 131; as only the beginning of danger to America, 105; revealing lack of modernization in Muslim world, 117–18; security elites caught unaware, 122
Sexual satisfaction, 10, 11
Shadid, Anthony, 157
Shantiniketan school, 197, 257n8
Sharia law, 214–15
Shiller, Robert, 49
Shiva, Vandana, 187
"Sick man of Europe," 242, 243
Sistani, Sayyid Ali Husaini al-, 100
Skin color, 21, 22
Slumification, 20
Somavia, Juan, 195
South Africa, 97, 102
South Asia: Afghanistan, 103, 123–24, 165–66; Tibet, 18, 19, 24, 26; *See also* East Asia; India; Pakistan

Soweto uprising, 97
Spain, 230
Spectrality, 185–86
Spivak, Gayatri Chakravorty, 172–201, 261
Stagnation, 46
"Starting gate equality" concept, 35
Stasi Commission, 169
State, the: attempts to find non-Western concept of, 78–79; being broken by globalization, 178–79; colonial compared to postcolonial, 75–78; cultural/religious versus political identity, 98, 99; defining public face of religion, 207–08; development of international law, 209; embodying notions of freedom and private property, 149; expectation of provision of basic services, 91; governmental technologies for differentiated populations, 90–91; model as market-driven management rather than redistribution, 178; modern expansion of power into individuals' lives, 159–60; pain and punishment as secular calculus, 217–18; reinforcing secular conception of religiosity, 158–59; religions adapting to, 211–12; as secular arrangement of power, 208–09, 210; secular role in religious conflict, 211; separation from religion, 160–61; social misery produced by economic policies, 217
Statistics on poverty. *See* Global poverty estimates
Sterilization, forcible, 195
Stiglitz, Joseph, 54–67, 261
Strauss, Leo, 127
Structural Adjustment Programs, 35
Subaltern studies, 74–78, 87, 191–92, 193–94
Sublime, religions of submission or "enslavement," 240, 241
Subordinate cultures of responsibility, 179–80
Subramaniam, Arvind, 48
Suicide bombers, 97
Sustainability, 195
Syria, 118, 121, 156

Taiwan, 125
Taliban, 146, 165–68
Terrorism: al-Qaeda as web of groups, 122–24; Contras, 103, 108; error of

"Islamic" label, 140–41; errors of cultural explanations for, 107; Hezbollah, 126; Islamist network formed for Afghan war, 103; as real threat to modern civilization, 124; relationship of state and nonstate terrorism, 96; Renamo movement, 102, 108; Saudi Arabia incubating, 120; sources in prejudice and injustice, 142; as strategy of U.S. in Cold War, 101–03, 108; suicide bombers, 97; Taliban, 123–24, 146, 165–68
Thailand, 56
Tharu, Susie, 192
Theological-political, the: definition, 225–28; difficulties of analyzing difference, 226–27; invention of race and religion, 233–34; need to confront enemy, 228–30; universalism and, 250–53
Think tanks. *See* Intellectual class
Tibet, 18, 19, 24, 26
Tolerance, 24, 151–53, 211, 213–14, 216
Torture, 220
Toynbee, Arnold, 133
Trade: breakdown of cultures, 21–22; closed Western markets, 54; colonialism encouraging production for, 17; commodity price swings, 46–47, 49; destruction of rural marketing opportunities, 21; favoring traders at expense of local producers, 19, 57; need to reverse process of centralization and urbanization, 25–26; as secondary economic goal, 18; U.S. trade deficits, 67; worker-friendly reforms of international system, 53; *See also* Development; Globalization
Translation issues, 188–90, 251, 257n6
"Tribes with flags," 118
"Trickle-down" economics, 59
TRIPS (Trade Related Intellectual Property Rights), 57, 63–64
Turkey, 156, 238

Ul-Haq, Mahbub, 4–5
United Nations: asymmetries of power in governance structure, 7, 142; as form of substitute "governmental technology," 91; Millennium Development Goals, 39–42; Statistics Division, 31, 33; Universal Dec-

laration of Human Rights, 219; as vehicle for critiques, 10

United States: actions subsequent to September 11, 109–10; advantages of spreading democracy by example, 119; advocating religious freedom for Third World countries, 209; Afghan war, 103; aid to allies, shoring up governments, 48; Carter administration, 121; causing debt crisis of 1980s, 43; Christian Right in heart of Bush administration, 206–07; CIA embrace of drug lords, 103; CIA global recruitment of volunteers for Afghanistan, 103–04; Clinton administration, 55, 57–58, 60, 112–13; "collateral damage" and relationship to terrorism, 101; coming to resemble Soviet Union, 105, 106; considerations of church/state separation, 206–07; costs of Cold War victory, 105–06; as dominating homogenized future, 223; as dominating through economic or military power, 83; at end of Cold War, 55; erosion of democracy in, 107; failure to analyze alternatives to Middle East policy, 130; geopolitics of oil, 134–36; hypocrisy at Israeli occupation of Palestinian territories, 121; ideologically empowered self-righteousness, 105; invasion of Afghanistan as self-defense, 123–24; Iraq War and lack of reference to Vietnam, 111; Islam as ideological enemy, 122, 156; lacking serious strategy for Middle East, 134; messianism in desire to spread democracy, 109–10, 111; near-global active military presence, 253; new forms of dominance, 82–83; opposition to conscription, 114, 115, 121, 134; policy of subverting militant nationalism in Third World, 106; Reagan administration, 43, 101–03, 104; ruthless prison system, 217; special relationship with Israel, 126–28; terrorism as strategy in Cold War, 101–03, 108; threat of war as necessary, 122; trade deficits, 67; U.S. Treasury, 59, 60; veto power at IMF, 56; "Washington Consensus," 59–60; *See also* American imperialism; American nationalism; Bush (G.W.) administration

Universal Declaration of Human Rights, 6, 219

Universalism, 250–53

Universities as corporations, 174

Urbanization, 19–22, 23, 25–26

Uruguay Round of WTO, 57, 63–64, 66, 255n1

U.S. Treasury, 59, 60

VAT (value added tax), 58

Veil/burqa: challenge to charge of oppressive symbolism, comparison to miniskirt, 168; as contentious issue in disparate societies and regions, 168–70; echoes of colonial fantasy to disrobe Muslim woman, 167; French Islamophobic ban on, 169–70, 252; as misinterpreted symbol in West, 167; not all Muslim women discarding, 167; as "portable seclusion," 145; status of, in Western history and colonial legacy, 165–66; voluntary adoption of, 168–70

Venezuela, 135

Vietnam War, 102, 111, 123, 132

Violation, enabling, colonialism as, 176

Violence: collateral damage versus torture, 220; decried when targeting Western power, 216; Hutu and Tutsi, 13, 95; jihad, 108; means of, as absolute military power, 83; of modern warfare as unprecedented, 219–20; need for civil society, 89; over competition for scarce jobs, 24; pain and punishment as secular calculus, 217–18; as principle of modern government, 81; secular societies allegedly less prone to, 211; with weakest as victims of conditions of war and starvation, 165, 166, 167–68; *See also* Terrorism

War: holy, 245–46; between states compared to insurgencies, 219–20; subjects' relationship to, according to Rosenzweig, 245–46; violence of modern conflict as unprecedented, 219; *See also* World War II

"Washington Consensus," 59–60

WDR (World Development Report, 2006), 33–37

Weber, Max, 117

Welfare state, 91

West, the: antipathy toward Islam, 212, 215; assumption of superiority of developed countries, 222; civilizing mission of colonialist era, 81, 82; claim to secularism, 227; having economic and military dominance, 253; Indians' interest in, 73–74; *See also* Europe

Westernization as consumer lifestyle, 21

White man's burden, 81, 115, 179

Wilson, Woodrow, 113

Wolfensohn, James, 6, 7–8, 34, 62, 67

Wolfowitz, Paul, 38–39, 64–65, 255–56n4

Women: Islam viewed as discriminating against, 141; native, colonialism "saving," 144, 147, 196; *See also* Feminism; Muslim women

Women's equality. *See* Feminism

Woodward, Bob, 131

Woodward, C. Vann, 114

World Bank: advancing capitalism, 177; advocating privatization of social security, 60; changes in leadership and approach, 6; defense of global poverty estimates methodology, 29–30; emphasizing governments' role in development, 62–63; Global Development Network, 37; governance structure issues, 6, 7, 38, 51, 65–66, 67, 142; harmful policies in health and education sectors, 34–35; inadequate estimates of global poverty, 27–30; legitimacy undermined, 66; loans to Saddam Hussein, 142; need for competition in development research, 36–38; need for transparency, 33; policies emphasizing systems of destruction, 24–25; problems of oversight of global poverty estimate process, 32–33; problems with agenda of human development, 5; purpose and funding, 55–56; questions of research budget and systematic biases, 36–37; questions of expenditures on universities and consultancy mills, 37–38; reforms, 62–63; responses to criticisms, 10, 34; "Washington Consensus," 59–60; Wolfensohn's influence, 6, 7–8, 34, 62, 67; Wolfowitz's influence, 38–39, 64–65, 255–56n4; World Development Report (2006), 33

World Development Report (2006) (WDR), 33–37

World War II: bombing of civilian centers, 217, 220; development following decolonization, 17–18

WTO (World Trade Organization), 55–56, 57, 63–64, 255n1

Yeltsin, Boris, 117

Zarqawi, Abu Musab al-, 123

Zia, Muhammad, 119

Zionism, 228–29, 233, 238, 244–50, 246–47

Zupanov, Ines, 250